THE SIXTH ALFRED I. duPONT – COLUMBIA UNIVERSITY

SURVEY OF
BROADCAST
JOURNALISM

THE ALFRED I. duPONT-COLUMBIA UNIVERSITY SURVEY AND AWARDS IN BROADCAST JOURNALISM

THE JURORS

THE SIXTH ALFRED I. duPONT – COLUMBIA UNIVERSITY SURVEY OF BROADCAST JOURNALISM

Rich News, Poor News

by Marvin Barrett

Thomas Y. Crowell Company

Established 1834 • New York

FIRST EDITION

Designed by Lydia Link

LIBRARY OF CONGRESS CATALOG CARD NUMBER: 77–95161

ISBN: 0–690–01740–5
ISBN: 0–690–01741–3 pbk

78 79 80 81 82 10 9 8 7 6 5 4 3 2 1

THIS VOLUME
IS DEDICATED TO
THE LATE LOUIS G. COWAN

Contents

APPENDICES

Foreword

In 1942 the late Jessie Ball duPont established the Alfred I. duPont Awards Foundation to honor the memory of her late husband by encouraging the best in broadcasting. This year for the first time the DuPont-Columbia Awards for excellence in broadcast journalism will themselves be the subject of a coast-to-coast broadcast, undoubtedly the most appropriate manner of honoring the men and women who exhaust themselves in the service of this demanding vocation. The following volume attempts to reinforce that occasion by relating some of the struggles involved in the heroic attempts by the broadcast community to inform us all.

—Marvin Barrett

THE SIXTH ALFRED I. duPONT – COLUMBIA UNIVERSITY

SURVEY OF
BROADCAST
JOURNALISM

1 • Introduction:
Money, Money, Money

"NOW THAT BROADCASTERS have all that money, what are they going to do with it?" *Broadcasting* magazine asked in a special report in its May 16, 1977, issue.

> Superlatives to describe the radio-TV boom year of 1976 are running out, but a few figures will suffice: The CBS/Broadcast Group exceeded $1 billion in sales for the first time, producing $215 million in pre-tax profit, a 20% gain over 1975, Capital Cities Communications' net broadcasting revenues reached $104 million, and its operating income from broadcasting reached $48.9 million, 29% above income in 1975. ABC's broadcasting revenues exceeded $1 billion, up more than $234 million from 1975, and pre-tax earnings of $150 million were more than double those of 1975.
> The list goes on. And as if 1976 weren't enough, first-quarter revenues for 1977 are bigger than ever, and advertisers are lining up to buy for next season at prices predicted to be as much as 17 percent higher than 1976's record rates. In a traditionally high cash-flow business, broadcasters' cups are running over.

Just how extreme the situation had become was underlined by an executive of Shields, Model, Roland, Inc., a Manhattan brokerage house. "Broadcasters who are up to their full station complements," vice president Anthony Hoffman told the magazine, "find themselves in the position of having to downgrade the overall quality of their company by investing in businesses that are generally less attractive than the one they're in. There is nothing as lucrative as broadcasting."

It was a little over half a century since Secretary of Commerce Herbert Hoover had told the first Washington Radio Conference in February 1922, "It is inconceivable that this potentially great public service and educational medium become a medium of commercial gain." In that time the number of radio stations has grown to over 8,000—7,389 of them devoted obsessively to commerce and representing aggregate annual revenues of $2.02 billion. In the last three decades, approximately 1,000 television stations have joined them on the air with the total revenues of commercial networks and TV stations for 1976 standing at $5.2 billion.

Commercial or not, average daily home TV viewing has gone up steadily, breaking all records during the bitter days of January 1977 by hitting seven hours and sixteen minutes, twelve minutes more than the previous high in January 1975. Radio listening was estimated at three hours twenty-one minutes per adult per day.

Another million American households, previously in that narrow margin still without television receivers, bought sets in 1976 and raised television's potential audience to 71.5 million homes, or an estimated 146 million men, women, and children. Color sets were introduced into 3 million more homes, bringing the total to 54.3 million, and households with more than one set stood at 33 million, 1.1 million more than the previous year. Radio sets in operation at the last tally had been estimated at 425 million, or 1.7 for every man, woman, and child in the land.

In network TV alone, there were sixty-two new advertisers among the 554 rich enough to fight each other for the most desirable air time, driving rates as high as $120,000 per minute for the choicest prime time positions.*

Still, the price of individual spots rose by 25 to 40 percent in the 1977–78 season. Already 65 percent more advertising availabilities than ten years before had been cleared by network juggling, and it was suggested that more spots be fitted into the already overloaded schedule, or that a fourth network be instituted to accommodate the needs of disappointed advertisers.

Looking at all these figures, *Variety* saw the reflection of "an economic health that is the envy of practically every industry in the country."

In the generally jubilant chorus there were, however, a few discordant voices. FCC Commissioner Margita White told a group of advertisers at Manhattan's Plaza Hotel in February 1977:

> Those who are looking ahead recognize that television is entering a new era of competition with emerging alternative systems for delivering information and entertainment. And, I submit, it will be the public's perception of the quality of programs on commercial television today and in the next years which will determine whether the American people choose to continue to

---

*This did not include such special attractions as the Super Bowl, which in 1977 had cost $250,000 per commercial minute. Thanks to the fact that the broadcast had been moved up from 2 P.M. to 6 P.M. and thus spilled over into prime time, the price was increased to $288,000 per minute for 1978.

rely upon commercial television or turn increasingly to new program sources. . . . It is these viewers who will determine the future of commercial television—not the rating of network shows against each other, but a rating of the quality of commercial television against potential alternatives.

A study of public attitudes toward television and television programs in 1976–77, instituted by McHugh and Hoffman, Inc., and KPR Associates, Inc., consultants and market researchers, came to similar conclusions. After interviewing a sample of more than 1,500 adult viewers, they summed up the results in quasi-academic jargon.

> The years from 1967 to 1977 have marked a period when the TV audience has "come of age," grown more mature and sophisticated in the value judgments it sets for the medium and more demanding that the medium serve its needs—rather than they serve the medium. At the same time, through its news, information and entertainment programs, the medium has become a major interactive force between the public and the social, political and economic institutions of this country—a fact the significance of which the audience itself is becoming increasingly conscious. During the last ten years, the failure of the TV programmers to stay in step with the audience's maturation and to remain sensitive to the societal force and functions of the medium, have caused a serious "loosening" of the audience commitment to the medium. Whether this continues or not depends on the degree to which the industry can meet the expanding responsibility placed upon it, and the changing attitudinal context in which it is operating.

Ms. White, former White House assistant press secretary, might be dismissed as a bureaucratic spoilsport. The researchers, whose living depended on selling advice to troubled broadcasters, could be accused of having their own axes to grind. Less easy to shake off were the words of Paul C. Harper, Jr., chairman and chief executive officer of Needham, Harper and Steers, an advertising agency which billed 98.6 of the millions of dollars flowing into broadcasters' coffers.

"We all know the viewing statistics," Mr. Harper told a New York audience in accepting the 1976 Human Relations Award of the American Jewish Committee:

> What we don't yet have a final grip on are the cause and effect relationships between what people see on TV and what they do and feel. But there is more and more evidence that what is seen on the tube blends with the real world, so that many people,

particularly the young and the troubled, find it hard to distinguish between the two. Given the content of much TV programming, this can obviously have a desensitizing and brutalizing effect on a whole generation. . . .

The basic content of TV programming must be changed so that, with rare but notable exceptions, the choice is not between silliness and socially destructive programs. It does little good for a network spokesman to get up and say, "Police shows reflect current reality and current concerns. We give the people what they want." This is sheer sophistry.

My wish for the three network heads is that they seek from their respective boards of directors broad charters to rebuild the content of network programming—drastically increasing the informative and drastically reducing the sensational. We have all seen the new figures on what the public feels about violence on TV. Eighty per cent express some degree of concern. Even the general public is beginning to sense how TV programming is eroding national values. This could easily translate over the next few years into pressure for yet new kinds of regulation—this time encroaching on freedom of speech itself.

My basic wish for the network heads is that they fix things themselves—before somebody tries to fix things for them. This could be tragic for all of us.

The good news in broadcasting in 1976–77 had to do with profits. The bad news, as Commissioner White and Messrs. McHugh, Hoffman, and Harper indicated, had to do with the quality and nature of most of the fare with which the profits were earned.

Somewhere between the good news and the bad was "the news," the principal concern of this volume.

For many years now the most important and craftsmanlike programming on the commercial air had emanated from the news departments of networks and local stations. Journalism was the one activity that seemed to bridge from the present back to those more hopeful younger days of broadcasting when the obligation of serving and informing the public had loomed large. Nor had the news been insulated from the prosperity of broadcasting in general. It was thriving as well.

The McHugh and Hoffman report stated that "interest in news-oriented information and public affairs programming is high. Sixty-two percent of those interviewed selected this programming as one of their favorite types," while 64 percent used TV for news and entertainment both—an increase from the 28 percent who saw TV as an informational medium in the early 1960s.

In the biennial Roper poll, TV still outranked all other media by a wide margin as the preferred source for the nation's news. Fifty-one percent found TV most believable, compared to 22 percent naming newspapers and 7 percent radio.

According to a survey of "key decision makers in politics, business, and the professions" published by *U.S. News and World Report* in April 1977, only the White House ranked above television in "the amount of influence it has on decisions or actions affecting the nation as a whole," and TV newsman Walter Cronkite was judged in the same survey as ninth among the nation's most influential men.* In a Lou Harris poll in January 1977, 66 percent of the respondents ranked TV news along with consumer protection groups as "the most ethical of U.S. institutions." At the bottom of the list were the men who ran the nation's corporations—including, one had to assume, the heads of the three commercial networks.

And it was not just a matter of claiming a preference and then ignoring it when a choice was made. People were actually tuning in the news.

Viewership of network news was reported to be up a spectacular 9 percent in 1976 over the previous year. Gains by local news shows in many instances were even higher. A headline in the April 27, 1977, *Variety* read "News Turns Into Network Money Maker," reporting that from "a 15 percent loss position in 1972" news rose to contribute "1% of the total three-web profits in 1975 and 1976, the latter an election year with all the attendant financial burdens."† Despite *Variety*, none of the networks reported profits from their news divisions in 1976. But NBC's president Herbert Schlosser predicted "marginal" profitability for news in 1977, which made him possibly the first network president in history to allow that news and public affairs might be more than a prestige-winning loss leader.

There was no such ambiguity about the profitability of news operations at most local stations. Frequently news was the only local programming of substance. In many instances it was the station's biggest money maker and audience builder.

"Within the last decade we've all realized that a local station can't be number one in its total programming unless it is also number one in its local news program," William Sheehan told the *Wall Street*

---

*George Meany, President of the AFL-CIO, was the only nongovernment figure to rank above Cronkite.
†Total news budgets for the three networks were set at $218 million, of which $45 million represented outlays for political coverage. Total entertainment budgets stood at $1.25 billion for the same period.

Journal shortly before he was deposed from his top position at ABC News in one of the major shake-ups of the broadcast journalism year. The *Journal* went on to state that a high-rated local news show could produce as much as 60 percent of an individual station's profits. In 80 percent of the TV markets, local news drew a bigger audience than the network newscast carried on the same station, and, in fourteen out of the top thirty-three, news rated in the top ten of all shows, national or local, carried on the station.*

At three-fourths of the nation's commercial stations, news budgets and staffs had been increased. The typical local newscast was no longer a thirty-minute rip-and-read time filler, but an elaborately equipped, manned, and presented operation running, in many instances, an hour or more. News had never been so important, nor so well heeled. But, under such apparently favorable circumstances, was it allowed to do the best job it could?

In broadcasting's most profitable year the networks, anxious themselves to expand their evening news, had not been able to persuade their affiliates to permit an increase beyond the long-established thirty minutes. The aborting of the sixty-minute network news concept was one of the most disappointing episodes of the 1976–77 broadcast season. (See Chapter 1.)

Although the failure of hour-long network news was a major setback for the forces of responsible broadcasting, there were other ways that radio and TV's burgeoning wealth might have bolstered news and public affairs. In many instances they were ignored.

The regular weekly prime time commitment to broadcast journalism remained on two networks—ABC and NBC—at zero. At CBS for a few weeks, when the network put its ill-fated interview show "Who's Who" into Tuesday evening prime time, the commitment stood at two hours, the high-water mark for the seventies. "Who's Who," which was more expensive and supposedly less demanding of its audience than "Sixty Minutes,"† failed to attract the ratings that network programmers thought they would get opposite TV's two most popular shows—"Happy Days" and "LaVerne and Shirley."

"Which is like Dennis the Menace competing with Attila the Hun," said *New York Times* critic John Leonard in a highly favorable review of the new hour. "The outcome is not in doubt," he added cynically.

*At WBTV, Charlotte, N.C., fourteen out of the top twenty shows in the February–March 1977 ratings were news and public affairs. "Sixty Minutes" rated second only to "The Waltons" as the market's favorite network program.
†The "Sixty Minutes" budget was reported to be less than half the $330,000 per hour which CBS was currently spending on entertainment shows.

His colleague John O'Connor was more sanguine. "CBS News is offering a clear alternative for viewers not hooked on inane situation comedies," he wrote in his critique. "If audience acceptance is encouraging, the make-up of both prime time schedules and network news departments could be radically altered. Some NBC executives are already musing aloud about the possibility of the 'Today' format expanding into a prime time slot."

"The fate of 'Who's Who,' " O'Connor affirmed, "could turn into the most significant TV story of 1977."

Despite the best CBS and three highly accomplished reporters—Dan Rather, Barbara Howar, and Charles Kuralt—could do for it, after just twenty times on the air "Who's Who" disappeared at midsummer 1977. Once again, "Sixty Minutes" was the solitary prime time network news hour on TV.*

Although the other two networks made no solid prime time news commitments, NBC announced that it was moving its lively TV journal "Weekend" from late Saturday to the early 6 P.M. Sunday slot, where CBS's "Sixty Minutes" had waited for several seasons before it moved forward into prime time. Again, the affiliates objected and the network reneged, at least for another season.

ABC had upped its news budget by 25 percent and taken a number of steps to dramatize the network's new commitment to broadcast journalism. One was the guarantee of a monthly airing for its award-winning "Close-Up" series of documentaries, which had been cut back by half in the less prosperous year of 1975. Despite the network promise, the Close-Ups tended to be clustered outside the month-long rating sweeps, and most of those aired lacked the impact and courage of the original series.

Counterparts to "Close-Up" on the other networks did not do any better. Thanks again to predictably low ratings and the sweeps, CBS managed to get only nine "CBS Reports" on the air during the 1976–77 season. This low score led to rumors that Bill Moyers, brought over from public TV to replace Dan Rather as anchorman, was unhappy and thinking of leaving "because of underwork." Moyers stayed on, but admirers of CBS's decade-long series of extended TV essays were distressed to hear that management was thinking of a revised magazine format, which could spell the beginning of the end for the one-hour documentary on the network which had brought it

*As consolation, CBS promised that during the 1977 football season the NFL games would no longer be permitted to appropriate "Sixty Minutes" air time, an occurrence which frequently in the past had reduced the network prime time news commitment even below the one-hour-per-week level.

to its finest flower. NBC's periodic hour-long prime time Reports made it on the air just ten times during the same period.

Local stations, many for the first time boasting budgets and staffs capable of putting together a respectable half-hour- or hour-long TV essay, chose the less demanding magazine and minidocumentary format.

The most spectacular expenditure and the most massively reported event of the broadcast journalism year was ABC's hiring of NBC newswoman Barbara Walters at 1 million dollars per annum. (See Chapter 2.) Of this provocative gesture, Karl Meyer, TV critic for *Saturday Review,* said:

> My wish for Miss Walters is that she will use the influence of her new position to improve network performance. Her contract stipulates that she will produce a series of ABC documentaries. I propose two topics. One would be a program called "How Much Is Enough?" in which Americans of all social strata would be asked about the amount of money they need for a fulfilled life. A second topic would be the economics of television. It would be a realized dream if television turned its cameras on itself and posed fully, fairly, and comprehensively the issues raised by the privileged positions the networks have in American life.

Mr. Meyer's suggestions might, with equal aptness, have been directed to either of the other networks. A six-column story in the *New York Times* in June 1977 promised a wild and extravagant broadcast season ahead. "This is the year of the jugular . . . scrapping for every time period every single night." Over 1 billion dollars would be spent for prime time entertainment programming alone.

"While the intensified battle for ratings promises to treat viewers to a greater array of glittering mass appeal programs than usually occurs in a season, its effects may be deleterious to types of programs that cannot be expected to draw massive audiences." Exactly what that meant was made clear in a quote from Irwin Segelstein, executive vice-president of NBC programming, who explained that since every week would be a separate ratings race, "this might mean fewer news programs in prime time, because no one will want to give away a single time period to the competition."

Certainly, of the 100 hours of special prime time events that Mr. Segelstein's own network had announced two weeks earlier to spearhead its drive for ratings supremacy, none could properly be labeled "news and public affairs."

If one believed Mr. Segelstein, the good news (record profits) for broadcasting in general meant bad news (still less prime time) for the electronic journalist in particular. In less affluent days, when profits had been disappointing or when government agencies suggested regulatory action that might limit network money making, news operations were the first to be threatened and curtailed. The complementary assumption had been that when things looked up again the news would benefit. Now it seemed that prosperity, far from promoting news and public affairs, could actually militate against it.

The position of broadcast journalism, embedded as it had always been in an enterprise devoted principally to entertainment and commerce, was ambiguous at best. To industry executives the recent success of TV and radio news with audience and advertisers alike was half vindication, half embarrassment. To news departments it was even more of a mixed blessing, inviting unwanted attention and intrusion by a management charmed by the money news suddenly was making. Add to this the fact that month by month the big news more and more frequently had a direct bearing on big business, an area of high interest to broadcast journalism's patrons and proprietors, and you had the potential for big trouble.

Speaking of the press as a whole, British journalist Henry Fairlie commented in the *New Republic:*

> The root of almost every weakness of the American press just now will be found to lie not with individual journalists, although some of them seem to have become careless of the standards of their profession, but with a management whose concern with profit has become no different from that of any other corporation.

In the *Wall Street Journal* James Ring Adams wrote:

> Three of the most profitable companies in America, the commercial networks, produce a steady stream of news reports, documentaries and detective shows in which business men play the heavies.

The confrontation between business and broadcast journalism, on and off the air, obviously could produce a string of problems for electronic journalists that would make the Watergate years seem clear-cut and easy to sort out by comparison.

2 • Pope Barbara and the Greening of ABC

AT APPROXIMATELY 8:35 A.M. on April 23, 1976, Barbara Walters squared herself with the cameras on NBC's "Today" show as she had morning after morning for a dozen years and began to read in her sharp-edged Eastern seaboard twang. "It is rare for a newsperson to have a story about herself. After considerable soul searching on the most important decision of my professional career, I have decided to accept the very challenging offer of the American Broadcasting Company. ABC has asked me to co-anchor the ABC Evening News with Harry Reasoner as well as to host a number of special prime time interview programs and to make additional contributions to other programs. Few newsmen could turn down such an opportunity, and for a newswoman it is unique and most exciting."

Self-serving and inconsequential as this item might seem, Ms. Walters was fully justified in including it among the morning's headlines. In a career which had contained its share of scoops and journalistic dazzle, this was probably the most significant news, so far as the broadcast industry was concerned, that she had ever put on the air. But only the tip of its import was evident in her brief, carefully worded statement.

Ms. Walters, who had been around TV for over two decades ending as the most conspicuous presence on NBC's top-rated early morning strip, had become a full-time network anchor person. She had arrived at this eminence with a contract in her fist which made her the highest-priced piece of talent in journalism, at $1 million per annum guaranteed for five years.

"I know that my friends here at NBC, and you, my friends out there, understand my decision and wish me luck," Walters wound up her statement. "Now let's go on with this program." Fade out and into a fertilizer commercial and then, sixty seconds later, Walters was back, selling us Revlon's Touch and Glo moisturizer, "the intelligent make-up." One good reason, certainly, for moving on.

Ms. Walters's decision, however, involved more than getting away from the reading of commercials (a form of primitive TV hucksterism that "Today" was one of the last network news and public affairs programs to require its reporters to engage in), or, for that matter, a million a year.* Her dramatic transition from one network to another summed up a great deal of what is happening in the world of TV and particularly its news departments these days. What it conveyed to anyone with a concern for broadcast journalism was exciting and conceivably ominous.

There were the positive aspects of the announcement. Walters's elevation meant that finally the intelligent, effective newswoman was being given, if not her due (conventional wisdom said that, however you cut it, no newsperson was worth $1 million per annum), then at least the remuneration, exposure, and responsibility long denied to all women in her profession and to all but a handful of men. (For the overall picture of women in broadcast journalism see the report on pages 151–67.)

Walters's arrival at ABC also could be interpreted as an earnest of that network's growing prosperity and confidence as well as of a larger commitment in a field, news and public affairs, where traditionally it ran a lackluster third. The bold new commitment was bound to stimulate others in the highly competitive network news field.

The promises emanating from the ABC news department accompanying the Walters hiring were impressive indeed. It was upping its news budget by 25 percent which, according to available figures, meant ABC news and public affairs would have several million more to play with than either of the rival networks.† Elton Rule, ABC president, announced "a major capital spending program for network electronic news gathering equipment over the next five years." News personnel would also be increased by one quarter, adding strength to both editorial and production staffs. This would include twenty-four additional writers and news producers in Los Angeles, Chicago, Washington, New York, and London and nine correspondents stationed around the globe.

Some of the other circumstances surrounding Ms. Walters's new employment, however, were less encouraging.

Most conspicuous was the response of the news media themselves.

*Big salaries had become the hallmark of ABC in 1976. Jumping from third to first place in the ratings, its top executives had received huge raises (up to 273 percent) and two of them were on *Business Week*'s list of the ten highest paid U.S. business leaders. Elton Rule, ABC president, stood fifth with $1.23 million and Leonard Goldenson, chairman, seventh with $1.06 million.

†News budgets were carefully guarded secrets, but 1975 estimates published in *Time* magazine put them at $47 million for CBS and NBC, $44 million for ABC.

Never before had the publicity value of electronic journalism been so dramatically acknowledged. Following weeks of rumors and inside stories, Ms. Walters's announcement of her decision, modest though it was, was greeted with headlines in newspapers coast to coast, and, most impressive of all, all three network news programs carried items on her change-over, a distinction TV seldom granted, short of death or scandal, to its own. It was true that Walter Cronkite for years past had stood at the top of the polls indicating the high esteem in which Americans held him, and local TV news figures in most of the fifty states had become the focus of personality cults promoted by their employers in the hopes of increased ratings and profits. But Walters set a new mark for coast-to-coast pan-media visibility.

Not all the commotion was friendly. *Newsweek*'s cover story struck a note which was echoed elsewhere. "To many, Walters' celebrity price tag raised disturbing questions about the distinction between news biz and show biz. Even the industry's most stalwart defenders were upset by the deal's 'that's entertainment' quality."

Richard Salant, president of CBS News, the one commercial network news department not directly concerned in the negotiations—and so, presumably, spared strong emotional involvement—said, "I'm really depressed as hell. This isn't journalism. This is a minstrel show. If this kind of circus atmosphere continues and I have to join in it, I'll quit first."

Salant's senior savant, Eric Sevareid, devoted his evening commentary to the matter. "The trouble now in TV news is that the reporter has been forced to cross the line and has joined those who are constantly reported about. . . . Inescapably, this [TV] is the most personal form of journalism. So the struggle has been to keep the packaging from dominating the contents of the package . . . and the intramural worry is that maybe the struggle has been lost."*

Senator John Pastore, head of the Senate Communications Subcommittee for twenty-one years before he turned the position over to Senator Ernest Hollings in January 1977, said, "The networks come before my committee and shed crocodile tears and complain about

---

*Actually, although Sevareid had spent all his thirty-eight years in broadcasting at CBS, talent slippage in network news departments was no novelty. In earlier switchovers CBS had lost to ABC two of its ranking male newsmen—Howard K. Smith in 1961 and Harry Reasoner in 1970. At the time of Sevareid's commentary there were persistent rumors that NBC's anchor man John Chancellor was being wooed by CBS as Sevareid's own replacement when he retired at the end of November 1977. When Chancellor signed on again at NBC, Harry Reasoner was mentioned as the hottest prospect. Later Bill Moyers, spirited away from public TV, was offered this job and turned it down. And so it went.

their profits. Then they pay this little girl a million dollars. That's five times better than the President of the United States makes. It's ridiculous."

Charles B. Seib, ombudsman and internal critic for the Washington *Post*, who had seen two neophyte reporters on his staff become overnight millionaires and the heroes of a hit movie, said: "We might as well face it. The line between the news business and show business has been erased forever." His colleague Sander Vanocur, former NBC correspondent and, for the time being, TV columnist for the *Post*, added, "Walters has not done anything to television journalism that it had not already done to itself."

A year later Vanocur had signed up as vice-president with Walters's new network at twice his *Post* salary to head ABC's recently established Washington unit for political and investigative reporting.

And what did the network Walters abandoned have to say?

An NBC news executive who asked not to be identified told *Broadcasting* magazine, "We have all learned a lot from this painful and embarrassing experience, and that is that we can't do business with journalists as we would with Redd Foxx.* It is important to deal on a professional basis with journalists so that the inmates don't end up running the asylum."

In the heat of the final day of negotiations, an NBC "spokesman" told the press that NBC had withdrawn its contract offer because of the "circus atmosphere. It got to the point where it was getting unseemly. There were things that one would associate with a movie queen, not a journalist, and we had second thoughts." There were references to a hairdresser, limousine, and press agent.

Walters made it clear that she had turned down a million-dollar offer from NBC in a clear decision in favor of ABC. The deciding factor was not money, or a hairdresser, limo, or press agent—she had had them all along—but the "unique and exciting" place alongside Reasoner on the evening news.

Walter Cronkite, perhaps farther above the battle than any of his network colleagues, had an interesting reaction to the affair which he related to a meeting of CBS affiliates in Los Angeles in May 1976.†

The Barbara Walters news did shake me up at first, as it did us all. There was a first wave of nausea, the sickening sensation

---

*Mr. Foxx, star of "Sanford and Son," NBC's highest-rated series, had been lured over to ABC three weeks earlier with guarantees of his own comedy-variety show and development money for other projects for his production company.
†For the full text see Appendix I.

that we were going under, that all of our efforts to hold network television news aloof from show business had failed. But after sleeping on the matter, with more sober, less hysterical reflection, I came to a far less gloomy view.

Perhaps thinking about his own salary, the most generous in TV news until Walters had come along, Cronkite saw some justification other than show biz for such jumbo pay checks.

What we on-air broadcasters do comprises a dimension beyond the skills required by the newspaper reporter, writer and editor. If we do our jobs well, we do things—reporting, writing, editing—as well or better than the print journalist, but beyond that we have to have special skills, talents, if you please, to present our material through the spoken word and, in a visual medium, frequently to think on our feet and to be right the first time with no editor imposed as a protective buffer between us and the public.

We must be able without reference to written works to pull from our heads the background of a given story, complete with the historical reference when relevant. We have to balance the moral and the immoral, the appropriate and the grossly inappropriate, the acceptable and the offensive, the right and the wrong, even as facts are tumbling in upon us, and there are no second guesses. With a certain degree of immodesty, I suggest that those of us who can do that are worth a little more than the print journalist . . . or, perhaps, a lot more.

In this attempt to justify Walters's price tag as well as his own, Cronkite had given an eloquent picture of the ideal TV anchor person —a picture that resembled few practitioners of the art currently visible.

Indeed, *that* turned out to be the burden of Cronkite's message. Making it clear he did not include Walters in his stricture, he went on:

What I do have some problem understanding is why an anchor person who does *not* have those qualifications still draws down such large compensation.* In fact, I wonder if those stations that hire the young and beautiful, but inexperienced and calloused, to front their news broadcasts are not getting ripped off.

---

*In 1976 pay for anchor people in the top twenty-five local TV markets was reported to have hit the $200,000 level.

Broadcasting magazine's editorial comment summed up the Walters affair as accurately as any. "Whatever else Miss Walters' million dollar standard means, it bespeaks the expanding role of journalism in the television business. Any time a network makes a commitment on that scale, news has become a principal commodity."

Ed Murrow, who set many of the standards for broadcast news practice, had said two decades earlier, "If news is to be regarded as a commodity, only acceptable when salable, then I don't care what you call it, I say it isn't news." To the news purist who attempted to follow in Murrow's footsteps, some of the circumstances of Barbara Walters's arrival at ABC were particularly disturbing. They could be interpreted as proof that network news departments, which had heretofore doggedly withstood the intrusion of outside consultants and entertainment-oriented network executives, might not be able to hold out much longer.

The idea of an anchor woman, innocuous enough in itself, arose back in 1974 when Av Westin, then vice-president in charge of ABC news and public affairs, was seeking a means to attract favorable attention to his low-rated evening newscast. By the time it was instrumented, Westin had resigned. Among the reported reasons for his departure: the cutting back by half of the much praised monthly "Close-Up" documentary series; the hiring of news director Steve Skinner, formerly of KGO San Francisco, the ABC-owned and -operated station, famous for its "kicker, guts, and orgasm" news formula; and the arrival on the network scene of consultant Frank Magid to doctor the network's ailing "A.M. America."

A year after Westin's departure the network returned to the idea of a female anchor, this time reinforced by Magid research which told them that 46 percent of the American public would like to see a woman heading a network newscast (41 percent did not care, and only 13 percent admitted to an outright preference for a male). Walters topped the list of possible prospects, first because, thanks to a series of headline-producing interviews with statesmen, politicians, and big name personalities, she was undoubtedly America's best-known newswoman; second because, if ABC got her away from NBC and the "Today" show, it might weaken the competition for ABC's own program, now in a livelier and more "entertaining" incarnation, called "Good Morning, America."

It was the kind of double whammy news consultants delighted in.

By now, according to industry reports, two more big guns had arrived on the news scene, heavy artillery who traditionally had no

business there: ABC Television Division president Frederick Pierce*
and Fred Silverman, ABC's new entertainment president, the man
responsible for bagging Redd Foxx. A substantial portion of Walters's
$1 million salary was reported to be coming out of the entertainment
division's budget.

The presence of ABC's high-powered entertainment brass and entertainment money gave substance to the fear that the network news
department was being taken over, if not by the inmates, then by an
extraneous and conceivably dangerous force.

Furthermore, Sheehan was reported absent from the table when
ABC faced Walters's representative, the William Morris Agency,
whose specialty was top Hollywood and Broadway talent. At the end
of the negotiations not only was Walters hired by Pierce and Silverman, but Sheehan's second-class citizenship as head of the news division was made clear. By this time the ABC story had taken on a
broader focus in which Barbara Walters was only one among several
protagonists.

In January 1977 Pierce was given overt responsibility for news as
well as entertainment, a bracketing that no other network heretofore
had risked. By the end of the season Pierce had moved Sheehan aside
to make room for his protégé, Roone Arledge, the phenomenally
successful president of ABC sports, who had no news experience.

In announcing his appointment of Arledge as president of ABC
News, Pierce said: "We want to change the perception of viewers so
that when anything happens they will turn to ABC first. . . . Mr.
Arledge will be able to accomplish this because he will bring a different perspective to the network's news . . . through the eye of a
production expert with journalistic leanings."

When Arledge said he intended to hire "the brightest, most talented, uncompromising, hard-nosed reporters available anywhere in
the world," partisans of old-style TV news were not particularly
reassured. *Broadcasting* magazine reported that "much of the press
reaction since Mr. Arledge's appointment has conjectured that the
Arledge style of sports coverage—with its flamboyant announcers and
technical gimmickry—might turn the news into a vaudeville act along
the lines of the operation depicted in the movie *Network.* " (See pages
123–24.)

With the scene thus set for fiasco, Arledge proceeded to rehire Av
Westin and engage Sander Vanocur, both news veterans with substantial credentials. They were followed by Catherine Mackin, NBC's

*At this time Pierce's concern was supposed to be strictly entertainment. Sheehan, as
at the other networks, reported directly to the big boss, Elton Rule, thus bypassing the
crasser aspects of networking.

crack Washington reporter; Wallace Westfeldt, onetime executive producer of NBC's Nightly News; PBS newswoman Lynn Scherr; and Sylvia Chase, the writer-reporter-producer responsible for CBS's first-class daytime "Magazine." There were rumors that Daniel Schorr, late of CBS, and David Frost, fresh from his encounter with Richard Nixon, would not be far behind.

"I am convinced that it cannot be done with cosmetics," Arledge told the *New York Times*'s Les Brown. "The news habits of people are hard to break. We have to first build a solid professional organization. One day something will happen and we'll be the best at covering it, and people will discover that we are the number one place to turn for news."

Already, Arledge reported he was beating the other networks to some stories. He was also better prepared and staying longer at presidential news conferences. ABC was suddenly the only network to do a prime time special after the New York blackout, to preempt regular programming to cover the return of the dead and wounded from the Korean helicopter incident, to carry President Carter live from Yazoo City, Mississippi. There were large ABC presences at the tragic Beverly Hills Supper Club fire in May 1977 and covering James Earl Ray's escape the following month and in Holland to cover the South Moluccan terrorists. On the other hand, there were rumors of dissatisfaction among the old guard at the sensational treatment of certain items and the new prominence accorded to Geraldo Rivera, a former local news star, who had had a network entertainment contract since 1974.

"I see it this way," said Arledge. "If all three networks delivered the same news in the same way, it would get down to which anchorman the viewer likes best. That's a contest Walter Cronkite would win."

"There's no reason," added Westin, "to imagine that in this day of advanced technology and instant communications and satellites, and tape and all of that, that we need tie the basic conveyor of news, that is the anchorman, to a seat in New York or Washington."

Which brought the subject back to anchor woman Walters, where all the excitement and activity had begun.

On her premier appearance on the ABC Evening News Walters had addressed her new audience:

> Most of you watching tonight are loyal viewers of Harry's and of ABC News. I hope, too, that some of you are friends from my early morning days at NBC. (I've missed you.)
> And there may be others of you tuning in for the first time out

of curiosity . . . drawn by the rather-too-much attention and overblown publicity given to my new duties, and my hourly wage.

It is to you that I'd like to take a moment for a personal note.

Harry and I are going to bring you the essential information you need to cope with the world today. We are going to do a news program.

I hope, too, to give you a closer look at the people who are the shapers of these news events. I find interviews a way to do this, and I will do them on this program when they are relevant.

Also, I'd like to pause, from time to time, as we shower news items on you, to say: "Wait a minute, what does this mean to my life . . . to yours?"

Whether it's understanding why every television news program gives the Dow Jones Industrial Averages and what it means to you even if you don't own any stock . . . or trying to understand the differences between the problems of Rhodesia and South Africa. . . . whether it's tying the national and international news more closely to its impact on your life or the quality of life we all hope to enjoy. And if some of the issues that are of particular concern to women have been neglected, I'll try to deal with those.

Which reminds me: People have asked if I want to be called an anchorman, or anchorwoman, or anchorperson, or even, as our producer refers to us, anchorhuman.

Titles aren't important. What is important is that Harry and I will try to bring you the best darn news program on the air. We hope if you've watched tonight out of curiosity, you'll return to watch us tomorrow out of conviction.

The sincerity of Walters's remarks was soon tested. The curiosity seekers did turn up in considerable numbers for her first appearance, at least in New York, Los Angeles and Chicago, where audience shares of 31, 28, and 36, much higher than usual, were reported. However, the first rating sweep to include the new ABC News was disappointing, and after two months there was still no noticeable change in the size of the audience. By then Walters had delivered several hundred news items, and conducted more than a dozen on-air interviews. There had been some loosening up of the newscast's format. Walters interviews and some softer features resulted in less hard news. "I said to the people at ABC when they hired me, 'Don't expect me to be a wonder woman,' " Walters commented. "My presence alone is not going to cause people to change their twenty-year viewing habits with television news."

As for the ratings, in the fourth month there were indications of a growth in viewership among the eighteen- to forty-nine-year olds, male and female, although there was still no noticeable increase in total audience.

The lack of audience growth was made all the more conspicuous by the fact that elsewhere on its schedule the network was having its most sensational year. Furthermore, since 1976 it had added sixteen new stations to its list of primary and secondary affiliates. Even more stations were expected to shift to ABC if their news picture brightened.*

There were other explanations for the lack of audience growth— rumors of a feud between Reasoner and Walters which supposedly made viewers uncomfortable; a grass roots resistance to the Walters big-city style, which some labeled "abrasive and cold." A strike of camera and sound men at ABC's New York studios did not help.

The most important reason probably was the one given by Arledge when he arrived on the scene. "A lot of people tuned in to watch and they didn't like the program. They have to like the product when they get there." Try as it would, ABC was still not delivering a first-class newscast.

Outside the evening news, Walters herself was doing much better, at least so far as ratings were concerned.

The first Barbara Walters Special, which included visits with Barbra Streisand and her consort Jon Peters as well as President-elect and Mrs. Carter, with a stopover at Walters's own pad, drew high ratings and the following comment from *Variety.* "If this is a preview of future Walters specials (three more are due this season), ABC may be getting a bargain at about $125,000 per hour show, but she may be doing irremedial damage to the reputation she's trying to cultivate as a journalist."

Barbara's fellow broadcaster Morley Safer was even harsher. On the CBS radio network he said:

> The interview with Governor Carter is really what ended Ms. Walters' brief career as a journalist, and placed her firmly in the ranks of—what? The Merv Griffins and Johnny Carsons? Well, sort of. Anyway, at the end of the Carter interview, Ms. Walters said, "Be wise with us. Be good to us." There she was, the first American female pope, blessing a new cardinal. . . . Apart from anything else, it is as if Mr. Carter had just become Louis XIV,

*The primary affiliate score for November 1977 stood at 215 for NBC, 201 for CBS and 195 for ABC.

and that without Pope Barbara's admonition, he might be dumb with us, and mean to us. . . . Perhaps it was a sense of financial superiority that made Barbara's benediction irresistible.

Safer's lofty dismissal, with its slight taste of sour grapes, was premature. Walters's one-hour interview with Fidel Castro (on Cuban TV it ran a full five hours), although it did not pull down the jumbo ratings of her first special, demonstrated her professionalism. Nor did the interviews she continued to deliver within the limited confines of the evening news indicate that she had lost her firm, persistent touch. Indeed, there were claims that she had already had an impact on the proportions of the news on the other networks. Anchormen Cronkite and Chancellor were reported increasing the number of interviews they engaged in from night to night.* NBC was doing some drastic tinkering with its format and had reinstated David Brinkley as Washington-based co-anchor with John Chancellor.

However, the most notable impact of Walters's new job as network anchor person seemed ironically to be the diminishing of the high regard in which that position was held. Richard Wald, then president of NBC Network News, had hailed a new era even before Walters's departure. "What we have always come to regard as anchor men will not work the way they work now. That is, our traditional sense of what a network anchor man is: in effect, the all-wise, all-seeing mouth, that person who knows everything and will tell it to you. That person really never existed, but because you now know the world to be as complicated as indeed it is, he can't exist in the popular fantasy. It may be that Walter Cronkite is the last of the great talkers.

"From here on," Wald continued, "anchor people will be Switching Central, not Ex Cathedra Central."

Before Walters's first season was over, Arledge, her new boss, was agreeing in word and deed. "The word anchor suggests stationary positioning," said Arledge, "when it should denote a top reporter. I don't believe anchor people serve a good purpose if they just sit in the studio and read the teleprompter."

Although he emphatically denied that he had any intention of downgrading Walters or Reasoner, other members of the Arledge team began to share the opening credits equally with the two anchors. Some evenings as many as five portraits were lined up on the TV screen during the introductory billboard. Before the summer was over

---

*Walters scored her most conspicuous scoop in November 1977, when she got Begin and Sadat together in front of TV cameras for the first time, beating out Walter Cronkite by a good two hours and John Chancellor by half a day.

Walters was being asked to give up her sedentary position for street reporting. And evening after evening the Reasoner and Walters total time allotment was half that given to Cronkite. The seat which had been the "unique" and "most exciting" reason for Walters to change networks, if not actually being pulled out from under her, was certainly being moved away from stage center.

Some months before he was hired back to cope with the multiple problems of ABC's Evening News, Av Westin, who in the interim had been free-lancing as a news adviser and documentarian, had commented: "The danger is that if ABC's ratings go up but its journalism does not improve, they will simply sustain the mediocrity they are now producing. And then the pressure will be on the other networks to go cosmetic. If Barbara works and personality takes over, TV news would become more entertainment and less journalism."

From that point of view Barbara's failure to deliver the ratings might be considered a blessing in disguise both to the journalistic profession and her own career.

However, Westin's evaluation of Walters's move and its significance was neither complete nor fair. First, it seemed to downgrade her abilities as a journalist, which were considerable. It also ignored, as did most of the accounts of Walters's disappointing performance, an element in the negotiations which had been crucial from the start.

Far from biting off more than she could chew, Walters had been denied the portion which in her mind gave her move its basic logic —the first hour-long network evening newscast in history. If Walters had been given what she had been promised when she made her big deal, she might have emerged not just as the nation's first female million-dollar anchor person, but as the heroine of a major breakthrough in TV news. Her disappointment and that of broadcast journalism were the same. Once more the need for profits had subverted good intentions; commercialism had defeated those who would serve and inform the public.

3 • The Sixty-Minute Hour

AT THE CLOSING of Walters's million-dollar contract, and apparently as a decisive condition to it, the American Broadcasting Company had indicated its intention of expanding its evening news, certainly to forty-five minutes, and more likely to a full hour. Thus ABC hoped to give its new anchor woman time to display her particular talent for the extended interview, and make back from the additional commercial income some of the money it was paying out. At the same time it would be stealing a march on CBS and NBC.

Expansion of the evening news had been a prime objective of TV journalists for many years. The last increase had taken place in the early 1960s, when network news had made the leap from fifteen minutes to a half hour. Since that extension the networks' evening news programs had assumed their preeminent place in American journalism. What a further expansion might mean to the conscientious broadcast newsperson was the subject of an eloquent speech by Walter Cronkite at the Radio and Television News Directors' Convention in December 1976.* This Miami statement, bracketed with Cronkite's Century City speech to the CBS affiliates seven months earlier, added up to a remarkably frank and accurate summary of the present shortcomings and possibilities of U.S. electronic journalism.

As will be seen in this and later chapters, the speech drew a more enthusiastic response from outside the broadcast community than from within.

Cronkite saw one primary flaw in the activity that gave him wealth and prestige:

> . . . the inadvertent and perhaps inevitable distortion that results through the hyper-compression we all are forced to exert to fit one hundred pounds of news into the one-pound sack that we are given to fill each night. . . .
>
> The cumulative effect is devastating, eating away at our credibility. Perhaps it will take a while for the masses to catch on— they usually are the last to know the truth. But among the informed, the opinion leaders, those whose views eventually will

---

*For the full text see Appendix II.

influence the masses, the awareness is spreading—the awareness that our abbreviated versions of the news are suspect. They or their friends and associates have been victimized by our truncated reports, and they spread the word.

. . . we fall far short of presenting all, or even a goodly part, of the news each day that a citizen would need to intelligently exercise his franchise in this democracy. So as he depends more and more on us, presumably the depth of knowledge of the average man diminishes. This clearly can lead to disaster in a democracy.

Cronkite saw more than one way out:

There are some remedies available to us. Of course, we could quit entirely. Simply admit erroneously that we cannot do an adequate daily news broadcast, turn the time back to the quiz shows and the situation comedies, and force the people seeking news back to their newspapers, also too frequently inadequate.

Or we could stop somewhat short of suicide and drop the pretense of the daily news summary by substituting a daily magazine format—one or two minidocumentaries in the fashion that "Sixty Minutes" does so well; backgrounders and special takeouts on past or future stories.

But both of these solutions are a denial of the great potential of television as a daily news medium and hence an abdication of the responsibility of those of us lucky enough to be in the business. They would represent an artificial blackout imposed by those of us journalists too honest to go on as we have, and on the other hand, too gutless to fight for and help engineer the one viable solution.

That solution quite simply is, for the network newscasts, more time, and for the local newscasts with enough time, a better utilization of it. In the latter case, in many of your cases, I think that comprises doing what you, as experienced news directors, would like to be doing rather than what consultants or non-news oriented station managers believe you should be doing. In other words, it means covering the meaningful, the genuinely important, relevant and significant news of your communities—city hall, county courts, the state house—whether there is a picture story there or not, whether the resulting story can be told in twenty seconds or not.

For the networks it means primarily: give us at least a two-pound sack for our hundred pounds of news each night. Now that will not be enough. There is no way we can ask the public to sit still in front of the box long enough to get *all* the news it needs. We always will be a complementary medium to print for those who would be fully informed.

But with another half hour, by doubling our time, we could take a long stride toward eliminating distortion through over-compression. We would not have many more items, would not present features and extraneous interviews, but we would take a little more time with each item—enough extra time for the explanatory phrase, the "why" and the "how" as well as the "who," "what," "when," and "where."

In his pitch for a sixty-minute early evening newscast, Cronkite conveyed at the same time clearly and simply the central challenges facing TV journalism at network and local levels. The networks, for all their money and expertise, did not allow themselves sufficient air time to do the job. The local stations, frequently with more time than they knew how to use, would for the most part skimp on resources. On both the local and network levels an opportunity was being missed. Despite the newfound willingness of the networks to provide an additional early evening half hour, the sixty-minute coast-to-coast newscast proved as unattainable as ever.*

If Walters's hiring demonstrated the mixed motives and strong-arm methods that could be involved these days in high-level network news and public affairs negotiations, what happened to the push for sixty-minute network evening news revealed how timid and easily discouraged these communications giants could be when profits, their own and others, seemed threatened.

As soon as ABC had made known its intention to go with an extended evening newscast as soon as possible, the other two networks had quickly spread the word that they had similar plans.

One-hour network news was given a cautious boost on May 4, 1976, when Arthur Taylor, then president of CBS, addressed his affiliates in Los Angeles. In the process, he gave a rare and revealing corporate acknowledgment of what TV could and should be doing, and wasn't.

Now let me deal with a matter where there are many concerns, and differing opinions. And I want to make sure you know that we are sensitive to your concerns. It is an issue in which there are commercial problems, financial difficulties, scheduling frustrations, regulatory issues. Despite all these problems, the goal of expansion of the network evening news is a worthy one for this industry. Let me tell you why I believe this is a worthy goal.

*No one seemed to count the excellent one-hour CBS Morning News as an extended network newscast. Its low ratings and clearances (thirty-two CBS affiliates refused it air time) made it all but invisible in the competitive network picture.

We live today in an incredibly complicated, incredibly fast moving world—a world in which a shot fired in Lebanon, a call for freedom in Africa, and, of course, a vote taken in Washington, can and does affect the lives of each one of your constituents —the people of your communities—whether that community is large or small.

You are the link, the strong, fast, and reliable link between your viewers and that world, so far away, and yet, because of you, so very near . . . that world of such urgent importance to the citizens of every community. I believe, and I think you believe, that it is your responsibility, and ours—our responsibility together—to bring the events of this wide world into sharp, clear focus to all communities. Communities which look to television as their major source of news. We are proud we provide this service, but with that pride comes a responsibility—to do the job in the best interests of the public we serve!

We do part of the job today—although it has been said, with perhaps some truth, that we provide not much more than a good headline service.

Why should we have a goal of providing more? Not for us. Not even for you. But for the man, the woman, who *must* know more if he is to live more.

Television has brought the world to the living room, but that is only part of the story. The world that it presents must be more than a superficial one. It must try to make clear the complexities of our time.

I hope it will be possible for CBS and its affiliates to work together to achieve this goal.

Taylor's call for sacrifice and high-mindedness had a cool reception. A more overt plea by Ms. Walters at the ABC affiliates meeting three weeks later generated even less enthusiasm. An advance poll tipped a negative response and a count of hands later in the convention showed 132 out of 156 affiliates attending opposed the change.

Nonetheless, according to trade publications, extended news was "the principal topic of debate" at all three affiliate conventions in the spring of 1976. The *New York Times* reported that "informal polls have found that roughly one-fourth of the 600-odd stations affiliated with ABC, CBS, and NBC concede it would be in the public interest for the evening news to run longer than a half hour." The number of those who felt such an expansion would be in their own interests turned out to be even lower.

The reason for affiliate reluctance was, as Mr. Taylor had anticipated, commercial, financial, and regulatory. Estimates as to the increased revenue to the networks from a one-hour evening news program five nights a week went as high as $100 million. Most of that, affiliates assumed, would come out of their own pockets. Also, along with the money, they would lose control of another half hour of prime time five days a week at an inconvenient and lucrative juncture in their schedules.

What the networks planned to offer the stations in exchange was ill defined. Would it be commercial positions in and around the appropriated half hour? Additional compensation for carrying the programs? Time elsewhere in the schedule to make up for that relinquished? No one was quite sure.

All through the spring and summer of 1976 comments from station managers were mostly negative.

James G. Babb, Jr., managing director of WBTV Charlotte, N.C., one of the nation's top news stations, said, "The networks are going to have to make adjustments or they'll have a royal battle on their hands. I've heard some stations say they're prepared not to clear network news—and might develop their own international news organizations. Many large group owners have embryo news organizations and know how to run an international news service. Of course, it would be expensive and time consuming and initially not as good, but it could be done."

Paul Raymon, secretary of the CBS Board of Affiliates and vice-president and general manager of WAGA-TV Atlanta, said, "It doesn't appeal to me worth a damn. . . . This would be a direct infringement on my local news programming."

John Conomikes, chairman of the board of governors of ABC affiliates and general manager of WTAE-TV Pittsburgh, said, "The affiliates have not heard any overbearing cry from the public for more news in the early evening." This perception seemed confirmed by news consultants McHugh and Hoffman, who despite an avowed enthusiasm for broadcast journalism, released figures in the spring of 1977 which indicated that only 30 percent of their sample favored longer network news.

News directors were considerably more friendly to the idea than their bosses. Of those commenting to the DuPont Survey, 60 percent were enthusiastic, 28 percent negative, and 12 percent guarded. Some of the comments:

> It is incredible to me as a journalist that broadcasters (local and national) have failed to assume this small sacrifice in profitability in order to increase the effectiveness of network news operations.
>
> *Rockford, Ill.*

. . . only if the networks compensate the local affiliates so local news won't suffer, and in some cases, so local news can too increase its time. If the networks' motives are pure (only to better inform the American public) then the networks should not object to the local affiliates' insistence that an increase in network time must not be made at the expense of local time.

Tulsa, Okla.

They should have done it five years ago.

Quincy, Ill.

Television should devote more time to news and education and less to entertainment.

Eau Claire, Wis.

I would welcome a 45-minute or an hour network newscast. There's no way the nets can do an adequate job with the time they now have. The news consumer ought to get the details he's missing now. Since TV is our major source of news, I should think having enough time adequately to inform the public would be of paramount importance to the people who make such decisions.

But as in most things with television, the public's right to know will take a back seat to local stations' greed for more money. They're probably right. They likely will make more from reruns of "Beverly Hillbillies" or "Get Smart" than from expanded network news.

Jonesboro, Ark.

I'm afraid the networks want to increase their news time at local stations' expense. They'll have to take our time to do it. But, in a pure sense, I'm for it.

Paducah, Ky.

If the networks would expand their coverage in a way that would better serve the information needs of the nation, I would be in favor of it. However, I am not convinced that would be the case. Secondly, expanded network news undercuts the economic base of my operation. And God knows I don't have enough money for the people and equipment I need now. So, I'm neutral.

Spokane, Wash.

Local news is better.

Miles City, Mont.

The networks persisted, CBS made a pilot of an hour-long newscast anchored by Walter Cronkite and sent it out over closed circuit TV to the affiliates in early August.* A second trial run was broadcast in October. The reaction, at least so far as CBS executives were concerned, was highly favorable.

NBC, reported to have offered Barbara Walters a part in a longer newscast if she would stay, was still sounding out stations as late as mid-September, promising the governing board of its affiliates at their November 1976 meeting a presentation of the network's "concept of a nightly news program which would not simply be an expansion of the present program but a program of revised form and scope." This would increase the hard news by four minutes, allow for backgrounding important stories, and add specialist reports from a variety of "back of the book" departments.

However, before NBC News had a chance to deliver its pitch for a bigger and better newscast, the network's top brass overruled the idea. "We decided," said a spokesman who announced in mid-October that all plans for an hour-long newscast had been shelved, "that it is wrong for us to impose our will on the member stations if they were so strongly against what we were trying to do. We felt we had to make an affirmative public announcement to that effect to convince them that we meant what we told them."

Instead of the persuasive presentation promised by the news department to the affiliates' board of delegates at their November meeting, the affiliates presented the network with a document commending NBC "on taking the leadership in deciding to drop consideration of expanding its Nightly News."

> The board fully appreciates the value of added news service and is aware of the constant need for cooperative planning in the network and local news and information services provided the public. However, we share the view of the great majority of television affiliates that expansion of "NBC Nightly News" in a time period programmed by affiliate stations would only have resulted in reduced local news programming, or certainly would have so negatively affected revenue bases that some local live or public service programming would have been impaired. The Board of Delegates congratulates NBC on its awareness of these problems, its consideration for the affiliate position, and its prompt and decisive action in the matter.

The announcement was timed so that ABC, which until that moment had been trying to convince its board of governors to go along with the plan for extended news, was undercut and gave up. Industry

*See Appendix III.

gossip said that timing of the NBC announcement was deliberately set for the night before the ABC meeting. "I hate to call this a stab in the back," said ABC News president William Sheehan, "but NBC has certainly hurt the cause."

"It's an awful blow," Richard Salant, president of CBS News, added.

And that was that. According to network president Taylor, the more that Americans must know in order "to live more," the more that would "make clear the complexities of our time" and avert "a disaster to democracy," would have to wait. The affiliates said no, and in the world of network presidents, given the kind of wildly competitive year they were embarked on, the affiliates had it their way.

Cronkite's plea for a two-pound sack of news, for all its honesty and eloquence, delivered as it was in mid-December, was a bit of Monday morning quarterbacking.

The thank-you note from NBC's affiliates had contained one particularly ironic and significant phrase, the one stating that expanded network news "would only have resulted in reduced local news programming or certainly would have so negatively affected revenue bases that some local live or public service programming would have been impaired." It was the same excuse and threat the networks had used so often—that anything affecting their profits would inevitably result in cutbacks in worthwhile programming. Now, in a face-off between parent network and affiliate, it was accepted that more news and public affairs on the one hand must result in less news and public affairs on the other. The status quo was maintained.

It would have been more honest to declare that neither the affiliates nor the networks were willing to sacrifice that small part of their profits which would make a full hour of network news a possibility.

Reduction of local news presumed that affiliates were programming an hour or more of their own early evening news. Although news commitments by local stations had grown steadily in the last five years, only 93 of the approximately 600 network affiliates actually put more than a half hour of their own news into the early evening slot —which in many communities was considered less important than the late news. Of those 93, 42 were in the top twenty markets, where the local news more often than not outscored the network variety. Five years earlier the prime time access ruling had given back to the stations an additional half hour in the expectation that it would be used for such worthwhile programming as extended local news and public affairs. In the fall of 1976 only a handful out of hundreds of prime time access hours every week had been retained by the affiliates in the top fifty TV markets for news and public affairs. It was hard to reconcile the hours devoted to game shows, "Hee Haw," Lawrence Welk, and stripped network reruns with the network affiliates' testimony to "the value of added news service."

As for the threat to local station profits which would inevitably result in the impairment of "local live or public service programming," that raised a familiar question. How large did profits have to become to ensure such programming? At what point would stations, in return for the use of the public air, feel obliged to reciprocate by broadcasting more than a minimum of programming in "the public interest, convenience and necessity" over that national resource? Network and affiliates would never have a more appropriate or painless occasion to make such a public-spirited gesture. Income, according to the figures quoted at length in the first chapter, stood at an all-time high and promised to go even higher.

Having been invited to sacrifice a portion of their profits for the public good and having regretfully declined, the affiliates responded with some countersuggestions that would offer the same opportunity to the networks.

Joel Chaseman, president of the *Post/Newsweek* stations, affiliated with CBS and ABC, put forward the idea that a full hour of news might run from 7:30 P.M. to 8:30 P.M. and that local stations, in exchange for giving up their half hour of prime time access, might be allotted control of the three hours preceding the news. That, he figured, would be a fair exchange for the millions given up by the affiliates. The networks didn't bother to respond.

They paid more attention to Donald H. McGannon, president of Group W, after the networks the nation's largest broadcaster. McGannon had a long-term reputation for commitment to the public interest and a feisty attitude toward the networks. All of his stations programmed at least an hour of early evening news and habitually preempted large amounts of prime time network programming to put on money-losing local public affairs. It was McGannon who had originally proposed the prime time access plan which had reclaimed from the networks five half hours of valuable early evening time every week.

As early as May 1976, McGannon had suggested a solution for the problem of superficial national TV news that he, a local broadcaster jealous of his air time, could live with. "Group W is in favor of an expansion of network news," said McGannon, "but not in a time period when there is substantial network and local news now being presented. The critical need is for in-depth news, analysis, and commentary on the crucial values and issues of our times during viewing hours when the largest potential audience is available.

"We strongly recommend that all three networks present such a needed breakthrough in electronic journalism on each weekday evening at 9:00 P.M. (8:00 P.M. central time). Because of the public need for this, Group W is prepared to clear such programming on its five television stations without network compensation."

"It is hard to justify a prime time schedule," McGannon continued, "that does not have any regularly scheduled news or public affairs. We have not adequately demonstrated that the free over-the-air system is superior to cable and inevitably, a pay system."

McGannon compounded this disloyal admission by saying, "We have been depicted as being excessively mass-audience oriented, and some believe the only solution will be a competitive system that will destroy, yes destroy, our present system. The networks must assume the giant share of this responsibility as they do the giant share of the power and the profits."

Again, the networks didn't bother to respond, insisting, according to McGannon, who followed up his statement with personal conversations at a high level, that he couldn't have intended his suggestions seriously.

That McGannon wasn't joking became apparent when on September 3, 1976, he filed a fifty-five-page petition with the Federal Communications Commission requesting the first inquiry into network TV practices since the industry-upsetting Barrow Study of 1955. The reason: the threat of expanded network news. The petition stated:

Group W recognizes the value and importance of national news and believes *the networks should do news programming in the evening hours they already control.* There is a great need for the networks to analyze and interpret important events and provide in-depth coverage of the national news—something that cannot always be done in a half-hour evening news program.

Unlike affiliated stations, the networks are not forced into choosing between unattractive alternatives in looking for a time period to expand news. The additional half hour of national news can easily be accommodated in the three hours of prime time (four hours on Sunday) which the networks now have available. Certainly there is no reason why they cannot replace one of their many "action" or other entertainment programs with a news and/or public affairs program. The networks are in a unique position to provide an important public service in this respect. The added cost would be a small price to pay relative to the riches currently being reaped from evening entertainment programming. Furthermore, it would provide an immediate reduction in the amount of violence and adult content in the present schedules.

If the networks use a present high-audience network period for any news expansion, local stations then will retain the time so important to the discharge of their local responsibility. The public will be the real beneficiary, because viewers will have the benefit of more discussion and explanation of the important national issues and the local news will not be preempted to a less desirable time period. While, of course, there is no obligation on any station to do this, Group W has offered to carry any such network news or public affairs program in prime time without compensation as a contribution to such an important project.

Group W had yet another suggestion.

While it will not be done, it would be possible for the network to structure an hour-long program into two half-hour segments and give affiliates the option to clear either a half hour or full hour of network news. This would be similar to the three separate half-hour feeds of the present news and would give affiliates the flexibility to provide the particular mix of network and local news programming best suited to the needs of their audience.

But McGannon had something else in mind beyond his recommendations for alternate plans for network news expansion. What he wanted the FCC to do was institute a study which would

. . . assess the impact of increases in scheduled network programming—both in the past as well as those planned for the future—upon affiliated stations and their service to the public.

. . . review current network practices which sharply limit and effectively foreclose the ability of stations to judge in advance the propriety and merit of network-offered programs, especially in the light of the social impact and community acceptance of those containing high levels of crime, violence and adult content.

. . . review the reasonableness of the networks' unilateral actions in virtually freezing compensation of their affiliates despite, on the one hand, expanded network programming and greatly increased network profits [and], on the other, sharply increased local station cost.

His petition went on to say:

The Commission itself in recent years has recognized the desirability of an updated review of these network practices. In October, 1973, the trade press reported that the Commission had tentatively decided to inquire into ways to reduce network dominance and influence in the television industry. Just a month later, after (and apparently as a direct result of) a particularly strident attack upon the networks by President Nixon, the proposed inquiry was dropped. Members of the Commission and its staff are said to have conceded that, in light of the White House attack, the Commission's motives in undertaking such an inquiry then would be suspect. No such impediment exists now. Watergate has passed into history, but the problems existing in 1973 have become even more pressing.

McGannon was saying, with a startling lack of sentiment, that the regulators put on the track of his adversaries—the TV networks—by Richard Nixon, and called off during the Watergate years, should resume the hunt.

McGannon also pointed out that, while network profits soared by 142.8 percent from 1969 to 1974 and their incursions on local time steadily advanced (up from 478 half hours to 516 half hours in approximately the same period), their percentage of compensation to affiliates actually shrank by 2.3 percent.

There was one weakness in McGannon's argument, pointed out editorially by *Broadcasting* magazine, a reasonably neutral referee, at least for such intramural industry quarrels.

> Mr. McGannon's call for government action portrays network affiliates as helpless victims of network domination. By his analysis . . . stations are doomed to become mere conduits for network programming and advertising if the networks are allowed by the government to go on their rapacious ways.
> Mr. McGannon's petition is somewhat weakened by the conspicuous omission of a recital of the profits of the VHF television affiliates that Westinghouse Broadcasting Co. owns in five of the biggest markets in the country. It must be assumed, however, that the group is making the most money in its history right now, unless it is running counter to all other major groups. Whatever may be said about network practices, television never had it so good.

ABC's answer to Group W's petition of inquiry further pointed out that "while direct station compensation may have shown only a moderate increase, the revenues from the valuable commercial adjacencies to network programs have increased in general ratio with the expansion of the television economy." NBC replied: "Since 1970 VHF affiliates' profit margins generally have been from three to six times higher than network profit margins." The ratio was, according to NBC, 29.5 percent to 4.4 percent in 1970 and a slightly more equable 28.2 percent to 12.5 percent in 1975.

Group W countered with its own statistics. "While 23.1 percent of network revenues went to stations as compensation payments in 1964, that figure declined last year to only 9.6 percent. This was a substantial decrease from the 13.4 percent return of 1975."

The Justice Department in comments urging the FCC's proposed inquiry pointed out the return for networks and their Owned and Operated stations—186 percent profit on the book value of tangible broadcast property—"was significantly above rates prevailing in other sectors of the economy" and "strongly suggests that the networks possess monopoly power and that competition is less rigorous in the TV industry than elsewhere in the economy." Justice also pointed out that network profits increased 124.9 percent between 1969 and 1975 on sales that had increased only 37.7 percent.

If the figures were confusing to the layman, the message was clear. Everyone was making pots of money. McGannon himself admitted "we are super profitable. It's unbelievable. We don't have heavy research and development costs. I think we ought to be very carefully and shrewdly investing in programs of certain types. Maybe we can break new frontiers. The American public is hungry for a new departure."*

Elsewhere McGannon commented, "We're not starving to death . . . that's not the issue. The issue is equity between the local stations and the networks." But the local stations, off the hook so far as the costly network intrusion into their early evening space was concerned, refused to join McGannon in his attack.

The affiliate position, already stated by NBC's board, was reiterated and expanded on by the CBS Television Affiliates Association—Cronkite's constituents. "The CBS affiliates believe emphatically," they told the FCC, "that . . . no governmental intrusion into the relationship between [affiliates] and their network is required for the affiliates to fulfill their public-interest obligations. To the extent that the Westinghouse petition may suggest that CBS-affiliated stations are unable

---

*Westinghouse's new departure for the year was a separate, locally produced strip magazine show at all five of its stations which occupied the prime time access slot five nights a week. A big risk and investment, it was already paying off. It was also the most dramatic demonstration to date of the creative use of the returned time which was McGannon's idea in the first place.

properly to carry out their responsibilities under the current arrangements, the CBS affiliates simply disagree."

The NAB's Hundred Plus Market Television Committee advised the commission to "steer clear of additional regulation of the network-affiliate relationship. . . . The present system—unencumbered by the tentacles of big government—works well." The group owners, other than Westinghouse, were for the most part in firm agreement with the networks.

Nonetheless, Chief Commissioner Richard Wiley, the retiring head of the FCC, mounted a plan of inquiry which was almost immediately dismantled when Senator Ernest Hollings, the new chairman of the Senate Subcommittee on Communications, refused to allot the necessary funds to staff it.

It was an empty victory for the networks, a strange conclusion to their high-minded push for the extension of network news service. Starting out to increase their newscasts, they had ended up by settling for a delay in a potentially embarrassing inquiry into their business practices. Nor were the affiliates much better off.

Broadcasting magazine commented on the irony in a bitter editorial entitled "Score One for the Marketplace," which pretty well summed up the whole sorry business.

Back in the spring, the conventional wisdom in broadcasting was that if one network went to a longer evening news form, the other two would have to follow. Then . . . one network (NBC) said it would *not* go to longer news. Domino-like, the other two now say they won't either. So much for conventional wisdom.

It may be just as well. Perhaps, as Rust Craft's Ralph Becker argues . . . , the reason television ranks first among the nation's news media is that it specializes in "abbreviated journalism." That he may be right is little consolation to those concerned that the president of the Radio Television News Directors Association has to advise viewers to read the newspapers.

Now that it's all over, we confess to a measure of disappointment. Not because we were anxious to see the networks increase their share of tube time, or to siphon more dollars away from their affiliates. (We have always had a quiet confidence in the ability of affiliates to negotiate a fair quid for whatever quo the networks would have asked for a longer news segment.) And certainly not because we wanted to see local news operations circumscribed in covering their beats. But because we felt those extra minutes—as few as 15, in the most probable configuration —might have made a significant difference in the quality and diversity of TV reporting. The network evening news, in the final analysis, is our national glue. All else being equal, we'd like it bigger and better.

TV Guide, which for years now has been keeping a jaundiced eye on network news and public affairs, concurred.

We really couldn't care less whether the stations or the networks profit from expanded network news. We do know that if television is to serve in "the public interest, convenience and necessity," which is what the Communications Act demands, network news must be expanded.

We respectfully request that stations and networks get off dead center, find a way to split the loot equitably, and pay more attention to the public.

4 • Business and Broadcast News

I. The Argument

RADIO AND TELEVISION news has become a big business within an even bigger business—broadcasting. In the years since Watergate this growth in prosperity and power has led to an increasing number of charges and countercharges between broadcast journalists and the larger business community.

One of the most important questions in journalism today is: How honest and thorough can radio and TV news be in reporting those stories which most concern broadcasting's management, advertisers, and fellow businessmen?

The relationship between the press and the government is, as it should be, adversary—a two-century tradition that has been strongly reaffirmed in this decade. But the relationship between the press and other less powerful institutions—business, the labor movement, education, religion, others—ought to be inquisitive and coolly interpretive and neither adversary nor promotional.

All too often, reporters dismiss the facts that managers are required by law to make public, preferring to get at "the real story"—with chicanery and power plays at the top of the list of desired stories. And too often, managers respond by taking refuge behind a wall of spokesmen when reporters call, isolating themselves and feeding the press suspicion and cynicism.

That's bad for business, which is not a cobra, and bad for the press, which is not its mongoose. The too-promotional reporting of business a generation ago has been replaced by a too-suspicious attitude today. The wave of distrust in political life has spilled over into the world of business and the result distorts what is happening in our economy.

We're not looking for "puff pieces," or phony buildups, or winkings at unethical practices, or gentle treatment of red ink. But we're not going to suffer silently while being blamed for the sins of the world by self-styled adversaries who substitute trendy distrust for objective standards of accountability.

The business manager is not the adversary of the person who works in the free market of news: We're on the same side and we ought to stop being uncomfortable about it.

This statement by David J. Mahoney, chairman, president and chief executive officer of Norton Simon, Inc. (Hunt Foods, Avis, Canada Dry, etc.) appeared on the Op Ed page of *The New York Times* in the summer of 1977.

A more frequent spokesman for the business community was the Mobil Oil Company, which for six years had paid good money for the lower right-hand corner of the same page to print its unsigned attacks on the media. A few weeks earlier Mobil had devoted the space to quoting Walter Cronkite's RTNDA speech (see Appendix II) and thanking the nation's favorite anchor man for confirming their worst suspicions—i.e., that TV journalism was superficial, dangerously ill informed, and "very largely responsible for public confusion and misunderstanding over America's energy problems."

Setting Mobil's contumely alongside Mahoney's invitation to tango gave some idea of the ambivalence of feelings between business and broadcast journalism in the days since Watergate.

In the spring of 1977 the DuPont Survey canvassed forty-five of the nation's business leaders concerning the treatment they and their enterprises had received at the hands of broadcast journalists. A third of them responded, a fact that in itself could be considered significant. Although the tone of the respondents was reasonable, there was virtual unanimity among them that broadcast journalism was superficial, ill informed, and biased in its treatment of those matters which particularly concerned the business community. Furthermore, their own personal experience with broadcast newsmen had been predominantly negative, their most common grievance being about quotes lifted out of context and interviews of up to two and three hours boiled down to a minute or less on the air. Still, they saw the situation as far from hopeless.

Some of these highly placed executives had quite specific advice as to how broadcasters could improve their coverage of business news:

(a) Assign reporters with appropriate training and background in business; (b) allow adequate time to cover complex and important stories; (c) seek out appropriate experts to represent differing points of view; (d) strive for excellence in preparing balanced, thorough and objective reports.

Hire more qualified business and economics reporters.

By improving the comprehensiveness of their treatment; by doing their homework.

Fill in for those who don't read the *Wall Street Journal* or *Business Week*—acquaint the general public.

By taking the trouble to understand both sides of an issue (the trade-offs) . . . then, hopefully, reflecting it in more objective, less snide reporting.

Train potential business reporters before throwing them into the assignment.

On the other hand, they seemed equally clear about their own shortcomings and how to overcome them.

Business people have to be candid with the media. They have to be available to the media. They have to speak out on issues, not only the issues impacting on their business, but also on all major issues of the day.

There must be increased effort by business management to understand media's needs.

Be patient, willing and learn how to deal with the camera as an audience.

Business is remiss in not taking the lead in making key information available.

By speaking out for what it believes in more lucidly, loudly and frequently.

Make an active effort to seek out and make contact with media reporters and producers. Try to anticipate certain needs and fulfill them when a story breaks. Have spokesmen available when requested.

More frequent contact. Greater access.

Make more of an effort to report views to the media and protest very strongly when there are misunderstandings or distortions.

Train MBA's and general management to deal with the pressures of TV format—all can handle interview with print, but have difficulty condensing thought process and with "being on the air."

The opinions of the business leaders on the new vogue for investigative reporting, which in recent months had been more and more frequently aimed in their direction, were mixed:

Watergate seems to have made every reporter an investigative reporter. We need investigative reporting, but sooner or later the media is going to find out that there aren't skeletons in every corporate closet.

It's good—the more there is, the better chance both sides of the story will be told.

The technique is good but the subject matter is poorly chosen.

Largely a witch hunt. We think the entire area could be improved; needed is more expertise and objectivity on the part of reporters.

Seems to have spawned a generation of careless, shoot-from-the-hip biased reporting with little concern for the journalistic canons of fact and accuracy.

True investigative reporting efforts should be encouraged. However, too many television stations are airing three to five part series that give the impression of in-depth reporting yet deal only with topics of questionable substance.

That the businessmen were genuinely concerned about the situation was evident in their estimates of the future:

I feel that much of the problem between business and the media has been due to the fact that a great many of the people in the business sections of the media are very poorly prepared for their jobs. They are generally without business experience or without understanding of how business operates. They are in a part of the press which is not very glamorous and the opportunities for misunderstanding and problems are tremendous.

I would hasten to offer that part of the problem is poor communication with some of the business community, based on lack of trust of the individuals with whom they come in contact in the media. I think most businessmen are trying to do a better job of communication, but others have been turned off because of poor reporting or particularly slanted programs on television which seem to be more interested in reporting the spectacular instead of reporting the facts.

> *John D. Harper*
> *Chairman and Chief Executive Officer*
> *Aluminum Company of America (ret.)*

Business and economic coverage by the broadcast media will not improve substantially until the mutual distrust between the two parties lessens through increased understanding of each other's roles. Businessmen will have to become more available, while broadcast reporters will have to become more knowledgeable.

> *Irving S. Shapiro*
> *Chairman of the Board*
> *E. I. duPont de Nemours & Company*

The good broadcasters (Cronkite, Sevareid, Chancellor) know it and say it . . . television is necessarily superficial at best, adversary and biased at worst. How does the public get its news and information unless it *reads?* TV is chasing the buck, not the truth or public service, and the public becomes more and more uninformed.

Any realistic p.r. person has learned not to be very trusting of the media . . . they will go out of their way to zing you every time. . . . There is no such thing as sympathetic treatment . . . it's adversary show biz, and if they can make you look like a fool, they will generally try.

> *Marshall C. Lewis*
> *Director of Corporate Communications*
> *Union Carbide Corporation*
> *(for W. S. Sneath, Chairman)*

Business cannot ignore broadcast journalism because of its importance in molding public opinion on matters of vital concern to business. We must work at the problem of improving the lines of communication.

> *George A. Stinson*
> *Chairman and Chief Executive Officer*
> *National Steel Corporation*

Business people have to be willing to meet the press and face the nation, to subject themselves to "live" interrogation under the "eyes" of the camera. Broadcast journalism has to be willing to devote more time to business coverage. You can't cover business in 90 seconds a night and an occasional half-hour show.

John D. deButts
Chairman of the Board
American Telephone and Telegraph

Business and broadcast journalism *must* learn to coexist. In order for the public to fully understand the business system—its achievements and its flaws—business and the press must understand and be sympathetic to each other's situation.

David Rockefeller
Chairman
The Chase Manhattan Bank

Some of the respondents enclosed extended statements further illuminating their feelings:

I believe business must be more open and responsive with the press—to explain its failures as well as its successes.

I believe the press owes, not business, but our entire society a continued effort to improve its mastery of the subjects of business and economics in order to add more professional sharpness to its reporting in these fields.

If business and economic news is more important news today, then it seems reasonable to assume that the resource allocated to those subjects in terms of top talent, dollars and training, should increase.

I think businessmen have a right—and a responsibility—to seriously question the assignment of a business beat to the reporter with no interest in business, no education or practical experience in business or economics, and who is not given the time to check his facts before his deadline. That can only lead the reporter to look for the most colorful feature in a story he doesn't really understand.

. . . the plain fact is that the future of our economic system rests as much with you in journalism as it does with us in business.

The corporation exists by public consent. And you are the day-to-day intermediary to inform people of what they are consenting to.

If you as an intermediary are informed, objective, and professional, no one in business can honestly criticize your reporting —however tough it might be.

Frank T. Cary
Chairman of the Board
International Business Machines

. . . the accent today is not on the evidence of progress in a multitude of fields; the heaviest emphasis is upon failure. The media, supported by some academic "liberals," would have us believe that things are not just going badly, they are growing progressively and rapidly worse. The dominant theme is the new American way of failure. No one wins; we always lose. Jack Armstrong and Tom Swift are dead. If an individual says anything important, it is either ignored or nit-picked to death by commentators. Logical argument has given way to sniping. We no longer have great debates. The accusatory has replaced the explanatory. . . . We daily see illustrated a point made by the jurist Oliver Wendell Holmes: "When the ignorant are taught to doubt, they do not know what they safely may believe." The media should beware of sowing the dragon's teeth of confusion.

> *Walter B. Wriston*
> *Chairman*
> *Citibank*

We in the insurance business, along with most other businessmen, greatly fear one-sided reporting. Too often a member of Congress, a consumer advocate, an environmentalist—or any other adversary—can make sensational charges to which there are factual, sober answers that are anything but sensational. Alas, these answers rarely get much attention. It takes time to assemble facts. Once the facts are in hand, the definition of "news" today militates against their widespread exposure in the media. . . .

Business executives often see facts wrongly stated or misinterpreted, usually as the result of misunderstanding by media people of how such facts fit into a broader context, how they should be properly qualified—or just because the reporter, editor, or commentator may be ignorant of economic cause and effect. I can truthfully say that I almost never read or hear an accurate media account of a business subject with which I am thoroughly familiar.

. . . Probably nothing haunts business-media relationships more than the commonplace evidence that so many writers, reporters, and commentators often do not understand the meaning, uses and benefits of profits. Opinion polls show the vast public misunderstanding of profit and profit margins has grown with the years, probably at least to some degree on the basis of media coverage. . . .

For their part, the press and air media have learned to be skeptical about the motives of all special interests, including business—maybe even especially business. They look for special pleading when business establishments defend themselves or seek out public attention and, unfortunately, they are too often justified in doing so.

And the men and women of the media are often frustrated

when digging for business news. They find many business executives excessively secretive and often inaccessible, or prone to double talk. Nor are business people noted for reducing complex matters to simple understandable terms. . . .

And so, all too often, the dedicated business executive and the equally dedicated newsmen and women meet in apparent harmony, discuss at cross-purposes, and come up with two different understandings of the interchange.

On both sides of the table, we are going to have to work much harder to alleviate this distrust. The public is poorly served by it in an era when matters of economics have come to dominate not only the news but, indeed, mankind's very future.

> *Donald S. MacNaughton*
> *Chairman and Chief Executive Officer*
> *The Prudential Insurance Company of*
> *America*

The journalists' side did not lack for spokesmen, nor did what they said make the situation seem any simpler. Among those on the record was Katherine Graham, the proprietor of one of the nation's great newspapers, the Washington *Post,* and one of its leading news magazines, *Newsweek,* as well as one radio and four TV stations.

. . . Believability depends on an intricate calculus involving words, performance, and the standards that are being applied. And this, I think, gets us closer to the real source of difficulty today—for in many areas of our national affairs, something has gotten out of line, the gaps between words and actions and standards seem to be unreasonably large.

It's hard to have much sympathy for public officials who systematically lie or mislead the people and the press—and then complain about a loss of credibility.

It's also easy to understand why large segments of the public automatically discount warnings from businessmen about the ruinous effects of environmental and safety rules. The auto companies have a consistent record of resisting tougher emissions standards—and then meeting them. The makers of vinyl chloride claimed that OSHA's rules would be impossible to follow—and then found ways to comply. And so on.

I don't mean to suggest that clean air and safe factories are cheap or easy to obtain. Nor do I think that industries are always wrong and regulators always right. Indeed, some regulations may be as costly and unreasonable as their opponents claim. Unfortunately, arguments to this effect have lost much of their force because executives have cried "wolf" too often.

Her advice to the business community:

> . . . inject more candor into all communications, and be more willing to explain policies and acknowledge mistakes. It seems almost too obvious to mention, but companies can avoid many problems by dealing honestly with reporters, consumers and investors, and by volunteering information about products and practices.

> . . . Too often corporate executives who are extremely up-to-date in other ways describe the free enterprise system, at least publicly, in terms that could have been plagiarized from the robber barons of the 19th century.

> . . . It would be a remarkable advance if we could describe our economic system in terms that better reflect the real complexity of these relationships. It would also help to discuss de-regulation the way we tend to lobby for it—selectively.

> Listen to criticism and respond.

> . . . Demand coverage that is accurate, fair, and grounded in real understanding of events. You can ask for much better economic coverage, an area in which much of the press has been quite superficial until recently.

> Credibility is the shorthand for the basic level of trust and mutual regard on which our whole economy and democracy depend. It is that foundation which enables competition to thrive, arguments to rage, and accommodations to evolve, however inefficiently.

One of the first newsmen retained by a network to devote himself exclusively to business news, ABC's Dan Cordtz, had his own bill of particulars:

> Every TV correspondent who has been assigned a business story can reel off accounts of corporate stalls, and outright refusals to cooperate. Companies won't give permission to film on their property and they won't make executives or spokesmen available for on-camera interviews. I suspect the companies hope that if they won't cooperate we'll abandon the story. Frequently they're right, but such tactics cut down on the amount of business news on television, and tend to confirm the worst suspicions of TV producers and correspondents—that business has a lot to hide.
> This is the main reason for whatever hostility towards business

exists in television. It's hard to feel all warm and snuggly about people who make it harder to do your job and then complain about the way you do it. The real problem, however, is not that television is against business. The problem is that television producers overwhelmingly are indifferent to business. They believe it's dull, and I sometimes think businessmen go out of their way to confirm that opinion.

. . . In more than twenty years of covering business, I haven't run into many situations too complicated for a normally intelligent adult to understand. And anything that is really too complicated wouldn't interest television anyway. . . . With twenty-two minutes to tell the day's news, the network evening news programs can't devote more than a couple of minutes to an average story. This means the spokesman for either side will have about 30 seconds to state his case. Executives frequently use this as an excuse for not going in front of the camera. "We can't tell our story in half a minute," they say. But their companies spend millions of dollars on commercials that are thirty seconds long. Are they just throwing that money away?

My own guess is that businessmen just aren't willing to do the very hard work of getting their thoughts so well organized that they can summarize their positions briefly. When they deal with their associates—especially their subordinates—they can take as much time as they need and overwhelm any opposition with the sheer weight of their words. But there's no way to do this on TV. If we gave them the time, they'd put the viewers to sleep.

And, finally, there was Cronkite himself, responding to John Connally, no great admirer of the news media, who had told the Houston Press Club that journalists today must assume "an educational role with a candid bias for the preservation of this political system. Enlightened self-interest lies in the performance of that role to protect the free enterprise system in its present incarnation." Connally's reasoning:

> Today's free press is a far cry from the fragile, almost endangered species whose perpetuations were guaranteed by the precious safeguards of our Constitution. The sanctity of the printed expression of thought was indeed vital to the fabric of an emerging democracy. . . .
> Big media has joined the nation's other institutional giants—big government, big business, big labor. They should be viewed for what they are: massive business empires built by entrepreneurs under the shelter of our free economic system. They are among the most profitable business enterprises in America.

They are corporate giants on a par, in terms of profit, with the major companies that manufacture automobiles and appliances, produce our steel, mine and refine our oil and gas and other resources, and market the multitude of products for American consumers.

There is no need to belabor the power of the three television networks. The influence of their news is so immense at this period of our history that I venture to guess that every person here has at least some concern about it. Any one of them has more influence on the public than the Speaker of the House, the majority leaders and the minority leaders of both houses of Congress combined.

Cronkite's response ignored Connally's appeal to big media's "enlightened self interest" and went back to basics.

It is not the reporter's job to be a patriot or to presume to determine where patriotism lies. His job is to relate the facts, to tell what's happening as clearly and clinically as possible. If we use a medical analogy, he's more like a laboratory technician than a doctor. He does not prescribe cures; he reports on the organisms he sees in the blood.

If he discovers a social disease, it may create all sorts of unpleasant problems for doctor and patient. But no responsible doctor or sane patient would want him to mask his discovery in the interest of politeness, or even of patriotism. And if he did so for any reason, he'd be a menace as long as he held his job.

Education with a candid bias is virtually synonymous with propaganda, which isn't always a bad thing, except for reporters. A reporter's prime responsibility to his country is to describe the things he sees swimming in the national bloodstream. To let patriotism get in the way of that function is about the most unpatriotic thing he could do.

Whether television was performing its prime journalistic responsibility or letting business, its own and others, get in the way was becoming increasingly difficult to determine.

II. Is TV News Anti-Business?

During two months in 1976, Kevin Phillips, one of the sharpshooters *TV Guide* had assigned to its weekly News Watch column, made a list of stories carried on the three network newscasts that he considered particularly hostile to business. Among the subjects treated:

> Pollution, auto emissions, new FDA labeling requirements, bans of Red Dye No. 2, false Geritol ads, Gulf Oil slush funds, FDA teething ring recalls, Bechtel's alleged Arab boycott conspiracy, Tenneco strip mining environmental damage, mislabeled grain exports, cancer-causing drugs, circumstances in the steel industry, confidential bank-report leaks, estrogen dangers in birth control pills, Kepone dangers, 240,000 people annually used for drug tests, Monsanto Corporation chemical fish contamination, paint and varnish remover linkage to heart trouble and arteriosclerosis, $6.5 billion Federal aid to railroads, oil company request to drill in a Houston park, the Vermont Yankee nuclear plant shut down for safety, soaring coffee prices.*

No less an authority than Walter Cronkite seemed to confirm that broadcasters were giving conspicuous play to anti-business items. "I think that in all broadcasting you'll find, and certainly at CBS News, we give a greater proportion of space to FDA and FTC actions than any of the printed press does. We don't have any back pages. Only a front page. If you give 15 seconds to an FDA or FTC action, it's a front page story. You don't find those in too many newspapers." Some of the FDA and FTC targets to which CBS News had given front page space since Phillips drew up his list were:

> the lead on MacDonald's drinking glasses, dangers connected with the use of Cope, Compoz, Miles Nervine, Tranquim, Quiet World, saccharin linked to bladder cancer in men, fluorocarbons, Laetrile, Red Dye No. 2 linked with cancer, genetic defects and miscarriages, estrogen may be causing cancer epidemic, in-

---

*Phillips's explanation for this bombardment, which managed to hit quite a few TV advertisers and even a broadcast proprietor or two, was that broadcasters were attempting to hype their news ratings. "Honest portraiture of American business doing its job, without overemphasis of the 5–10 percent wart factor would be boring. And low rated. And unprofitable." In other words, it was good business for TV to be anti-business.

creased risk of birth defects, breast cancer and cancer of the uterus, deceptive practices in the used car industry, abusive pressures in bill collection agencies, fat and oil in food products, women's apparel industry, food additives, land development fraud, ice cream.

And week by week the list grew longer.

It was not only on network newscasts that TV was hard on business. Documentaries, when they were fortunate enough to get air time, had been known to hit dozens of business targets in the sixty minutes at their disposal. Any TV program about food, energy, or the environment almost inevitably displeased several important members of the business community. Examples in the past two years that brought open objections from the business community included "The Politics of Cancer," "What Is This Thing Called Food?," "Danger: Radioactive Wastes," and "The Last Voyage of the *Argo Merchant*."

Over the years there had been a series of documentaries that the business community still remembered with pain, beginning with "Harvest of Shame" and including such notable troublemakers for businessmen and parent networks alike as "The Selling of the Pentagon," "Hunger in America," "Migrant," "Banks and the Poor," "Corporation," and "Pensions: The Broken Promise." There would seem to be some justice in the accusation that the network news departments looked on the U.S. business community with, if not outright hostility, a somewhat jaundiced eye.

At the same time there were important areas neglected by broadcasters where the oversight might come from a desire to ingratiate themselves to, or at least not to offend, the business community. On two recent lists of subjects inadequately covered or totally ignored by TV, 90 percent of the stories mentioned had to do with the nation's industry. According to a panel including Ben H. Bagdikian, Noam Chomsky, Victor Marchetti, and Jerry ter Horst, assigned to pick the "ten best censored stories of 1976," the list included "Jimmy Carter and his little-known relationship with the Trilateral Commission, an international policy making group; . . . corporate control of DNA; the sale of banned pesticides and drugs to third world countries; the conspiracy among oil companies, governmental agencies, and OPEC to raise oil prices; Mobil Oil's illicit dealings with the internationally condemned Rhodesian government; the missing plutonium and inadequate nuclear reactor safeguards; the widespread number of injuries, diseases, and deaths caused by work hazards in America's industry; . . . the questionable value of nonprescription over-the-counter drugs sold to the public; the illegal and unethical activities of gas companies and government agencies in creating a natural gas shortage." Of the ten only "the secret manipulation of the Strategic Arms Limitation Talks by Henry Kissinger" seemed not to directly impinge on the business community. All the rest were obviously stories which, if indeed they had any merit, businessmen must be grateful to see ignored.

A list of "the seven deadly taboos in the world of television documentaries," drawn up by investigative reporter John Culhane and published in the *New York Times* in February of 1977, claimed even larger territories avoided by electronic journalists. They were big labor, big business, big TV networks, the automotive industry, nuclear power, the military-industrial complex, and U.S. foreign policy. Again, if one assumed, as Culhane did, that a thorough job in any of these fields must be discomfiting to its subjects, TV documentaries were going easy on U.S. businessmen. Although the networks protested that they could cite documentaries in all of Culhane's categories, there was little question that they were few and far between.

One of the reasons Culhane reported for this dearth of business-oriented documentaries was lack of corporate cooperation. Nor did the documentary makers interviewed seem to blame the businessmen for being wary. "They would have to be out of their minds to let us near them," said Marlene Sanders, ABC vice-president in charge of documentaries. "The ABC Close-Up team has a reputation for investigative stuff. If I were a public relations officer for that firm, I would tell the company not to do it."

Jay McMullen, CBS's star investigative reporter, attempting an in-depth profile of a corporation, any corporation, after three false starts finally convinced Phillips Petroleum of Bartlesville, Oklahoma, to hold still. After filming began, the chairman of the board was indicted for illegal political contributions. This made a good story for McMullen, but probably insured that no other TV investigator would get a similar chance at a corporation for many seasons to come.

Whether TV's feelings toward the nation's business community were hostile or protective, there had been a steady increase in industry attempts to counter TV coverage which they thought either unfair or untrue. First there were the paid replies and counterattacks in newspapers and magazines, for which a company like Mobil might budget $5 million a year, plus the image ads in both print and electronic media aimed at subtle correction of impressions given by earlier coverage.

Of nearly 500 complaints received by the National News Council since its inception in 1973, a good number came from individuals angry at the TV treatment businesses had received. Accuracy in Media, a Washington-based defender of conservative causes, regularly challenged the networks on coverage it considered critical of business. Reed Irvine, a former Federal Reserve Board economist who headed the organization, had a file of dozens of cases which he contended showed a consistent anti-business bias on the part of broadcasters.

Equally convinced of TV's bias were such critics as Edith Efron and ex-Nixon aide Patrick Buchanan. Their principal forum, along with Kevin Phillips's, was *TV Guide*'s News Watch column, which reached 20 million American homes weekly.

There was a growing list of organizations dedicated to correcting media mistakes generally, or in specific areas. Some of them were: Morality in the Media, Media Watch of N.Y.C., Spotlight, Council for Agricultural Science and Technology, Atomic Industrial Forum, and the American Nuclear Society.

Watergate had certainly not helped the relationship between business and broadcast journalists. Accepted by a new generation of investigative reporters as an example to be admired and followed, in most stories concerning business it was worse than useless as a model. With Watergate, however elusive the story might have seemed, the press was able to dig out the truth and present it to the public. With the stories which gave journalists and business their worst trouble, it was frequently a matter of determining not what *had* happened, but what *might* happen, not intentional wrongdoing but inadvertent mistakes, not who was telling the truth, but who, if anybody, had the slightest notion of what the truth might be.

For several years now the American public had been subjected to a series of conflicting signals on any number of alarming topics by business and press alike. TV had given its audience the first scary word on a list of subjects twice as long as any Kevin Phillips or his fellow critics had compiled—the first scary word, and the second, and the third. Usually the business involved, as frightened as anyone else, denied them all.

In 1973 Pamela Hill, in her admirable ABC Close-Up "Fire," demonstrated vividly to TV viewers the dangers of inflammable nightwear for children with the implicit recommendation to seek out those garments properly treated with retardants. Not too long after, Americans were informed that such retardants could possibly induce cancer. A short time after that they learned that such substances might cause sterility as well. This was followed by news of the discovery of a fire retardant apparently neither carcinogenic nor sterilizing but as yet not completely tested. Then word came that a noninflammable fabric tested and proved safe in every way had been abandoned because nightwear manufacturers feared it would raise prices to non-competitive levels. At this point Hill, who had observed each twist of a story she had reported in indignant good faith, said, "It's precisely the kind of thing a reporter can't know. You are always dependent on experts." The feelings of the public and the businessmen involved went unrecorded.

The *Argo Merchant* oil spill off Cape Cod in December 1976 was one of the big stories of the year. TV played the possible environmental damage to the hilt in both documentaries and running news accounts. Three months later the National Oceanic and Atmospheric Administration announced "minimal biological and aesthetic damage from the spill." If the fact was buried by most of the media, Mobil Oil dragged it out and made it the subject of another of its ads, concluding, "Kinda makes you wish the press could get as excited about the end of a big story as it does about the beginning, doesn't it?"

Which was fair enough, except that it wasn't the end of the story. Another six months and the spill surfaced again with news of a million-dollar settlement to state and federal governments, with claims of several million dollars still pending from fishermen and environmentalists, "although little damage has been found to date."

And there was the matter of fluorocarbons, of supersonic transports, cyclamates, saccharine, and all those other items on Kevin Phillips's list.

John W. Hanley, chairman and president of the Monsanto Company, which had been recently involved in an imbroglio over the desirability of plastic soft drink bottles, commented:

> Our nation's scientific genius has become, in effect, a double-edged sword. Just as we now have the technology to identify infinitesimal trace quantities, we also know infinitely more about how human systems cope with toxic substances. But the issue becomes magnified and beclouded when we lose perspective on what these quantities mean when translated into human terms.

He had suggested five steps to set matters straight. First, a reconsideration and updating of the controversial Delaney Amendment, involved in the cyclamate, saccharine, and plastic bottle cases, which prohibits the use of any chemicals in foods that can induce cancers in test animals at any feeding level, no matter how massive.

> Second, we must put an end to regulatory policy established in an ad hoc fashion—whereby the conditions of acceptability

literally change overnight without full debate among the parties directly affected.

Third, risk-benefit analysis must be brought to the decision-making process. The costs throughout industry of the punitive measures I've described range into the hundreds of millions of dollars. In human terms—jobs and economic dislocation—the costs are often immeasurable.

Fourth, all of us must come to understand that these decisions cannot be reached by scientist battling scientist over interpretations of test data—even within the concept of a Science Court which would permit a formalized forum for scientific debate, and which I think has merit.

Ultimately, these are public decisions which should be made after deliberative consideration of benefit versus risk. Importantly, the consumer must be heard in this process.

Finally, industry and government, public interest groups and the scientific community must lay before the American people all the evidence relating to questions of product safety and human health in an open and forthright manner.

We must confront the question of consumer risk in a manner free from the old suspicion and irrationality that too often have characterized the debate over the proper interests of industry, government and the consumer.

The broadcast journalist could undoubtedly perform an invaluable service in laying before the American people all the evidence. But, obviously, not in Walter Cronkite's fifteen seconds, nor even Dan Cordtz's thirty. And who, once the evidence was laid out, was to be believed?

There was an increasing list of subjects where discovering the truth might be quite literally a question of life and death, and these subjects often were the ones where no one involved—journalist, expert, or businessman—seemed to be quite sure, or sure enough, to dispose of the subject once and for all.

Piracy on the high seas could be a matter of life and death to the almost 8 million Americans who owned ocean-worthy craft. "Sixty Minutes" and the *New York Times* Sunday magazine considered it important enough to cover at length on the same day, May 22, 1977. But they were unable to decide just how prevalent the crime was. And with good reason. "When a boat disappears without a trace," concluded the *Times,* "investigators are often left with no hard information and no useful leads. It's anybody's guess as to what happens in such cases, and the guessers include everybody from the Coast Guard, the FBI, the Drug Enforcement Administration, the local police, the State Department, to the insurance companies"—and, although the author doesn't say so, the *New York Times* and CBS News.

The stymied executive, the stubborn and self-righteous bureaucrat, the mystified expert who shrugged and looked off camera, had become staples of every TV documentary or investigation of more than limited scope. Ultimately even the most confident reporter had to be shaken, the most pugnacious partisan of free enterprise humbled.

Moreover, in those few instances where it seemed likely that the truth had been or was about to be isolated and pinned down, the very uses of that truth became a matter of dispute. In-depth reporting, true objectivity, investigators were told, required a knowledge of the trade-offs involved. Journalists must be concerned with matters other than life and death, such as loss of jobs, derangement of the economy, and the impact on the nation's international posture. "Corporate America has painted everyone into a classic dilemma," said Anthony Mazzocchi, legislative director for the Oil, Chemical and Atomic Workers Union. "Now it's job versus environment. The worker has a choice between his livelihood and dying of cancer."

Sometimes when one needed them most there seemed to be no experts even to contradict each other. In April 1977 President Carter was calling for "an independent information system that will give us reliable data about energy reserves and production, emergency capabilities, and financial data from energy producers." At the same time the Petroleum Institute was saying they "were anxious that the government take this over, and we're encouraging them to do it. We recognize that we have a credibility problem."

Nor if an unbiased expert were forthcoming were there many in journalism, according to Frank G. Zarb, former administrator of the Federal Energy Administration, capable of interpreting what he had to say. Exempting CBS's energy specialist Nelson Benton, Zarb observed:

> Often there was not another correspondent on the scene experienced enough to pick out the real news and to describe how one event fit into the ever-changing world picture; and the report was usually incomplete. The viewer was frequently shortchanged —and sometimes misled.
>
> It is a myth that television has a responsibility to "educate" the people about energy or any other major national matter. It does have a mission to report events and provide some in-depth summaries of vital issues . . . but this kind of coverage cannot be achieved unless major networks permanently assign one or more

correspondents who thoroughly understand the subject. If this is not done well, the result must be failure of television news to accomplish its primary mission—to know what is news, to report it and to inform the American people as to its significance.

Nor did the environmentalists have much good to say about media coverage of their subject, even when it seemed to be on their side. Neil Goldstein of the Sierra Club agreed with Zarb and then went further:

> The job of news is not to educate. It is to report spot news because, frankly, people would turn off the tube. They want to know what happened today. The truth is nothing happened today. The important stories are developing over time. It is not the biases of individuals or of the station. It is a bias in favor of what's news. Deer look pretty on TV. Trees look good. And what looks good is what makes a sexy story. I know how to manipulate the media. I can get them to focus on garbage very easily—but you cannot manipulate it on underlying issues. And you cannot manipulate the networks. Not unless you blow up the Alaska Pipeline, or ground a tanker.

Despite such discouragement from all sides, occasionally a reporter or a commentator broke free from indecision and spoke out. One summer evening in 1977 Howard K. Smith said:

> . . . the auto makers were given several years to meet certain emission levels by the coming model year. Foreign producers, like Volvo, have had no trouble doing it. But that great repository of American skill, Detroit, says it can't. Unless our elected representatives amend the law, they will simply not produce, throw half a million out of work, do great damage to our not fully recovered economy. It is not too harsh to call that blackmail. Government, naturally, is caving in. But it should accompany surrender with saying firmly, Never Again. It fouls the whole principle of democracy.

In this instance, except for a mild letter of protest from an auto company's public relations department, big business remained silent.

For a whole season Ben J. Wattenberg, an admitted partisan of free enterprise, held forth on the Public Broadcasting Service in a series entitled "In Search of the Real America—A Challenge to the Chorus of Failure and Guilt." The series opened with a segment on "There's

No Business Like Big Business."* No one from the opposite camp took audible exception.

A clearer demonstration of the problems involved in conscientious coverage of a prickly subject than Smith's commentary or Wattenberg's advocacy was NBC's highly controversial "Danger: Radioactive Wastes."

Considering the outcome, the preliminaries were remarkably serene. Of the two dozen utilities and other businesses asked to cooperate, only one refused. There seemed a general agreement among the subjects, the network, and the documentary team that an important topic was being given serious consideration. Joan Konner, the producer in charge, had handled a host of difficult subjects for the network before without unpleasant incident—including such highly controversial ones as abortion, marijuana, and homosexuality, "but never one that really involved business."

Scientists and experts of all persuasions ("I know a fact from an opinion," said Konner) were consulted along the way. After four months spent in research, filming, and editing, the program went on the air in January 1977. Its conclusion:

> Ever since man first split the atom, the problems of nuclear power have increased along with its benefits. With new technology, there is often a trade-off between growth and risk. With nuclear power now a part of the nation's energy future, it is important to consider whether the unsolved and little understood problem of nuclear waste should be a limiting factor. (Sound effects: geiger counter)

There was an instant reaction. The following morning William Doub, former AEC commissioner acting as a representative for the Atomic Industrial Forum, was invited onto "Today" and blasted the documentary. He confided later to Konner he had no problems with her reporting except that he felt there was not enough distinction made between what he considered a serious problem (high-level wastes) and a not-so-serious problem (low-level wastes). A second discussion was broadcast on "Today" some days later.

Among other reactions, there were 200 letters requesting a rerun since the program had been aired in the slot opposite one of the

---

*Wattenberg's series was one of three pro-business projects offered to public TV contingent upon outside underwriting. After many months the money finally came through for "In Search of the Real America." As of November 1977, two other series, Martin Mayer's "The American Gift," ten parts on the great achievements of industrial production in the U.S. and one featuring economist Milton Friedman and intended as a rebuttal to John Kenneth Galbraith's "The Age of Uncertainty," had not found the necessary backing.

installments of "Roots." The Environmental Protection Agency complimented the program and there was no criticism forthcoming from the atomic experts at the Nuclear Regulatory Commission or the Energy Research and Development Administration (ERDA). However, in succeeding weeks, as letters arrived from members of the Atomic Industrial Forum, the American Nuclear Society, and Accuracy in Media as well as employees of some large corporations involved in the manufacturing of nuclear hardware, the balance shifted. Six complaints were received by the National News Council.

Edith Efron and Kevin Phillips both had their say. After blasting the program, Phillips concluded that "television coverage of the nuclear-power controversy, demonstrably warped and biased, is blotting the professional credentials of electronic journalism." Pointing to such prejudicial effects as the ominous click of the Geiger counter and Paul Dukas's creepy *Sorcerer's Apprentice* on the soundtrack, he accused the program of "emotionalism, show-biz gimmicks and heavy-handed editing to create a classic propaganda piece in the guise of the news." Particularly offensive to some was a sequence where the head of the nuclear disposal operation at Richland, Washington, asked that the tape be stopped and that they start again. The embarrassing episode was left in the final program. Konner said it was included to indicate the uncertainty of the men in charge of nuclear waste disposal. Some critics said it was put there simply to discredit them.

To further stir up matters, both of the program's major sponsors, Textron and Northwestern Mutual Life Insurance Company, had substantial capital involvements with some aspect of nuclear power. The president of Northwestern Mutual Life, with millions invested in utilities (most of which operated nuclear facilities), was reported by Phillips to have "vigorously protested," stating "our confidence in NBC News' ability or willingness to treat controversial issues evenhandedly has been shaken, and we shall watch closely how future programs on other subjects in the NBC Reports series are handled." Another source claimed a company spokesman had said flatly, "It's an aggravation we really don't need. . . . I don't suppose we'll ever sponsor one again.*

The facts that the rating was only 5.8 and that the documentary was listed 608th out of a possible 610 on the roster of the season's specials did not help. Ten months later the National News Council issued its mixed conclusions. Why the Council took somewhat longer in its deliberations than usual might be indicated by the central documents it had to deal with—for instance, fifteen specific exceptions taken to

*Textron apparently was more philosophical. It was on board for the year's biggest energy blast, CBS's three-hour report the next summer.

the documentary by the Atomic Industrial Forum and NBC's fifteen answers. Neither side conceded the possibility of error.*

Whatever the merits of the case—and they might never, short of confirmatory disaster, be finally decided—the NBC Report was important for several reasons, most notably as proof that a network was willing to attempt a job on a critical and controversial subject not only directly involving big business, but with big business paying for the show. It was proof as well that if the broadcasters could dish it out, big business, at least some of it, was able to take it.†

However, in most instances, if network news and public affairs gave the appearance to some of being anti-business, it was usually a matter of inadequate information put on the air prematurely. If to others the networks seemed to favor big business, it was mainly by its omissions.

Retreating from the complicated world of networks and corporate giants to the simpler one of local broadcasting, where there was assumed to be more time and less suspicion on both sides, the relationships between news and business still remained ambivalent. There had been a definite increase in the coverage of business. Ninety-two local news directors confirmed that fact to the DuPont Survey so far as their own operations were concerned. One hundred and twenty-three, in addition, had begun or increased consumer reporting. Among those heard from:

> We have started a Monthly Economic Report, researched and produced by the News Department in cooperation with the local college. In addition, we strive to import significant business and agricultural news.   *Yuma, Ariz.*

> In 1975 [our station] recognized the importance of business and economic news and hired a full time reporter to cover that area. We provided additional training through the MBA program, the College of Business at the University of Utah, as well as Washington Journalism Center and other special seminars for economic journalists. Our commitment includes daily reports by the economic reporter, and occasional special stories, series, documentaries or mini-documentaries on the subject. The first economic reporter we had has now left us, but our commitment remains high as he was immediately replaced by another reporter

---

*See Appendix IV.

†Joan Konner might find some comfort in President Carter's offer ten months later in which, echoing Emma Lazarus, he volunteered to welcome the nuclear wastes of the world to our shores, and admitted at the same time that he and all his experts weren't as yet quite sure exactly how they'd dispose of them.

with training and background in the field of economics as well
as TV journalism. *Salt Lake City, Utah*

It has been one of our goals to increase substantive coverage
of business news, and I believe we have been able to accomplish
that to a limited degree. But we still react too much, and anticipate too little in terms of covering business. We very seldom
"break" major business stories, in large measure because we have
no one reporter specializing in this area. But I believe we are
doing a better job of covering the general business area, and
especially agriculture. *Minneapolis, Minn.*

We find business and financial stories much more numerous in
the general flow of news we cover. These stories are presented as
important local news stories which stand alone in the newscast.
. . . They are not lumped into a department headed business news.
Washington, D.C.

We are now doing a financial and business wrap up in newscast
once a week. *Cincinnati, Ohio*

Added a contributing reporter who specializes in economics
and the marketing places. *Dallas, Tex.*

We have become more aware of the importance of reporting
economic news in light of tight money, the recession and the oil
shortage. Since we are in the middle of the petro-chemical complex of this country we have found our reporting wrapped around
the futures of these companies, since their futures will to a large
extent save our cities and country's future. We do try to get
business to allow us to tell both sides of the story.
Baton Rouge, La.

We have made greater efforts to relate to our viewers just how
business activities directly affect their lives. In one particularly
controversial area, that of brown lung, we did a series of programs dealing with the disease and its causes . . . with full
cooperation of a textile firm involved in the dispute. .
Our major point of confrontation has been in the area of
organized labor, not a favorite subject in Carolina corporate
circles. Some pressure was brought to bear on a reporter doing
a report on the labor situation in one county of our area. Businesses contacted refused to provide spokesmen, and with corporate prompting, the local chamber of commerce and its president-elect urged our reporter to drop the idea entirely, without
asking what the thrust of the story was to be. When it aired, the

piece ran approximately seven minutes and, as planned, was neither pro union nor pro company.   *High Point, N.C.*

We have increased our coverage of the business and financial community in the Pittsburgh market over the last 12 to 18 months. Pittsburgh is the fourth largest corporate headquarters city in the United States and the activities of these companies are of major interest to a substantial part of the population we serve. Further, I think this increased coverage has added a new dimension to our consumer reporting. Besides the normal coverage of consumer frauds and tips and the activities of public utilities, we have been able to get the inside track on new products and services offered by area firms. As an example, we have been able to cover not only the problems of fantastically high construction costs, but also couple those stories with at least two new names which offer excellent construction at the lowest possible cost.
Pittsburgh, Pa.

No special features have been instituted, but increasingly business and financial news is appearing within the regular news blocks. In most instances, the stories are directly related to jobs, consumers, home buyers, and economic conditions, as opposed to the more traditional stock market and business reports.

The general manager will, from time to time, receive comments, but they have no impact on news coverage and such are not unexpected. I feel that the relationship between the advertiser and television management has become on the whole too sophisticated to follow such a crude approach. If anything, news management and agency people are more sensitive to this issue than to any other area of news coverage. I feel this very sensitivity to the issue has in part worked to defuse many situations which might have, in the past, become confrontations between station and advertiser.

Again, more sophisticated relationships have evolved between the sales department and the news department. The goal of a sales department is to court advertisers and that goal, by definition, will occasionally run counter to the needs and desires of news, but on the whole, if all concerned can deal openly and honestly with the issue, then the integrity of the news department can be both discussed and protected. The key is in the creation of an atmosphere for open discussion. If anything, the paranoia on the part of many news people tends to close down such lines of communication and thus eliminates a vital voice in station decisions. It has been my experience to find our salesmen extremely sensitive to this issue, and acutely aware of the necessary independence of the news department. I must also add that our general manager has given news his total support in maintaining what I consider a healthy situation. *San Francisco, Calif.*

In the wake of this increased commitment, news directors reported a positive response from local businessmen, particularly in those communities where big business was represented.

They, too, are becoming more aware of their role in the community and now realize that media coverage is a two-way street; they are now more open, and have hired p. r. people to deal with us on a professional level.

Baton Rouge, La.

Local business, for the most part, has been very cooperative. As long as they are dealt with fairly and given the opportunity to respond, there is very little pressure placed on the station in regard to coloring information.

Tulsa, Okla.

By and large most modern businesses are becoming aware of the fact that it is in their best interest to be open with the news media. Fair and accurate coverage tends to result in more cooperation from the business community.

Portland, Oreg.

. . . Agribusiness concerns have begun to recognize that their operations are no longer being "taken for granted," and have begun to become more open and more accessible to the public affairs department.

Some of that "openness and accessibility" has not been easy to come by, however. Some has resulted from business recognition of the power of the broadcast medium itself.

Des Moines, Iowa

Several of the major corporations have become more cooperative as they have come to realize the importance of local news coverage of national industries in the Pittsburgh area. The result of such cooperation is easier access to information and corporate spokespeople.

Pittsburgh, Pa.

I think there is a growing awareness among businessmen of the importance of television news, and a greater readiness to cooperate in the reporting of business news. But a great deal of suspicion remains on both sides, curtailing some efforts to increase coverage. Business still tends to view television as an adversary (because, I think, of our consumer reporting) and is fearful of opening its doors too wide to the television cameras. And there is still a tendency on the part of businessmen and their public relations advisers to disappear in times of company or industry crisis, when they or their firms may "look bad" in the public eye.

Minneapolis, Minn.

We have conducted a public relations campaign among many of the businesses in the state by issuing a brochure explaining how businesses should deal with news organizations. It seems to have had a positive effect and I think businessmen are hearing more and more from their own peers that they've got to quit hiding their heads in the sand when it comes to news organizations and that many of the complaints they have with news coverage of business are their own fault. As a result, we are finding greater cooperation, but there are still those who prefer to hide their heads when a reporter comes around.

Salt Lake City, Utah

All was not so calm, however, as these comments seemed to indicate. Objective coverage of the business scene and such subjects as energy and the environment led in many instances to fairly primitive responses from local businessmen and their friends in broadcast management. In the past two years, news directors reported to the DuPont Survey over 150 incidents in which they had been attacked directly or indirectly through management by irate businessmen. They mentioned fifty-eight threats of cancellation of advertising and thirty-one actual cancellations resulting from disapproval of broadcast news. Several benefactors were reported to have withdrawn their support from public TV because of displeasure over reporting. In addition, there were thirty-six threats of suits with damages going as high as $6 million.

Some typical incidents reported:

A year ago we did an in-depth series of reports on professional tax preparers called "Many Unhappy Returns" in which we investigated the work of randomly selected tax preparers. As a result of this series, one major national company threatened to withdraw a substantial advertising budget the next season, a threat which was never carried out. Also, a local grocery chain was so irritated by one of our health inspection reports that it not only withdrew its advertising, but urged its suppliers to do the same.

Minneapolis, Minn.

S.F.'s Bechtel Corporation cited two Newsroom stories as unfair to Bechtel and the reason Bechtel would not consider supporting KQED's "World Press" program. The stories, both of which I consider solid, fair and complete, were on Bechtel's tacit compliance with the Arab boycott and Bechtel's efforts to win big government contracts to rebuild Vietnam. What might have particularly annoyed Bechtel was that both stories drew on internal Bechtel memos our reporters had obtained.

San Francisco, Calif.

One instance was a mobile home dealer complaining because a civil defense official had stated that mobile homes could be very dangerous in Oklahoma because of high frequency of tornados. Dealer complained, since he was an advertiser, that the station should not have aired the civil defense expert's remarks. The dealer did not threaten to cancel his advertising, but was given an opportunity to advise viewers on how to avoid dangers.

Tulsa, Okla.

Hearing aid company was upset over story on new regulations requiring a physical exam. Auto dealers get upset over almost any story we run about cars. Sears manager has complained about stories on electronic TV games. Local pet shop owner upset over story on decline of rabbits and chicks as Easter gifts.

Eau Clair, Wis.

Chemung County Republican Committee dropped entire campaign package following investigative series on "patronage" insurance set-up.

Elmira, N.Y.

Alyeska Pipeline Service Co. greatest perpetrator of threats for pipeline coverage. They feel could hurt their eight member companies in the bond market. Currently have a disagreement going with them over pipeline employment levels and cost of the pipeline.

Fairbanks, Alaska

Have had at least two sit-down sessions with particular companies to discuss charge of "anti-business bias" with no specific examples. Sessions very rewarding in that we could establish poor public relations policies which have prevented us from doing positive business and industrial features or a good hard news version because of a "no comment" policy or a policy of relying on a piece-of-paper press release approach, resulting in an on-camera "reader" story with less impact than a filmed piece would have had.

Milwaukee, Wis.

A local fast food hamburger chain threatened a cancellation because of a story showing misleading advertising; a national transmission repair chain brought pressure through the sales department and threatened cancellation because of a consumer complaint story. (In both of the above the story did not run.) In each of the above, these cases went to management (as they usually do) and in the case of the hamburger chain, the story was dropped because of management pressure.

Salt Lake City, Utah

In some instances news directors reported a pro-business bias on the part of management resulting in front office intrusion.

"Front office must" stories frequently arise . . . despite important opposition to them by the news department.

Mobile, Ala.

When we do a touchy topic, management becomes "keenly" interested in every aspect.

Springfield, Mass.

Once or twice have had what could be described as a "trial" in general manager's office over news coverage.

Phoenix, Ariz.

In the last eight months since I started in news one of the salesmen asked not to use a story about a local restaurant being closed due to Erie County Board of Health closing establishment due to dumping raw sewage in a local creek. It was not that big of a story. I did not use it.

Buffalo, N.Y.

The management has requested that the news department film grand openings, remodelings, etc. and use them as local news.

Sterling, Colo.

How do you define pressure? Certainly we are aware each time an advertiser cancels because of a news story, but station management has not said "Run this," or "Don't run this."

Spokane, Wash.

It was subtle pressure—so subtle, in fact, that if challenged to prove it, I'm not sure I could. "Why aren't you covering this?"

"What do you mean it's not news?" "Do you know what's going to happen if you run that story?" FYI, the answer to those questions is I'm the news director and advertisers will get the same treatment from my department as anyone else.

Greensboro, N.C.

We don't crap on any business. The boss says they put groceries on my table.

Dodge City, Kans.

Before our consumer reporter left, he published the list of wholesale prices that Missouri car dealers paid for their inventory. They became upset and we lost our auto dealer advertising for several weeks.

St. Louis, Mo.

Last year news began the Consumer Reports TV service reports with great opposition from sales and programming. First report infuriated two auto dealers sponsors who threatened cancellation and I don't know if they did or not.

Recently, a similar situation from a sponsor, with sales department screams over a rinky-dink issue. Then, one of top station men jumped on it.

At the end of our contract year we will not renew consumer reports. Two reasons: lack of public response to the series itself; we can use that money on other projects.

Second, it's exhausting to fight week-long battles several times a year over a concept. News, of course, feels it is the station's obligation to present such unbiased product comparisons. Other station segments say "Caveat emptor."

It is my feeling that the day will come when television stations will have to make the effort to balance the imbalance created by advocacy advertising. Impartiality and nonbiased comparisons will be run on the air as public service announcements.

Hopefully, it will not be necessary to have government require this, but given the nonprogressive attitude of many stations, that probably will be necessitated. The Fairness Doctrine, which requires that all positions be aired in news and public affairs, may come to advertising. As it is now, other points of view are smothered by dollars.

Monroe, La.

Such pressure occasionally was conspicuous enough to receive attention off the station premises. Among those instances reported by DuPont correspondents:

KTVV-TV held a party for advertisers. Told news people to cover it and put film of the band that played on the news. Details were confused and management and news people gave conflicting stories. Anchorman and News Director left the station immediately thereafter.

Austin, Tex.

Blue Cross-Blue Shield attempted to squash a series of stories produced by KSL-TV's economic reporter which showed a serious deterioration in the company's reserves. The company enlisted the help of the state insurance commissioner, but the station resisted the pressure and aired the stories.

Both Utah Power and Light Co. and Mountain Fuel Supply Co. kept up a barrage of criticism against all the stations, accusing them of misunderstanding and misinterpreting rate increase requests.

Salt Lake City, Utah

WJW-TV news director, Virgil Dominic, killed a story that would have embarrassed the Cleveland Electric Illuminating Co. The reporter, Jim Cox, was fired soon after the incident.

Cleveland, Ohio

Addressing the Association of National Advertisers on the subject of "Business and the News Media: Can We Find a Better Channel?," J. L. Ferguson, chairman and president of General Foods Corporation ($129 million in TV billings including local news and public affairs) ended a fairly harsh consideration of today's journalistic practices so far as the business community was concerned with a short litany which began by eliding I Corinthians 13, verses 1 and 2: "Though I speak with the tongues of men and of angels, and have not charity . . . I am nothing."

Ferguson continued in a more colloquial vein.

The reality is that we are all in the same boat. The reality is that we are all being whipsawed by change that has come too fast. There is no further profit in a search for Bad Guys. The solutions we find will be solutions we find together. The benefits that accrue will accrue to everybody.

To date, neither business nor broadcasting, network or local, seemed quite ready to accept the admonitions of Saint Paul, or those of the head of General Foods.

III. Is TV Business Anti-News?

Mr. Ferguson was restating a truth already voiced by Mr. Mahoney and Secretary Connally: broadcasting was big business. But, far from being an advantage in covering business, in several ways the big business success of broadcasting remained a handicap. Broadcasting's business nature and its responsibilities as the nation's leading purveyor of news and information were frequently and painfully at cross purposes.

One way in which broadcasting's business nature had militated against thorough coverage of any subject, including business, was demonstrated in Chapter 3 in the matter of extending the evening news. The bottom line in that encounter between networks and local stations was all too apparent. The unwillingness to risk profits had done the nation's viewers out of the sixty-minute network news. They would continue to get most of their TV economics in thirty-second takes.

There were other less obvious reasons why broadcasting, the big business, had difficulty in covering big, serious, hard-to-grasp stories about its colleagues in American industry, or in being totally convincing when it did so.

For one thing, as broadcast news became increasingly important to the American public there had been, rather than an enthusiastic acceptance of this added responsibility, a steady resistance to it on the part of network and local stations.

This was understandable. Unlike the newspapers and news magazines whose circulations and advertisers electronic journalists were appropriating, broadcasting early in its history had acknowledged itself a primarily commercial enterprise whose first concern was not journalism, but the assembling of audiences in the interest of moving merchandise. To this end, first radio and then TV had become the world's largest purveyor of entertainment; and it was to this activity that broadcasting owed its enormous success. If the people of America had chosen to make television their overwhelming choice for information as well as entertainment, that was a fact that broadcast management accepted with some uneasiness.

Indeed, to a powerful group within the broadcast business, news and public affairs had always seemed inconvenient, expensive, and frequently an embarrassment, tolerated mainly for reasons of vanity and prestige, or as a sop to congressional and bureaucratic busybodies. They knew the time could be more profitably employed.

By the eighth decade of the century, management realized, along with everyone else, that TV news had become a force potent enough to be credited with destroying presidents, stopping wars, and accelerating social revolutions. It had developed other uses too, namely making money and collecting audiences. The people in charge were hesitant to act on the facts.

Nor could one blame them for caution. As the president of the Prudential Insurance Company of America, a long-time broadcast client, said, "Sixty seconds on the evening news tonight is all that is required to ruin a reputation, turn a politician out of office, or impair a company's profitability. The power of the press with today's methods of mass communications has become, in short, the power to destroy." And, of course, it hardly needed saying, the power to enlighten the public and to invite retaliation from damaged politician and impaired advertiser alike.

Other complications for the broadcast journalist were implicit in broadcasting's business success. Over the years, as a result of their good fortune, broadcasters had assimilated or been assimilated by enterprises which frequently had nothing to do with commercial broadcasting (except possibly as clients for advertising space) or with news and public affairs (except as promising subjects for investigation).

Being embedded in a proliferating corporation or conglomerate had few advantages for the broadcast newsman.

In its early days, broadcasting was all CBS was concerned with. In 1976 broadcasting represented a little more than half of CBS's business. The budgets of the news divisions of the three networks, even in a year with political conventions, campaigns, and the Bicentennial, amounted to less than 3 percent of the annual expenditures of their parent organizations.*

With individual stations the proportionate investment in the news could fall much lower. Even at Westinghouse, the nation's most important broadcaster after the networks, and one particularly dedicated to news and public affairs, news budgets were a small fraction of the corporate balance sheet.

Being a part of such rich and extensive corporate families might seem to have advantages for the news operations. Such was not the case. Corporate ownership was being blamed for the milking of broad-

*See Appendix V.

cast operations, the hiring of news consultants to jazz up the news in the interest of maximizing profits, and the manipulation of news items and ad schedules to benefit other members of the corporate family. As early as 1945, when Aviation Corporation (AVCO), one of the nation's largest manufacturers of airplane parts and farm equipment, decided to acquire Cincinnati's famous clear channel radio station WLW, nervousness about corporate ownership of broadcast properties was expressed by the four FCC commissioners who approved the transfer. In a communication to Congress they sent the following caveat:

> The dangers inherent in licensing a radio station to a company whose principal business interests lie in other fields are, of course, that the station will become a mere adjunct to the principal business and be operated to forward that interest at the expense of public service, or that its operations may reflect only the social, economic, or political views of its owners, or that the stations will be operated in the way calculated to return the largest revenue without regard to public service.

A quarter of a century later, in 1969, with the nation's major market stations rapidly passing into corporate hands, the commission finally instituted an inquiry into the actual effects of conglomerate membership on radio and TV. Preliminary findings showed that some of the practices outlined in the 1945 communication might indeed have developed in the intervening years.* The inquiry was expanded to cover an additional thirty-one conglomerates owning broadcast licenses, both those starting in broadcasting and branching out into other fields and those buying into broadcasting from outside.†

In 1976 the commission belatedly announced that the study had been completed three years earlier and that for reasons of business competition and confidentiality only portions of it would be available to the public. Its findings, they said, had already been incorporated in various unspecified rulings and no further action was contemplated.

Despite FCC reassurances that nothing further need be done, the possibly negative effect of conglomerate ownership on broadcasting operations surfaced again—most notably in the case of General Tire and its wholly owned subsidiary RKO General.

General Tire, the fourth largest rubber company in the nation, had

---

*AVCO, one of the six conglomerates selected for the preliminary inquiry, was found to be recommending preferential use of its broadcasting facilities which by that time totaled twelve (five TV and seven radio stations) to its other subsidiaries. By 1977 it had divested itself of all its broadcast properties.
†See Appendix VI.

been charged in 1970 with reciprocity agreements* with RKO General, which, in its turn, was proprietor of seventeen radio and TV stations. Although the parent company settled its differences (including antitrust and federal securities violations) with the Department of Justice, license challengers who had accused RKO's Boston station of inadequate service to the community in 1969 persisted. In 1975 they aired evidence that General Tire had made illegal donations to Nixon's 1972 campaign. The SEC followed up the challengers' investigations and in the summer of 1976 accused General Tire of paying bribes in Chile, Rumania, and Morocco and to the Arab League; violating foreign currency laws; having unrecorded slush funds; overbilling foreign affiliates for supplies; making illegal contributions in the U.S. (to persons undisclosed); and paying "gratuities" to military and civilian employees of U.S. agencies with which it did business.

Although it was difficult to demonstrate that misbehavior on the part of the parent corporation, even if proved, could affect its stations' news and public affairs, in September 1976 General Tire requested that it be allowed to spin off RKO General along with all its broadcast properties—an admission of vulnerability, if not of guilt.†

The license challenges continued.

Nor was General the only organization that might anticipate such harassment by license challengers. Dozens more U.S. corporations had admitted to the Securities and Exchange Commission that they had paid bribes or had "questionable" expenses overseas. Add to those the names of corporations which had political slush funds and made questionable campaign donations and the list swelled to 400. On this list were some who, if they did not own broadcast properties outright, were under the same corporate umbrella.‡

More frequent than accusations of news distortion, suppression, or special treatment were complaints that top-level management maximized and diverted profits from thriving broadcast holdings to the less prosperous parts of conglomerate operations or used them for outside acquisitions, thus depriving viewers of the desirable public services which employment of such surpluses within the broadcast operation might have brought them.

---

*Free commercial air time worth $22,750,000 in exchange for goods and services.
†A similar concern had been given credit for the withdrawal of ITT's bid for control of ABC in 1968.
‡Thirty-five of the nation's top 100 advertisers (with hundreds of millions in annual TV billings) were on the SEC list, a fair portion of them underwriting news and public affairs. Although the morality of accepting advertising from the badly behaved or for products of questionable social value was a problem as old as journalism itself and not one that TV journalists were likely to solve soon, it did produce some odd effects when negative news and positive advertisements followed closely upon one another.

Siphoning of profits, specifically from the news, with a resulting ceiling on budget and staffs, had been mentioned with increasing frequency by DuPont correspondents and news directors reporting to the DuPont Survey in recent years. In some instances the managements were those for whom news quality should have been a paramount concern, namely the media magnates who had begun their empires in print and found themselves depending more and more on broadcasting properties, not only for profits, but as a means of keeping their print operations afloat.

The fact that journalism was supposed to be a major concern of big media was not an inevitable benefit to individual TV stations. On the NCCB's list rating broadcasting group performance in news and public affairs, two of the five lowest-rated broadcast groups were newspaper-owned.

Media cross-ownership, which had been labeled a danger to the fundamental First Amendment requirement of diversity, obviously posed other threats to the quality of a community's news service.

Journalistic representatives of media conglomerates were subject to other embarrassments which surfaced during the energy crisis of 1973. When oil companies were criticized on the air for their dramatic increases in profits while the rest of the country suffered inconvenience and deprivation, spokesmen responded by pointing out that in most instances their profits were substantially lower than those enjoyed by the reporters' own employers, an argument still being used as late as John Connally's remarks to the Houston press.

This "Why me? You too" syndrome had other manifestations so far as broadcast journalists were concerned.

In November 1976 Thomas A. Murphy, chairman of General Motors, told a meeting of New York businessmen:

> I want to contribute a note of urgency—that the clock is running on free enterprise and it is later than we think. I want to make certain that we recognize that all the fault does not lie elsewhere—much of it lies in our own business community, and perhaps in our own organizations.
>
> We know that every shoddy product, every neglected service, every reason for complaint is worse than bad business: it invites more regulation by government. Adverse public opinion, the antecedent of government regulation, has been shaped to a great degree by the failure of business to satisfy the customer. Other factors are involved, but much of the public's antipathy toward big business is rooted in the American consumer's own bad experiences in the marketplace. To the extent that it is rooted there, it can be remedied only there.

Although a consumer revolt by TV viewers was not yet indicated by the ratings, there had long been ominous rumblings of discontent from special interest groups, accompanied by threats of tougher regulations. Concerned broadcasting executives might, like Mr. Murphy, point to a similar decline in product and services dispensed by their networks and individual stations. Degradation of public taste, the corruption of innocents, and incitement to violence were just three of the more lurid accusations that critics had listed when enumerating broadcasting's shortcomings.

Even those who were reticent about laying such responsibilities at broadcasting's door had to admit that the TV viewer was getting increasingly shabby merchandise for his recycled dollar. And the advertiser, who was handing the public's money on to the broadcaster, had other justifications for the complaint that he was paying more for less.

In a study of the network flagship stations in Manhattan, among the nation's biggest money makers, presented to the Association of National Advertisers in February 1977, it was disclosed that 22.5 percent of all time on the air, four and a half hours per day, was nonprogram material.

This included advertisements, promotions of station and network offerings, and a comparatively small number of public service messages. The study also showed that the average broadcast hour contained thirty separate visual elements, adding up to one programming interruption every two minutes. Pile-ups of as many as thirteen of these elements without any program content intervening sometimes occurred. Promos, one of the most frequent elements in these many-layered nonnutritional sandwiches, were a product of interstation and network competition. If broadcasters had paid for them at the rates they charged outside advertisers, they would have cost approximately $634 million per year.

Nor was the news exempt from this infuriating barrage of messages. The worst program monitored, in terms of frequency and length of interruption, was the ABC flagship station's Late Saturday News. This half hour contained 37.8 percent nonprogram material and averaged sixty-six separate elements per hour for the viewers to assimilate. WNBC's late news was the second most cluttered program logged.

The responsibility was not all with the broadcasters. Even with such evidence of glut, some advertisers, left out in the stampede for TV time, were clamoring for an additional advertising minute every half hour. However, the broadcasters had not given them a definite no.

"Good business" meant bad news for the news in yet other ways.

Although network money was being spent on new programming at a higher rate than ever before, budget and time preferences went to the biggest potential money makers, which did not include news and public affairs. Even when a news division program such as "Sixty Minutes" proved a winner and was brought in at half the price of an hour of entertainment, the networks had a hard time bringing themselves to act on the evidence.

NBC and ABC had both murmured about developing their own prime time news magazines to follow CBS's lead. NBC had actually tried out a couple, but none had gotten onto the 1977 network schedules. CBS, which made the attempt to follow in its own footsteps with "Who's Who," gave up after five months. Although NBC renewed its promise of a weekly TV magazine for the 1978–79 season, no further experimentation in prime time informational programming was imminent. As for documentaries, figures showed a drastic drop on all three networks, even as their profits climbed. According to the *New York Times,* CBS had aired twenty-eight documentaries in 1975 and only fifteen in 1976. ABC was down from eighteen to eight, and NBC from fifteen to thirteen. The budgets involved in putting these programs on the air were substantially less per network than the cost of a half hour weekly situation comedy.

Although all three networks claimed an increase in their commitment for "next season," more and more frequently good business practice dictated that the special reports which represented this increase be slipped to the far end of the evening schedule beyond the late news where the costs of preemption and the audiences were minimal.

That a ceiling on time for news and public affairs had been reached nationwide despite climbing profits was demonstrated by FCC figures released in June of 1977. They showed that nonentertainment/nonsports programming between 6:00 A.M. and midnight stood at 24.2 percent for 1976 against 24.6 percent in 1975. For 6:00 to 11:00 P.M. 1976 had 19.4 percent against 22.4 percent in 1975. Locally produced nonentertainment programs between 6:00 A.M. and midnight had stabilized at approximately 8 percent of total programmed time over the past three years.

There were other practices which in the competitive atmosphere of big business were considered necessary to survival or at least to ensuring profits. When associated with the gathering and dissemination of news, they took on a different coloration and dramatized further the need for absolute insulation between the business and the journalistic aspects of broadcasting.

Paramount among these was lobbying, an activity in which big business and big broadcasting frequently made common cause. Nothing that broadcasting did seemed more directly opposed to the pledge to serve the public interest, convenience, and necessity than its lobbying presence in the nation's capital. Considering the network vice-presidents assigned full time to the Washington beat, the legal firms and lobbyists retained by station groups and individual station owners, and the national and state trade organizations (including the NAB), few other industries had such a large and potent group plugging their special interests with the nation's legislators, administrators, and regulators.

While the reporters and newscasters at home pursued objectivity as best they could, the lobbyists for their employers were pursuing preferential treatment motivated by their own desire for legitimate corporate gain. Again, it was impossible to prove that the urgent positions of the Washington wheelers and dealers fed back to the nation's most important newsrooms.

That the lobbyists and the politicians they dealt with were aware of those newsrooms and the power they wielded was, however, quite obvious.

In a narrower context there were lobbying efforts against the limitation of energy advertising and against regulatory measures within the FTC, FDA, and the FCC itself which might directly impinge upon the broadcasters' profitability—and certainly were the raw material, as Walter Cronkite indicated above, with which their news staffs back home must deal. When California broadcast management zeroed in on Washington to protest the saccharine ban in the name of a large group of their advertisers, one had to wonder if a similar pressure had been exerted within their own news organizations.

Probably most disturbing of all was the broadcasters' closing ranks with big business in one of the most massive lobbying efforts of the year against the establishment of a national consumers' agency—a body which, if one accepted what one heard night after night on the evening news, was long overdue.

All of the concerns which broadcasting shared with big business would seem likely to result, if not in "puff pieces, or phony buildups, or winkings at unethical practices," at least in a softening of broadcast news as it impinged on the business community.

The continuing complaints coming from big business and its partisans about what got on the air suggested that this was not the case. The final paradox to those that saw the press-business confrontation as unresolvable was the support of TV by big business.

The growth of corporate advertising on TV, the ultimate accolade of the business community, was celebrated in the fall of 1976 at the Television Bureau of Advertising's first corporate advertising workshop. There representatives from 180 of the nation's big businesses heard testimonials for television, and particularly for TV news, as a means of getting a favorable image across to the public. The testimonials were delivered by spokespersons for such industry giants as General Motors, United States Steel, International Telephone and Telegraph, Textron, and Union Carbide, all sometime patrons, critics, and subjects of TV journalism. TV, the meeting was told, had been the leading medium for corporate advertising for the past five years with ad billings growing from $67 million in 1970 to $118 million in 1975. That that was good news for the broadcast industry, and good business, everyone could agree. As for broadcast journalism . . .

5 • The Year in Broadcasting

THE BICENTENNIAL of the American Republic, the nomination and election of its thirty-ninth president, the first soft landing on Mars, a half dozen "minor" wars, a plague of hijackings, terrorism, and multimillion-dollar scandals . . . It sounded like a bumper year for journalists and yet, on the home screens across the nation, it came through fragmented and repetitive, as though it had all been seen and heard before, or that finally the limitations and idiosyncrasies of television had infected not only the viewers but the very events the medium chose to cover.

Even the great occasion, July 4, 1976, with its tall ships and bursting rockets, came off unfocused and listless in the day-long coverage of the three networks, as if there were no adequate way to celebrate such an august occasion, or at least to convey it on a screen whose dimensions were not much larger than the hand-written parchment document that began it all 200 years before.

The Political Year

The 1976 nominating conventions of the two great political parties also struck many viewers as perfunctory and out of focus. This failure to be bright and to the point could hardly be blamed on the broadcasters—except insofar as the rule of giving them what they want, broadcasting's equivalent of the second law of thermodynamics, seemed to restrict and blur events as never before. At the end, network heads said gravely, once again, that gavel-to-gavel coverage of the conventions must be reevaluated, perhaps rotated, perhaps turned over to public TV.

As for the presidential campaigns that followed, few risks were taken, and the real issues were infrequently explored. Thanks to federal subsidies each candidate had $21.8 million to spend. Of this total Ford spent $2.5 million on network TV, $3.88 million on spot TV, $1.49 million on radio and $1.29 million on print media. All Ford production costs (mainly for radio and TV) totaled $1.65 million. Carter spent $7.2 million on TV air time, network and spot; $1.26

million on radio time; a little over half a million on print media, with a half million total for all production costs, print and broadcast.

Broadcasting budgets for both Republicans and Democrats were up substantially over Nixon's and McGovern's. The 1972 candidates had spent $6.9 million and $6.8 million respectively. Thanks to the federally imposed ceilings, expenditures for grass roots organization, mailings, and all other nonbroadcasting expenses were down on both sides.

In congressional and local politics (owing to the expanded use of TV) the cost of running for office had gone up steadily. Still, it was impossible to prove that any amount or particular way of spending money on TV and radio could guarantee a politician victory.*

Even the presidential debates—the first such confrontations since the historic Nixon-Kennedy broadcasts of 1960—failed to create much excitement. The fact that they took place at all was testimonial to the persistence and ingenuity of the League of Women Voters and the somewhat grudging cooperation of the three commercial TV networks. The whole undertaking seemed threatened at one moment by CBS News president Richard Salant, who objected to the manner of selecting newsmen for the panel. He saw it as an opportunity for the candidates to manipulate the proceedings. The difference was resolved, but not before the broadcasters made it clear that they felt matters could have been handled more professionally had they been in charge. The second conspicuous contretemps, a technical failure which interrupted the first debate for twenty-seven minutes, clearly demonstrated that the occasion, far from being the genuine news event it was billed as (in order to get past the FCC's equal time restrictions), had obviously been staged for television and (at least so far as the networks were concerned) would have been better handled in a proper studio with cameras panning the audience.†

Howard K. Smith evaluated the campaign at midcareer in one of his increasingly acidulous commentaries:

> The campaign has been, in a word, banal. . . . The public has the feeling of being nibbled to death by ducks, not addressed by titans as should be the case in a contest to choose not only our

---

*According to former FCC Commissioner Nicholas Johnson, "The power of the broadcast industry is reflected in the fact that it takes money from elected officials rather than giving it to them. It's probably the only business that does this. They don't have to pay politicians. The politicians pay them. The politicians take the little brown bags of money they get from corporations, and turn around and give it to the broadcasting stations."

†League ground rules forbade cameras to move away from the principals to pick up audience reaction.

President but the *ex officio* leader of a troubled Western civilization. The men have but thirty days to dissolve the impression visibly growing but which we all dread to accept: neither has the stature for the job.

For all the lack of excitement the network commitment to political coverage was as high as it had ever been, with the three networks claiming costs of $45 million for a total of 193 hours on the air, including the conventions, election night coverage, and the presidential debates.

The oddness of the relationship between politicians and press was caught in Iowa public TV station KDIN's "See How They Run," one of the few TV documentaries of the year that attempted critical self-examination. The program began its observations three months before the Iowa caucuses of January 1976, touted as "the nation's first political test." The caucuses were covered by all three networks and a covey of the top political reporters "as if it were the election itself." In the half hour that followed, the documentarians clearly demonstrated their thesis that "the power of political bosses and machines . . . has been passed on . . . to the press."

> In that transfer of power, the press, once a mere viewer of the political process, has become an active participant.
>
> In a way, the growth of television contributed to that transfer of power. The first broadcast of President Eisenhower's press conferences, for example, brought the immediacy of politics into living rooms across the country. Television began to set the standard—not only for the reporting of events, but often for the nature of the events themselves.
>
> News conferences were scheduled by candidates to gain maximum exposure on television's early-evening newscasts. And even the settings for political concession speeches were dressed so that the "television cameras" could catch a glimpse of what, for the candidate, would later become a forgotten dream. . . .
>
> Television in recent years has contributed to the growth of a curious phenomenon: a phenomenon which holds that the reporter is a star.
>
> It doesn't mean, necessarily, that the *style* of political reporters has finally triumphed over the *substance* of their political reporting. It simply reinforces the notion that reporters are participants —and, as such, a few of them stand on equal footing with the candidates themselves—both groups recognizing that the process demands performance as well as substance.

Dick Stout, who had covered three presidential elections for *Newsweek* magazine and in 1976 was press secretary for candidate Morris Udall, commented for KDIN's camera:

> Every political reporter should be locked up in a room for six weeks after a campaign is over and be forced to read everything he has written, or view everything he has done on television, or listen to everything he has done on radio for six full weeks through the whole campaign, and I think he'd come out a cleaner man.

However fascinating and devious the events behind scenes, on the screen the campaign was anything but fascinating. The repetition and amplification of candidates' slips, Carter's unfortunate remarks about his interior lusts and middle income taxation, Ford's disastrous comment about the temper of Eastern Europe, the homely details and daily routines, the endless polls and prophesying of results that TV would itself help to fulfill, all added up to a contest with little sense of suspense or climax.

However, the curtain was ceremoniously rung down at the inaugural gala, for which CBS had paid $1 million, $250,000 to the inaugural committee, the rest to the producers. It ran from 9:00 to 11:30 P.M., was fully sponsored, and with the presence of such high-priced talent as Shirley MacLaine, Muhammad Ali, Leonard Bernstein, and Lily Tomlin did well in the ratings, topping "Baretta" and "Charlie's Angels."

By that time it was clear that Carter's use of the media would be dramatically different from that of his immediate predecessors. The only evidence needed was his walk up Pennsylvania Avenue, with his wife Rosalynn, following the inauguration, an inspired bit of TV-wise business and an obvious follow-through on his campaign vow to keep in "direct, intimate relationship with the common man."

Shortly thereafter came his "fireside chat" on energy. Sitting in a cardigan by the fireplace in the White House library (FDR actually did the original "fireside chats" at a desk in the basement) Carter was relaxed, serious, sincere.

The president and his advisers had other innovative ideas for the use of the media, including radio phone-ins, town meetings with the president in attendance, televised cabinet meetings, and talks with literary and artistic giants—"a conversation about alienation" with Nobel Prize winner Saul Bellow was mentioned as a possibility.

Some of the plans materialized, others didn't. On the afternoon of March 5 from 2:00 to 4:00 P.M. (EST), CBS radio carried the first Carter "phone-in." Nine million Americans placed calls to the president and forty-two got through, asking unrehearsed questions about everything from Idi Amin to Laetrile. Although turned down in its request for a simulcast, PBS played a video tape of the event later in the day. On radio the show got the highest rating ever measured by Arbitron, 30 percent of all in-home listeners. "I liked it," said Carter. "The questions that come in from people all over the country are the kind that you would never get in a press conference."

Not that Carter was timid about meeting the press. His promised schedule of press conferences, one every two weeks, was rigidly adhered to, making him the most regularly available president in recent history.

In March, Carter went to Clinton, Massachusetts, to attend a town meeting. Television also attended, PBS live, ABC on a delayed basis. (A later presidential town meeting in Yazoo City, Mississippi, was covered by ABC.) March also saw two more Carter press conferences, his first appearances before Congress (aired by all four networks) and the U.N. (aired only on PBS).

On April 14, NBC News put on a special NBC Report entitled, "A Day with President Carter" (the first since "Beware: Radioactive Wastes" and with the same sponsors). Carter had cooperated because, according to an adviser,

> it seemed ideal for purposes of bringing the President closer to the people and because it was a way to make good on Mr. Carter's campaign promise to open up the government. There isn't any way we can open the White House to millions of people to let them see what the President does all day and what an incredibly busy schedule he keeps. We believe there's a lot of interest in how the White House functions, particularly in the wake of Watergate.*

The program, with a 12 rating, was number 480 on *Variety*'s list of TV specials.

By his third month in office Carter's TV appearances had been given credit for building "the image of a sincere, dedicated, common-

---

*Nixon opened the White House to Americans via NBC News in January 1972. There had also been TV visits with Lyndon Johnson and the Kennedys.

sense President." His popularity in the polls stood 12 points higher than at his inauguration and he was being called "the first TV president" and "master of television." The *Wall Street Journal* said:

> Inevitably comparisons go back to Franklin Roosevelt's practiced use of radio. But television is infinitely more potent than radio as a communications tool and perhaps, fortunately, the country hasn't until now had a President able to tap its true potential.
>
> Television was just becoming widespread under Harry Truman, Dwight Eisenhower's straightforward honesty was effective on TV, but he didn't employ the medium very often. John Kennedy was a TV natural, but never had time to exercise his talent fully.
>
> Lyndon Johnson was a disaster on the tube, while Richard Nixon went hot and cold—sometimes highly effective, often far too contrived. Gerald Ford did well in unrehearsed appearances, badly in more formal ones.

The long-standing fear that TV was giving the president an unfair advantage over Congress was revived. "The networks simply aren't going to give remotely comparable coverage to congressional leaders," the *Journal* concluded, "and only in the most unusual circumstances will they devote very much air time to congressional hearings or debates." (See pages 135–36.)

Said *Broadcasting* magazine, "Like Julius Erving on a basketball court, or O. J. Simpson on a football field, Jimmy Carter, before a camera or microphone, seems to move with the grace and style of a natural."

David Broder of the Washington *Post* was quoted as saying the president "has transformed himself from the very shaky winner of a bungled campaign into a very popular President whose mastery of the mass media has given him real leverage with which to govern."

George Reedy, press head for Lyndon Johnson, said, "Carter is not a man of words. He gets in trouble when he uses them. But he is sending complicated messages by purely symbolic means. When he wore a sweater, it was more than a stunt. He told people there was no magic solution to the energy problem, that they should dress warmly. And when he walked down Pennsylvania Avenue with his wife, he announced the end of the imperial Presidency."

Already by the end of March, however, there was talk of overexposure. In early April, when the president announced a speech on the energy crisis would be "available for live coverage," CBS declined.

"We didn't think it warranted an interruption of our programming," said a CBS executive. At this point Carter formally requested broadcast time from all three networks and got it. Said a Carter spokesman, "He knows there is a distinction between what is news and what isn't, and he recognizes that the networks have a final say on that distinction, but he felt it was a matter of national urgency. If he had not felt that way, he would not have asked for the time."

As the year progressed Carter continued his full TV schedule, although the televising of cabinet meetings and talks with distinguished intellectuals did not materialize. Nor had his way with a camera and microphone helped to protect him against the drop in popularity with press and public alike which inevitably follows the first few hopeful months of a presidency. By November his ratings in the polls had fallen to 55% approval and Washington correspondents and commentators had long since sharpened their knives.

Before Carter went on the air for his first postinaugural appearance, Republican chairman Senator Bill Brock had wired all three networks for "free television time . . . to permit an appropriate Republican spokesman to respond to and to express points of view other than those which may be expressed by the President in his fireside chat on February 2nd which you have agreed to broadcast."

In their own fashion broadcasters had already anticipated Brock's request. Even though official out-of-office party pronouncements never attain the attention of a White House resident's, certain Republicans, particularly the veterans of Watergate, had been in high demand. Nor were they performing, like the president, for free.

Foremost among the highly visible was Richard Nixon, who returned under the aegis of British entrepreneur/showman/interviewer David Frost. Turned down by all three networks and public TV as well, "The Nixon Interviews with David Frost," four ninety-minute shows edited out of twenty-eight hours of film, went on the air on a pick-up network of 165 stations, capable of reaching 95 percent of the American TV public, at 9:30 P.M. (EST) on May 4, 1977.

It had been a slow sell. In February the syndicator said, "I'd be naïve not to suppose that some advertisers are reluctant to associate themselves with Nixon or for that matter with any program that might be controversial." Of the 165 stations (19 independents, 146 network affiliates), 28 waited until the last week to sign up. Advertisers were equally slow to get on board at $125,000 a minute. However a full complement was on board for the premiere, including Datsun, Alpo, Colego, Greyhound Bus Lines, Weed Eater, Hilton Hotels, and Radio Shack. They got a good buy. Nixon and Frost talking about

Watergate managed to divert an estimated 45 million viewers from their usual TV prime time fare. It was the biggest audience ever recorded for a syndicated program.

Although the appeal of the four-part series declined after the premiere, Nixon still achieved a victory against his old adversaries the networks by helping reduce their ratings for the important May rating sweep by a full seven points. He also demonstrated the feasibility, at least on a one-shot basis, of a "fourth network," a long-standing advertiser and TV syndicator's idea whose time, many now claimed, had finally come.

Ad Age commented:

> While the form and timing of the fourth network remains hazy, the change in competitive outlook seems irreversible. Having acquired some know-how, and tasted the sweet fruits of success, independents are bound to intensify their efforts. Their ability to earn handsome profits for Mr. Nixon has not gone unnoticed. So their access to other properties will improve, and so will their alliances with advertisers.
>
> Advertisers have longed for a fourth national TV advertising alternative as a hedge against the continuing rise in prices on the established networks. But in the absence of the prospect of value received, they have been reluctant to invest. Aggressive creative programming by the independents provides the missing ingredient, and that hedge now seems attainable.

Herman Land, executive director of the Association of Independent Television Stations, added:

> The Nixon-Frost interviews demonstrated that the audience no longer cares, very much, about whether a station is affiliated, independent, UHF, VHF, or whatever. If it knows that programming will be there, which it thinks will be exciting, interesting to watch, it will watch it. And so it is perfectly possible to get the rating on an independent station with the right show. This is a significant development.

Although there were only thirty-three markets with unaffiliated stations to form the nucleus of a fourth network, Nixon and a six-hour Hollywood-produced version of the Taylor Caldwell novel *Testimony of Two Men,* shown on ninety-five stations simultaneously the same month, gave independent producers hopes of something big ahead. Louis Friedland, president of MCA-TV, one of the oldest and most successful producers in TV, told Les Brown of the *New York Times,* "I truly believe this is the wave of the future and that we're going to take a big bite out of the networks." If he was right, Nixon might enjoy a belated revenge.*

No other program, entertainment or otherwise, during the season received such a build-up. If the networks had rejected the series, they were not averse to calling attention to it. The Sunday before air date Mike Wallace spent a third of "Sixty Minutes" pumping David Frost about what was coming three days later, and all the evening news shows covered the event, although there was a supposedly permanent embargo on clips of the actual performance.

Newspapers and magazines were equally attentive with breathless coverage at each stage of the series' development. Karl E. Meyer reported indignantly in the *Saturday Review:*

> . . . The first show was heralded with an orchestrated barrage of leaked stories written in tones that suggested a Second Coming of the San Clemente exile—lead stories in The New York Times and The Washington Post, and almost identical cover stories in Time ("Nixon Talks") and Newsweek ("Nixon Speaks").
>
> Each interview was followed by panel discussions in which the precise degree of Nixon's truthfulness was weighed. There were news reports and more magazine articles, followed by hints that there would be a fifth show making use of the leavings on the cutting room floor.†
>
> Thus in the Nixon interviews a national tragedy was repackaged as home entertainment, with sales messages from makers of spray deodorants and the newest dog food. What was truly remarkable about the interviews was the degree to which print journalists (who look with scorn on television) allowed themselves to be used to promote a pseudo event. One has to congratulate Richard Nixon. He made his adversaries look foolish. What will the old entertainer do for pin money when he no longer has the press to kick around?

Other notices ranged from shrilly indignant to grudgingly admiring. Anthony Lewis wrote in the *New York Times:*

---

*News and public affairs was not promoted as major fare on such an interconnect. However, "Between the Wars," a half-hour documentary series with Eric Sevareid as narrator and sponsored by Mobil Oil, another network adversary, was scheduled to begin on a fourth network beginning in January 1978, and Capital Cities' energy program, "We Will Freeze in the Dark," was seen on a network of 156 stations coast to coast.

†There was: aired on September 3, 1977.

... shameless, grasping, freakish ... People talk about whether David Frost or someone else can extract "the truth" from him, as if he had any notion of truth. Our fascination actually lies in knowing that there is no limit, and never has been, to what the man will do. And so we watch him on show in our society's well-paid equivalent of a barrel.

The first Frost interview made this dreadful creature seem pathetic.

Richard Ben-Veniste and George Frampton, Jr., two former Watergate prosecuters, pointed out:

But for Gerald R. Ford's pardon, Richard M. Nixon might have been obliged to answer Wednesday night's $600,000 question* for free, in a court of law. Nixon's trial by television, a bizarre, uniquely American spectacle, was not the real McCoy, but did demonstrate that the former President has no credible defense to the Watergate evidence against him.

Nixon seemed to have two objectives: first, to prove his innocence by casting David Frost in the role of "prosecuting attorney," himself as the lawyer for the defense, and the American people as the jury; and, second, to rehabilitate his image by gaining the sympathy of a nation-wide audience.

In the first, Nixon failed. Frost, though disadvantaged by time constraints, was better prepared than Nixon expected. More important, the evidence itself was overwhelming. Many of Nixon's fumbling explanations proved the maxim that the man who chooses to be his own lawyer has a fool for a client. . . .

Realizing he had been defeated by the evidence, Nixon steered the interview toward his second objective: winning sympathy by throwing himself on the mercy of the television jury. . . . To earn the audience's sympathy, Nixon did make some significant admissions . . . but mostly it was vintage Nixon. The bionic smile . . . Time and again Richard Nixon has rescued himself from the facts with this kind of maudlin self-exposure. He undoubtedly evoked a good measure of sympathy from a large segment of the viewing public; it was good television.

David Halberstam in *Rolling Stone* was particularly scornful, not only of Nixon, but of Frost as well:

He passes for a journalist at a time when the lines are blurred and when journalists, because of television, have become celebrities, and celebrities, because of the power and the money, have

*$600,000 was Nixon's original guarantee.

become journalists. So he is a figure of our age: the celebrities probably think David Frost is a journalist and thus someone important, and the journalists probably think he is a celebrity and thus someone important, and Frost is not telling. . . .

He is bright and he is talented; he is very shrewd and he does not really care, which is a great advantage. If a kind word were to be used he might be called a media hustler, or, in a less generous phrase, a media racketeer. His essential instinct is not, I think, to inform, to break new ground. One cannot imagine David Frost going against the accepted social grain of a story because of some interior set of values, some sense of right and wrong. If he does not know what is right and what is wrong, he does know what is up and what is down. He is a man driven, I think, to promote himself and make a very great deal of money. The best journalists I know respond to interior ethics and values that are more a part of them than they know. They almost cannot help being honorable. But David is of a different breed, a man who intuitively knows when journalism becomes theater, and who can ford that particular canyon without a hitch.

Thus, he was a far better choice for this assignment than anyone might have expected, since theater it was, and theater it always demanded to be.

As for the interviews:

What was at stake was not something called facts. They are long past and forgotten. . . . What was at stake was theater. . . . The record would entail a long series of network documentaries, often tedious, the interviewing of 20 or 30 people putting together the whole history. It might be gray; it would take up a lot of expensive network time; it would not sell very much Alpo. There was no reason to do the record. The record would mean memory and television has no memory. Television allows you to be what you are today, it is never haunted by what you were yesterday. Television and Nixon arrived at the same time.

It is, in that sense, why Frost was such a good choice for the interviews. His motives were much the same as Nixon's. He could tap-dance away from the strict narrative as readily as the ex-president. A man of more serious intent, more compelled by the past and by Watergate, and more mindful of the Constitution, might not have played the role as well. Another man might have been too difficult, too obsessed or, more likely, too serious and too technical, caught up in minutiae . . .

The Frost interview will not change a single vote, or a single mind; the only thing about it that will affect people is that Nixon is being paid a million dollars for it. . . .

At the May 4 banquet of the American Society of Newspaper Editors in Honolulu, Ben Bradlee, executive editor of the Washington *Post,* who had seen a preview, said, "The interview provided little hard news, but it was perhaps the best television I've ever seen. I thought it was very moving. When Nixon said he 'let the country down,' he came closer to an apology than ever before. I think he was genuinely trying to say he was sorry."

Gerald Warren, editor of the San Diego *Union* and former deputy press secretary to Nixon, added:

> Nixon really said what he truly felt all the way through the interview. It was powerful stuff. I think he went a long, long way. I think that he's probably gone farther than ever before in revealing his true feelings. I think he was taken aback by Frost's shotgun approach. I felt his discomfiture. But I felt the bottom line was the important thing. Here was a man not able to get his point across—but I think he ultimately did.

Whether or not he made his point, Nixon had been paid well over a million dollars and the end was not in sight. David Frost had signed with NBC-TV to develop what he called "a sort of documentary done in outrageous comedy terms which we're calling a docucom."

Other Watergate alumni who made lucrative TV deals included John Dean and John Ehrlichman, for TV rights to their best-selling books, *Blind Ambition* and *The Company.* The latter in its TV incarnation had the distinction of opening ABC's TV year in the fall of 1977, a commercial TV accolade second to none.

Henry Kissinger, after having been rumored as everything from William Paley's to Eric Sevareid's replacement, finally was announced by NBC as a special consultant to NBC News. He would be paid up to $1.5 million over five years. His duties would include answering news correspondents' questions from time to time and presiding over a documentary on foreign affairs scheduled for the winter of 1977–78.

President Ford did not do quite so well. For "close to $1 million" he had agreed to participate in at least one documentary or news special a year for five years, with the TV option to his memoirs thrown in. Mrs. Ford, in exchange for taking part in two programs in the next two years on any subject she might find interesting—"dance, mental health, cancer research"—plus an unspecified number of appearances on the "Today" show, would receive "nearly half a million dollars."

The two other networks sniffed at NBC's contracts. Said Richard Salant, president of CBS News, "Our basic policy is to keep journalism in the hands of journalists. I think there is a sharp line to be drawn between political writing and journalistic writing, and we insist that they [commentators and newsmen] have established journalistic credentials."

William Lord, vice-president in charge of ABC's TV news, said:

I'm not convinced that someone who was in the public eye in government is automatically qualified to be a newsman. And I haven't been convinced that it's that easy for a politician to divest himself of the trappings of having been with the government—of past situations he was involved in or was aware of. I think those of us in the broadcasting business have to be very careful about where these people are coming from.

Richard Wald, president of NBC News, responded, giving the rationale for such extra-professional hiring:

. . . If we are successful in doing this—presumably we will be —other similar occasions will arise in the future.

At the change of this administration, four or eight years from now, we will be interested in doing the same thing with the people who are then the major figures in the field, because I think that they do have something to tell us, and that it's indeed within the purview of television to help them say it, and that we are now in sufficient command of our own resources and our own abilities to be able to do it.

It was not unusual for major figures in public life, after they retired, to write books, not necessarily memoirs, to write newspaper articles, to write series for newspapers, et cetera. It was unusual for such figures to do television programs because television was not around for very long.

Had Jack Kennedy survived and lived out eight years, probably in the Presidency, I think he would have wound up doing something in television. He was a natural for it. . . . Johnson tried it, but it didn't work out quite right. He died before he really got into his stride with that sort of thing.

I think television has come of age. I think it is quite possible for television to deal with public figures as if they were of interest and worth talking to. And I think that what NBC is doing is of value.

There ought to be a way, regularly, of talking to prominent public persons after they leave office, and about topics that are of general interest.

Later it was reported that the decision to hire the Fords and Kissinger was made by NBC president Herbert Schlosser, not by Wald. A former newspaperman, Wald was said to be fearful of the effect such huge cash commitments might have on the networks' more serious journalistic endeavors. Wald's opposition, combined with corporate anxiety about network news ratings, was also said to have had a great deal to do with his departure from the NBC News presidency in the fall of 1977, the second network news head to fall in less than six months.

Other Republicans who found regular jobs in broadcasting included ex-presidential contender Ronald Reagan, whose commentary series "Viewpoint" was sold in more than 280 markets; ex-Secretary of the Treasury William E. Simon, who had become a syndicated radio commentator on economic issues; and ex-New York Senator James L. Buckley, who had undertaken a biweekly stint on National Public Radio's award-winning "All Things Considered" at $65 per appearance and was working for Group W as well.

Foreign Affairs

After a decade of large national, international, even cosmic events, a certain parochialism (localism it was called in broadcast jargon) was reasserting itself across America. Potential cataclysms in Southeast Asia, Africa, and the Middle East and creeping wars on four continents commanded less and less attention from the American people and were even turning off some sophisticated newsmen. David Brinkley, for example, told the RTNDA convention in December 1977:

> Television is a mature and serious news medium, and it is time we who work in it had our own standards of news judgment instead of those handed down to us from the newspapers.
> It is time to do things our own way, to meet the needs of our audience and the strengths and the weaknesses of the medium we work in.

Which seemed reasonable enough, except that once again television's weaknesses seemed to be dictating the terms more than its strengths. "We should not put a story on the air," Brinkley contended, "unless we believe it is interesting to at least 10 percent of the audience. Preferably more. But at least 10 percent."

Brinkley's example of misjudgment was a two-minute story about the Lebanese civil war on the NBC Nightly News.

> There was a little military skirmish on the front line and we ran two minutes on it with great confidence and assurance that this was important news.

But, was it? That night I spent a little time thinking about it. Why did we put that on the air? Who, in this country, really cared about it? Who really cared about it? Lebanese living in the U.S.? Even if they do, they're a tiny fraction of one percent of our population. Americans who have business or other interests in Lebanon? How many can that be? A fraction of one percent? Foreign-policy specialists, government and private? How many can that be? A fraction of one percent?

Ordinary working Americans like the rest of us? A fraction of one percent? That is not enough.

The Middle East is of great interest to Americans, but Lebanon is peripheral to the area we're concerned about. It has very little effect on the lives, hopes, problems, needs, fears or future security of Americans sitting at home looking at television. In my judgment, 99.9 percent of them did not give a damn.

What I concluded in thinking about it that night was that practically nobody was interested in our story from Lebanon and that the two minutes we devoted to it were an utter waste of effort, money, and air time.

So why did we put it on? Because nobody stopped to ask all these questions. Because the decision was made by habit, by rote, unthinkingly. Wars are always news, aren't they?

Well, no, they aren't. It depends on who's fighting whom and what they're fighting about and what the consequences are likely to be.

We couldn't even use the excuse that the story was easy to get. It wasn't. It was hard, dangerous work for a correspondent and a camera crew and it was sent to the U.S. by satellite, which is expensive.

And, in the end, after all the work, danger, time, and money, who really wanted to see it? In my opinion, almost nobody.

But even so, we do that kind of thing frequently, if not every day.

Because we continue—in radio and television—making news judgments by habit, by rote, and formula developed over the years by the newspapers and inherited by us.

Brinkley's reasoning could be challenged, but his point was significant. Foreign news is expensive to collect and transmit, and its appeal to the great American TV public, except in very specific instances, is measurably limited. Prime time news specials dealing with overseas subjects regularly rate even lower than those devoted to domestic matters. The item Brinkley mentioned as presented on the air may have seemed inconsequential. But the failure conceivably lay in not allowing sufficient time to explain its significance and put the Lebanon crisis into perspective. That failure and lack Brinkley shared all too frequently with his fellow TV newsmen, and not just in the matter of foreign news.

Foreign news had had a slow year. In-depth coverage of extranational stories was infrequent. Of the individual programs, local and network, screened by the DuPont jurors, one in thirty took the viewer overseas. With the exception of a spate of programs on Cuba, including such admittedly interesting items as Barbara Walters's interview with Castro, Howard Smith's Close-Up "The Castro Question," and Bill Moyers's highly controversial essay on terrorism and the CIA, there was no extended prime time coverage of Latin America on the networks. Although coverage of Africa picked up as the year progressed, with the exception of "Who's Got a Right to Rhodesia?" on CBS and exhaustive three network coverage of the rescue at Entebbe, the continent for the most part was left to the kind of expendable day-by-day coverage Brinkley deplored. Asia, now that the Vietnam war had been terminated, fell from the networks' prime time concerns. On the TV magazines, "Sixty Minutes" and "Weekend," one out of four stories came from abroad. In the first twelve weeks of NBC News's "Segment 3," eighteen of the sixty topics dealt with foreign affairs.*

Nor were the TV networks alone. The whole foreign news establishment was experiencing a set of painful contractions. The total of foreign correspondents, according to a survey by Dr. Ralph E. Kliesch of Ohio University, had dropped from 563 in 1969 to 429 in 1975.

There were several possible reasons for the decline in interest in foreign news, among them a post-Vietnam reaction on the part of the public and a preoccupation with pressing matters such as inflation and energy closer to home. An important factor may have been the growing inhospitality of other governments to the Free World press. In the past five years the number of nations who boasted an uncensored press had fallen to forty-two, representing under 20 percent of the world's population.† In June 1977, ABC's William Sheehan, appearing before the International Operations Subcommittee of the Senate Foreign Relations Committee in hearings on "The Role and Control of International Information and Communications," testified that TV's greatest problem in covering international news is censorship:

*Nowhere was the networks' declining commitment to international news more conspicuous than at the U.N. In TV's early days coverage of the General Assembly and Security Council were network staples, going on during important occasions for hours at a time. In recent years only PBS gave any time to live coverage of the U.N.
†Fall 1977 saw a sudden surge in overseas coverage on the evening newscasts, thanks principally to the hard news coming out of Africa and the Middle East.

. . . Censorship takes many forms. The old-fashioned censor with the snipping scissors often appears in more sophisticated disguises today. Thus we have censorship by visa, censorship by facilities, censorship by filming permits, censorship by customs official, and, at least in one instance, censorship by excessive hospitality.

Among specifics mentioned by Sheehan:

Many countries, particularly Third-World countries, require a listing of subject matters before visas are issued. If the subject is not to the country's liking, visas never arrive.

Often local foreign television facilities break down just prior to satellite deadlines if the story meets government disapproval.

In Israel all scripts must be seen and rubber-stamped by the government censor, as must our film.

In Egypt citizens will interfere with filming if they feel their nation might be embarrassed, i.e., one incident in which the background of a "stand-upper" incidentally showed the filth of Cairo.

In Angola an ABC crew found itself greeted, placed in a government guest house and chauffeured, all under strict supervision . . . censorship by hospitality, excessive hospitality.

Nor was the situation for foreign correspondents improved when stories began circulating that certain foreign correspondents, with the blessings of their highest corporate officials, had been doing double duty for the CIA.

Such handicaps made NBC's documentary on human rights, "The Struggle for Freedom," a particularly notable achievement. The program took the viewer to Russia, Poland, and Czechoslovakia, introducing him to the life of dissidents in those three countries and examining what had happened to the handful who had left for the West. Timed to coincide with the opening of the Belgrade Conference on the Helsinki Accord of 1975, it was preceded by an even more unusual TV occasion, "Human Rights: A Soviet-American Debate." In a historical first, three spokesmen for the U.S. met three from the Soviet Union for a debate on human rights—first proposed to NBC by the Russians—in an auditorium at Georgetown University in Washington. There were apparently no holds barred. They had at each other for a fascinating ninety minutes with NBC's Edwin Newman acting as referee. The rhetoric was predictable, but what was not were the glimpses of common humanity, such as an emotional admission by one of the Russians that his mother, a churchgoer, was probably praying for him at that very moment. When the confrontation was over, the principal winner was the TV audience.

That creeping localism could affect more than foreign news was dramatically demonstrated by the demise of NBC Radio's News Information Service. After it had been in operation just two years, with losses of over $10 million, NBC abandoned its ambitious project intended to furnish broadcasters with a forty-seven-minute-per-hour news feed, twenty-four hours a day. Aiming at 150 subscribing stations and 750,000 listeners to break even, at its best moment it had a network of sixty-four representing an audience of 200,000 listeners. Plans had included thirty different categories of material to be covered and during the two years on the air the service undertook such ambitious projects as an eighty-segment feature on cancer and a three-day-long Labor Day weekend documentary made up of 300 separate items on the labor movement.

The principal reason given for the failure of the service was that it was too "national" in its coverage and that local radio required something that related more directly to its listeners' lives.

Terrorism and Other Violence

One subject which never lacked for coverage during the year was terrorism, national and international. Beginning with the hijacking of an Air France plane with Israeli passengers on board at the Athens airport and the subsequent Israeli raid at Entebbe on July 4 (this was covered extensively in hard news reports, documentaries, and docudramas), a steady procession of international terrorist incidents marched across American TV screens. Most frightening were the sequence of crimes in West Germany associated with the notorious Baader-Meinhof gang of terrorists: a series of kidnappings and murders culminating in the hijacking of a Lufthansa plane, its successful recapture on an airfield in Mogadiscio, Somalia, by a German commando group, the alleged suicide in prison of three leaders of the terrorist gang, the cold-blooded retaliatory murder of the German industrialist, Hans Martin Schleyer, and the open-ended threat of more violence to come. A series of kidnappings and shootings attributed to Italy's terrorist Red Brigade singled out six journalists as victims.

The three-week-long occupation by South Moluccans of a Dutch school and commuter train with more than 160 children and ordinary civilians taken hostage received as massive attention as any of these disturbing events. More than 300 reporters, cameramen, and technicians congregated in the small Dutch towns of Bovensmilde and Assen to cover the story, sixty of them from the U.S. TV networks. Craig Whitney, in a special to the *New York Times,* described the scene:

> The lavish resources of the American television networks here have fascinated the frugal Dutch reporters. . . .
> ABC's contingent has been close to 30 people, the biggest here. The exact number seems to embarrass ABC's correspondents. Right now there are 23 here—four correspondents, three producers, two assistant producers, four camera crews, two radio correspondents, and several drivers and motorcyclists as messengers.
> . . . Armed with walkie-talkies [and] jet planes to rush films to big-city studios for satellite transmission to the United States at $80 a minute, the television people, like the rest of the press, spend most of their time waiting in frustration for the news.

"Professor Jan Bastiaans," Whitney reported, "a psychiatrist at the University of Leyden who is advising the government on how to treat the hostages to avoid psychological damage after they are freed, said, 'I think the newsmen should undergo the same kind of therapy— they're all under a similar sort of tension.' "

How involved journalists could get in terrorism was even more vividly demonstrated at home. Domestic disorder and violence, particularly the taking of hostages, occupied more air time than ever before, and caused more serious behind-the-scenes concern from the broadcast community. The symbiotic link between TV and the material it covered had never been more unpleasantly apparent. During two months early in 1977 three incidents in three different communities involved broadcasters in ways other than as objective observers and brought a spate of harsh comments from electronic journalists as well as their critics.

In February 1977 Anthony Kiritsis, an out-of-work car salesman in Indianapolis, held the local TV stations and at least one of the networks hostage while he kept a shotgun wired to the head of a local banker for sixty-three hours, walked down the main street of the Indiana capital, and shouted obscenities and insults at the camera. Less than a month later, Cory Moore, an ex-Marine, seized two hostages in suburban Cleveland. His demands included extended television coverage and a phone call from President Carter. He released one hostage in exchange for a television set on which he viewed the coverage he was getting, including a press conference in which the president said he would grant Moore's request for a telephone conversation following his surrender.* The call was made. Moore gave himself up and policemen stood by while Moore conducted a final press conference.

Frightening as these two instances were, it was a massive act of terrorism in the nation's capital two days after Cory Moore got his telephone call from the president that brought the media to full attention, first in their coverage, and second in a discussion of how to deal with such an apparently out-of-hand situation.

On the morning of March 9 a dozen members of a splinter group of the Black Muslims called the Hanafis began occupying three conspicuous premises in downtown Washington, including the District Office Building, the headquarters of B'nai B'rith, and the Islamic Center. They took 132 hostages, killed 1 man and injured 16 others. Their demands: that a film based on the life of Muhammad which they considered blasphemous be blacked out; that the men convicted of murdering the five children of the sect's leader, and the leader of the triple invasion, Hamaas Abdul Khaalis, be taken from jail and turned over to them; and that $750 in legal fees resulting from a contempt of court citation be repaid to Khaalis.

Thirty-nine hours later, the Hanafis, having won just one of their demands (the opening of *Mohammed, Messenger of God* had been postponed at Manhattan's Rivoli Theatre), released their 132 hostages and surrendered.

Even beyond the fact that the one fatality, Maurice Williams, twenty-four, was a radio reporter from the Howard University station WHUR on a routine assignment at the District Office Building, electronic involvement in the events was disturbingly deep. Commenting on the dozens of phone calls which were placed by reporters to the Hanafis throughout the siege, Bruce MacDonnell of Washington's WRC-TV said, "Folks, we were talking about the lives of 140 people here, and we were talking about some people who were not showboating, but were perfectly capable of snuffing these people. These calls went on from the beginning to the end of this story. It was madness."

Another WRC-TV newsman, Jim Vance, called his colleagues of

*Moore might have gotten his ideas from another disgruntled Cleveland veteran who the preceding summer had taken fourteen people hostage and said he would release them when his demands were broadcast on network television (he had already gotten extensive local coverage). Nine hours later, immediately following the network evening news which had carried stories about him as a regular news item, he surrendered.

the press "disgustingly irresponsible. It was shameful . . . an arrogant disrespect for human life . . . made me wonder when and if some of us are going to realize that there are some things more important than putting every little piece of information on the air." Among those items which could have endangered human life were the report that several councilmen were hiding in their offices three floors below and the rumor, untrue, that the owner of a building across the street was allowing the police to use it for surveillance.

One radio reporter who phoned in suggested to Khaalis that the police were trying to trick him—a suggestion which prompted him to select ten of the older hostages for extermination should it be true and forced the police to remove sharpshooters from two adjacent buildings to placate him.

A disk jockey who got Khaalis on the phone asked him what deadline he had set for the meeting of his demands. No deadline had thus far been mentioned, which the police had taken as a hopeful sign. Fortunately Khaalis did not seem to register the question.

Other evidence of the direct effect of persistent radio and TV intrusion into events included the interruption of an on-air phone conversation between Pat Mitchell of WTTG-TV's "Panorama" and Khaalis, at police request, and a complaint from the police when Delores Handy of WMAL-TV finally hung up after a twenty-five-minute interview with Khaalis's son-in-law, Abdul Azia. On Wednesday afternoon Khaalis had called WTOP radio reporter Jim Mahannon and told him that if he did not apologize on television for calling his sect by the wrong name, "I'm going to kill someone and throw him out the window." Mahannon promptly complied.

Hostages reported later that Khaalis was screening calls for impact and importance. According to Charles Fenyvesi, editor of the *National Jewish Monthly* and a hostage, Khaalis bragged, " 'Everybody in the world is trying to talk to me.' He was elated as he informed us —and our guards—that newsmen called him from as far as England, France, Africa, Australia and, of course, from all over the United States." "I am not interested in publicity," Khaalis told the hostages at one point, according to Fenyvesi, "I only want justice. If I was interested in having my face on TV, I would have held you prisoner in a place where TV cameras could take our picture." However, when a small radio station in Texas asked for a phone interview he told them, "You are not worth talking to. I don't talk to a radio station with less than 50,000 watts."

Fenyvesi described the hostages' feelings toward the attention they were getting:

While being held captive—and since then—many of us felt that the Hanafi takeover was an absurd happening, guerrilla theater, a high-impact propaganda project programmed for the TV screen. From beginning to end, there was an air of unreality to what happened to us—an atmosphere of exaggeration and role-acting one associates with television. . . . Khaalis forced the world to recognize him and his small sect and to pay him the homage of stunned attention.

And he devised as his press release, as his publicity gimmick, an elaborate, bloody, media event unpredictable from one moment to the next—a mock ritual of holy war and human sacrifice.

Beneath the resentment and anger of my fellow hostages toward the press is a conviction, gained these past few weeks, that the news media and terrorism feed on each other, and that the news media, particularly TV, suggest ways to earn fame and recognition. Reporters do not simply report the news, they help create it. They are not objective observers, but subjective participants—actors and scriptwriters and idea men.

This goes beyond the Nixon-Agnew indictment of newsmen as specialists in ill tidings and as the liberal-left shock troops against the status quo. It is a gnawing suspicion that the news media awaken, legitimize and—to use a Nixon word—stroke fantasies, particularly fantasies of violence which might otherwise lie dormant, repressed; and that on a level deeper than any court can probe, newsmen are responsible for a climate congenial to terrorism. . . .

I am against government regulations for the press—for all the classical reasons. But I think concern for life should be absolute and the public's right to know *need not.*

The hostage-press polarization was nowhere more obvious than in the coverage of the captives' release when, according to a detailed account in the Washington *Post:*

> . . . the hostages, many pale and weak from the strain, shrank from the glare of lights, while print and broadcast reporters and camera crews swarmed around them from vantage points. There was shoving and elbowing. Hostages who ran were literally chased by cameramen. Some hid their faces behind their coats and sweaters to avoid the cameras.
>
> One hostage's husband punched a photographer in the face while the wife, in tears, shouted, "Animals! Animals!" at the journalists.

Once the furor created by the story had died down, the importance of the bigger issues involved quickly surfaced.

Commenting on the Hanafi incident, Dr. Frederick J. Hacker, an authority on international terrorism, declared, "It can hardly be denied that the news media is a major influence in the spread of these sorts of incidents. Television especially is a medium of contagion. It is obvious that what is being shown is also being imitated. Television sells deodorants and breakfast food: why wouldn't it sell violence?"

U.N. Ambassador Andrew Young accused the media of "advertising to neurotic people that the way to get attention is to do something suicidal or ridiculous." Young recommended a clarification of the First Amendment, a suggestion which brought indignant response from the press.

In an April Gallup poll 47 percent of the respondents believed terrorist coverage was overemphasized and 64 percent believed coverage incites other acts of terrorism. Another view was put forward in a 661-page Justice Department study from the federally funded Task Force on Disorders and Terrorism:

> As a whole, the development of public understanding . . . is best fostered by a news media that provides [sic] more, rather than less, information to readers, [listeners] and viewers. The media can be most influential in setting the tone for a proper response by the civil authorities to disorders, acts of terrorism, and political violence. It can provide an outlet for the expression of legitimate public concern on important issues so as to act as a safety valve, and it can bring pressure to bear in response to public sentiment in an effective manner to redress grievances and to change official policies. . . . As a whole the development of public understanding of the phenomenon of terrorism, quasi-terrorism and disorder . . . is best fostered by a media establishment that provides more, rather than less, information to readers and viewers.

ABC News correspondent Ted Koppel, in a commentary on his network, concurred:

> The psychiatrists . . . are probably right. The promise of publicity almost certainly is one of the principal factors that induces desperate people to engage in open acts of outrageous protest. What is far more debatable, though, is the implied suggestion that the media would be rendering a public service by selectively ignoring certain acts of protest violence.
>
> The question, of course, becomes who sets the standard? And by what criteria? There were many, in the early sixties, who argued that the media should have ignored the civil rights protests. A few years later, there were just as many who felt that the

media gave too much coverage to anti-war demonstrations; and it was easily arguable in both cases that the demonstrations were largely designed for the media's benefit. Pouring blood on selective service files may have been an act of conscience; but it was also a premeditated piece of theater. Governments almost invariably prefer that their opponents be relegated to obscurity; so does what is generally referred to as the Establishment.

Once the media begins making qualitative judgments based on the presumed effects that [their] coverage will have, there will be no end to the arguments that can be mustered against covering acts of violence, protest, civil disobedience and, ultimately even, political opposition. The most insidious threat to free speech is to limit it because of its possible consequences, because there can never be complete agreement on what those consequences will be.

Since the media were incapable of ignoring such manifestations of violence and terror, even if that had been desirable, the treatment of terrorism became a subject of general discussion.

CBS was among the first to draw up explicit guidelines. Issued April 7, 1977, over the signature of CBS News president Richard S. Salant, just a month after the Hanafi Muslim siege was lifted, the guidelines were prefaced by two paragraphs:

> Because the facts and circumstances of each case vary, there can be no specific self-executing rules for the handling of terrorist/hostage stories. CBS News will continue to apply the normal tests of news judgment and if, as so often they are, these stories are newsworthy, we must continue to give them coverage despite the dangers of "contagion." The disadvantages of suppression are, among [other] things, (1) adversely affecting our credibility ("What else are the news people keeping from us?"); (2) giving free rein to sensationalized and erroneous word of mouth rumors; and (3) distorting our news judgments for some extraneous judgmental purpose. These disadvantages compel us to continue to provide coverage.
>
> Nevertheless, in providing such coverage there must be thoughtful, conscientious care and restraint. Obviously, the story should not be sensationalized beyond the actual fact of its being sensational. We should exercise particular care in how we treat the terrorist/kidnapper.*

Of the news directors responding to the DuPont Survey nearly a quarter had been involved in at least one instance of terrorism in their

*For complete guidelines see Appendix VII.

own communities, some more than once. A sampling of their comments:

> We try to avoid live coverage. In one instance, we offered a reporter as a mediator for a troubled young man believed to be holding a hostage. But we broadcast nothing until he surrendered.
>
> *Atlanta, Ga.*

> Stephen Coleman, suspected bank robber from Louisiana, was holding hostages at gunpoint for four hours in Brush, Colorado. All news organizations, including wire services, withheld information until Coleman was shot and killed by FBI sharpshooters about 25 miles west of Sterling.
>
> Richard Turner, escaped convict, suspected of killing five persons, shot himself and died on a county road about thirty miles from Sterling. Information on his whereabouts was withheld until he committed suicide, even though he had three hostages and raped one of them.
>
> *Sterling, Colo.*

> A three-hour hostage situation was covered in the same manner we would cover any other news story.
>
> *Rockford, Ill.*

> We had at least one incident involving "hostage taking" where 13 people were held at gunpoint by an individual who attempted to make a plea for help for Vietnam veterans. He was Ashby Leach and he asked for his list of demands against the Chessie Railroad System to be aired on local and later national television. We covered the story, but did not give him command of our coverage. Contrary to some of the other television stations, we covered the story like any other story of major importance.
>
> *Cleveland, Ohio*

> Four county-city jail inmates took a federal marshal and a jailer hostage, holding them for 6½ hours. We used natural sound ENG of the scene at the building on the 10 P.M. News, an update at 11:17 P.M., and a report on the sign-off news, including a report from the scene plus additional information. A 7½-minute report on ENG was aired at 7 A.M. The inmates had viewed the 10 P.M. News and saw riflemen stationed atop nearby buildings. The inmates demanded that police remove the riflemen . . . that our station show a clip of the buildings when the riflemen had been removed. Because of darkness, this made the question of

doing this moot. But police did issue a statement that officers had been removed from the buildings and this was carried at 11:17 P.M. on a special report.

Lincoln, Nebr.

Views from stations in the same market sometimes differed.

We report incidents fully, generally reading excerpts of terrorist communiques that help explain their motives and identity—but not going through all the rhetoric. On the one occasion we broke into regular programming with news of a terrorist communique, we did so out of a concern for life and property. Communique said bomb was about to go off at a utility power station in San Francisco. We called police, power company and went on the air with the information. Police discovered bomb minutes before detonation and said it was a big one.

San Francisco, Calif.

We let the police handle it, and covered the police handling it. Other stations in the market became directly involved . . . resulted in our being praised by police for not interfering with the situation.

San Francisco, Calif.

A motel rooftop sniper held a large section of the city at bay for three hours one morning. We did one live insert describing the situation and telling people to stay away, then cut in as soon as possible after the capture to assure people that the situation had returned to normal. The rest of the coverage for the evening newscasts was done on film in the usual manner.

Portland, Oreg.

Two film teams covered a motel roof sniper. We covered from a reasonable distance behind police lines. When the incident ended we ran a bulletin from the newsroom. We did no live coverage [from] the scene. That night we did a report compiled by 2 reporters of the incident along with background on the person during his stay at the motel and from his hometown in California which we collected by phone.

Portland, Oreg.

Miami news directors had a special problem.

We are a Cubanized area. Anti-Castro terrorists regularly threaten businesses that lean to reconciliation with Cuba. Cuban

> leaders are gunned down. A Cuban newsman opposing terrorism lost his legs when his automobile was rigged with a bomb. We report . . . we film . . . and we editorialize. We also receive threats. So far we have survived.
>
> *Miami, Fla.*

> Political assassination of Cuban terrorist exile leaders and Cuban terrorist threats and bombings. Our coverage was comprehensive and in-depth—we tried to explain for a predominantly non-Latin audience what these events mean.
>
> *Miami, Fla.*

And from the nation's capital:

> Hanafi takeover of three buildings in the District of Columbia . . . produced two hour-long specials, cut into programming throughout day and into the night with studio and live updates. Essentially, had everyone on staff working at least 18 hours a day (with attendant large costs for overtime).
>
> *Washington, D.C.*

Assessing our coverage of the Hanafi takeover . . . determined that this type of story, while it might never again be quite so dramatic, would be with us for a long time. Washington, because it is a world capital, would appear to be especially vulnerable.

We did not want to frighten our audience into thinking that a terrorist lurked around every corner, but we did believe that terrorism could strike anywhere. The experts in the field that we consulted bore this out.

"When Terror Strikes" ran for five consecutive evenings on the 6 P.M. and 11 P.M. editions of News Seven.

What we wanted to do was to explain to our viewers what terrorism was, who the different kinds of terrorists are and what the viewer could do when terror strikes. We were also able to show what law enforcement agencies were doing to combat terrorism including a first-ever filming of a meeting of the State Department's Task Force on Terrorism.

Also for the first time, the FBI permitted its top expert on terrorism, Patrick Mullany, to discuss its strategy for defusing terrorist situations.

Because the role of the news media is so controversial, we devoted one segment to this topic. Journalists and ex-hostages were featured.

The single most dramatic segment was the interview with five ex-hostages. They talked about their own experiences, what they might have done differently, and they provided some practical advice to viewers on what they should do if caught up in a hostage situation.

We obviously have not halted the spread of terrorism in its tracks with this series. However, we have provided our viewers with a better understanding of what terrorism is and how they can deal with it.

Washington, D.C.

Washington was not the only community where incidents led to an extended on-air examination of the subject of terrorism. Similar programs were reported from San Francisco, Cleveland, and Los Angeles, where in a single five-week period there were nineteen different incidents involving sniping at passersby or holding hostages. One station avoided live coverage and the possibility of inciting some of its viewers to similar actions by packaging all the episodes in a two-part analysis which attempted to put the epidemic, conceivably media inspired, in perspective.

Many local stations developed their own guidelines, frequently closely patterned on those issued by the networks or growing out of a desire to avoid repeating mistakes of the past.

1. Report the incident as simply and as factually as possible avoiding a sensational approach.
2. Avoid becoming a part of the story, such as serving as negotiator with terrorists or [having] direct communications with them.
3. Do not violate law enforcement ground rules in the area of the incident.
4. Report demands if they are relayed but avoid becoming a broadcast platform for the terrorist. Do not seek deadlines from terrorists.
5. Cooperate with law enforcement to the extent that lives are at stake. However, our credibility with the public is important. To knowingly broadcast half truths or fabrications would not be in our or the public's interests.

Lincoln, Nebr.

They are simple. No live coverage unless approved by me [the news director].

Atlanta, Ga.

We define "terrorism" as an act to overthrow or control a government agency or representatives. Anything else is a crime story. It helps us get it in its proper perspective.

Los Angeles, Calif.

Standards and Practices: Terrorist Activities

The receipt of any information regarding possible terrorist activity should be reported immediately to law enforcement officials. This includes notification of bomb threats or any kind of planned and disruptive activity.

Any notification of a bomb threat involving [the station] should be reported immediately to the security office and the Building Services Department.

The coverage of any terrorist activity will be carefully considered and shall be subject to constant review by news management.

Generally speaking, the News will not carry extensive live coverage of terrorist activity. Live situation reports will be broadcast along with carefully edited and written summaries of such incidents. We can not and will not allow ourselves to be used by terrorist organizations to further their own causes and great restraint must be shown during coverage of any terrorist activity. Station competition in the area of live coverage must not have any bearing on a decision involving the coverage of such situations.

The outbreak of any terrorist activity in our coverage area must be reported immediately to the news director and no live coverage of such activity will be carried unless authorized by the news director or his/her designate directly.

Boston, Mass.

In response to a query from *Television/Radio Age,* Pat Polillo, head of Group W's news operations and responsible for policy decisions, not only in Boston, but in four other important TV markets, said Group W's guidelines were

> . . . based largely on two considerations. One is for life—of our newsmen, and of possible hostages. The other is for our stations. We don't want any of our facilities taken hostage in the sense that its people might be blackmailed into having to let it become a mass mouthpiece for some group's propaganda, hate messages, obscenities, or what have you. . . . We've projected ourselves into just about every hypothetical life-threatening situation we can think of and have a set of alternatives to meet each possibility. But we don't like to say more than that for the public print, because once we tip our hand a potential terrorist knows our counter moves, our position becomes weaker and his stronger, just as in international military intelligence. So we keep our specific tactics to ourselves.

Any reporter who is suddenly forced into reluctantly becoming part of the story instead of part of the coverage, ceases, for the duration of that particular life-threatening situation, to be a reporter. He becomes a source and we assign another newsman to finish covering the story until the danger is over.

The news director of WIFR Rockford, Illinois, told *Television/Radio Age,* "Our coverage should be available to those who wish to promote changes in society as well as those who oppose such changes, but we must avoid becoming a tool for those who want violence. . . ." Jim Connor, executive producer of WKYC-TV Cleveland, said:

> We have had three such situations. We've learned from each . . . that caution is the best approach. During such hostage coverage we have had to deal with overwrought police who wanted to use our van as a screen—so we pulled our van away from the scene—and with competitors who have jumped on the air with each flurry of activity, once causing a gunman to call off an agreement to surrender. We've also had to deal with the arrival at the scene of self-important politicians who want to show the folks they're out there trying.

Of the news directors reporting to the DuPont Survey, several said they chose to have no guidelines. Some of the reasons given:

> We will make decisions on the minute-to-minute situation and not by a set of predetermined guidelines. The most important question is whether we are being used by a particular group and whether we escalate a condition.
>
> *Dallas, Tex.*

> It is a news story and to be covered like all other news stories.
>
> *Washington, D.C.*

> We are not a bulletin-happy station. We do not have live on-the-scene capability. If we should be so unlucky as to face the problem we will attempt to play it cool.
>
> *Springfield, Mass.*

> Such stories should be handled with intelligence and restraint on a case-by-case basis. Guidelines can't cover every circumstance. We have to rely on our professional standards, not guidelines.
>
> *Miami, Fla.*

> We are journalists. If we are to remain a free society, we cannot enter into prior restraint agreements. Our coverage must be

based on the judgment of the news director and top news department supervisors. We cannot allow anyone to dictate news policy. Each story is treated independently. There is far more danger in collusion than from terrorists.

Miami, Fla.

We have developed a very good and close working relationship with FBI and local law authorities. Our guidelines are to cooperate with those authorities in the instance of a terrorist act and to follow the basic guidelines of good responsible journalism.

Tulsa, Okla.

Such close working relationships were not universal. A survey of police chiefs in the nation's thirty largest cities conducted by California State University at Northridge showed that 93 percent of the respondents believed live coverage encouraged terrorism, and 67 percent said TV journalists should communicate with terrorists only "with official consent." Half thought on-the-scene reporters weren't doing a very good job, and 27 percent thought there should be no coverage of such incidents at all.

One chief responded, "Widespread publication of details of incidents can foster future incidents or be utilized to improve future attempts. . . . Also, details of how officials successfully concluded an incident can be utilized by those inclined to perpetrate a future incident."

TV's concern with violence was not limited to the growing problem of terrorism. One of the major stories of the year was the endlessly delayed execution of Gary Gilmore. Since it was the first execution following the Supreme Court decision to lift the ban on capital punishment, there was no way that responsible news media could ignore it. However, the nature of Gilmore's crimes and his attitude toward them, and the circumstances surrounding his imprisonment and imminent execution, almost dictated sensational treatment. CBS and NBC responded with specials. The mood of the local Salt Lake City stations was conveyed by one newsman speaking of the possibility of getting an eyewitness view of Gilmore's death. "We might go to a lot of extremes to get the story. We are considering using paragliders, long lenses, helicopters, maybe even a dirigible, but I doubt we could show it."

Dan Rather's way of bringing "Who's Who" viewers close to the event was to interview a man who had been a member of a Utah firing squad seventeen years before and ask him to relive his distant experience in painful detail. NBC's Jack Perkins, who had spent the week before the execution in Utah with a crew of twenty-five, opened his special half-hour prime time report on the night following the execution with the grim words:

> As recently as ten years ago, most people in this country were not in favor of capital punishment. That's what surveys said. So courts and legislatures stopped executions. For ten years. But now, surveys show, we have turned around—by far most Americans again *do* want capital punishment.
> Today, here, they got their wish.

Prison officials reported they had been besieged by last-minute requests to bring in TV cameras, two from TV networks, but they refused.

In Texas, there were indications that newsmen might be allowed to broadcast an execution. Robert Excel White, scheduled to die in Huntsville, Texas, in June 1977, had already received his death sentence on camera—a chilling TV first. Later he announced he wanted to die on camera as well. "The public should see it."*

In January 1977 a Dallas district court judge ruled in response to a lawsuit filed by Tony Garrett of KERA-TV that broadcasters be permitted to air the next execution in the state. The reactions of local newsmen were instructive.

Ray Miller, news chief at KPRC-TV in Houston, who had asked to be present at White's execution, said, "We are not in the business of *not* covering the news. We'd like to have a camera there, but whether or not we'd put it on the air is something else."

KVII-TV Amarillo, responding with enthusiasm to the possibility of a "live" execution, noted that some advertisers might pull their ads, but big ratings would more than make up for it. "We are in the ratings game," the station manager, Jim McCormick, explained. "If KAMR [the NBC affiliate in Amarillo, one of three Texas stations that said it would air the execution] does it, we want to, too. . . . Of course, I would want to alert people of the event, and I would really want to air it live and hope that it would be at a late hour. I would not want to run it in what was known as the family viewing hour."

The Dallas Power and Light Company was asked if it would pull its commercials from news coverage of an electrocution since that would seem to represent a conflict of interest. The company responded:

> If DP&L were given an option as to pulling its advertising from a newscast that included a live execution, it would give the matter

*As of December 1977, White was still awaiting execution.

some thought. However, we traditionally have taken a stand that advertisers have no right and no business commenting at all on news coverage. That is a matter of news judgment the station must make and not one we make for them.

Several Dallas banks queried on the same matter said they would not hesitate to remove their ads from such coverage.

If crime and violence were conspicuous in the hard news on the air, they were also the subject of some of the most ambitious and effective documentaries of the year, as well as some of the most highly rated. At the top of the list in terms of ratings, if not of quality, were NBC's three-hour special "Violence in America" and the ABC Close-Up "Sex for Sale: The Urban Battleground," the two top-rated documentaries of the year.

More impressive in terms of craftsmanship and imagination was "Murder One," a co-production of Georgia Educational Television, the University of North Carolina Television Network, and WNET/13. The sixty-minute TV essay directed by Tex Fuller brought the viewer into direct contact with six convicted murderers (half of them condemned to death), as well as some of their families and the families of their victims. The objectivity of the TV camera matched the detachment of the murderers themselves as they described their crimes. The viewer was left with a compelling and noncommittal statement with no simplification and no special pleading on the central issues of capital punishment and its human components.

Slightly less chilling was "The Police Tapes," a remarkable ninety-minute essay on night life as seen by the policemen of New York's Forty-fourth Precinct in the South Bronx. It was made by Alan and Susan Raymond (also responsible for the most controversial series of the 1973 season, "An American Family"). The husband and wife team used a half-inch black and white video tape camera, which was not only cheap (total budget $20,000) but allowed them maximum mobility with minimum light. The result was the year's most interesting example of cinéma vérité on television.

Star of the show was Anthony Bouza, at the time Bronx borough commander, who described with remarkable insight and subtlety the policeman's lot. "A policeman is taught to help people, but he is regulating human behavior and is resented. He's shocked by this. . . . The policeman has great difficulty assimilating this knowledge. . . . he becomes a bit cynical, a bit hardened."

Bouza spoke for the poorest of Bronx residents as well:

We're conditioning people to fail, to be violent, and we give them no mechanism with which to cope . . . the poor are more ignored now than they have ever been. . . . To the degree that I succeed in keeping it cool, am I deflecting America's attention from this cancer? Maybe I'd be better off failing, and confronting America. . . . We are manufacturing criminals . . . because we don't want to face the problem.*

Bouza added his message to another outstanding documentary, Bill Moyers's CBS Report on "The Fire Next Door," which started with the South Bronx's incredible arson problem (over 30,000 buildings abandoned and burnt in the past ten years) and branched out into the problems all around. Bouza, who changed jobs between the first and second programs, had not lost his eloquence. Labeling the South Bronx "a society out of control," he said, "we're creating here what they had in Rome, a permanent under class of disaffected and poor . . . educators that don't educate, a bureaucracy that doesn't respond —police that don't police. . . . I'd like to rub America's nose in this. . . . America is too decent a place to let this go on."

Another remarkable essay on crime was WNET's thirty minutes entitled "Rahway Sta'way," which showed a group of supposedly hardened convicts (several of them imprisoned for murder) doing their best to warn a group of teenagers in trouble away from the criminal path, and commenting on the bleakness and futility of their own lives with brutal eloquence.

KSD-TV Salt Lake City's "The Trial of Bobby Ferguson" explored in five sad installments another kind of criminality, that of the individual who breaks the law to get himself locked up. For a week WNBC's News Center Four visited Manhattan's violent, overcrowded Riker's Island with reporter Felipe Luciano, who had himself once been an inmate.

White- and blue-collar crime had their innings in Marilyn Baker's ironic multipart pursuit of the "Bay Area Tow Car Fraud" on KPIX-TV San Francisco. WFAA Dallas's talented investigative team took on illegal trucking, the Teamsters, and the latest ramifications of the Kennedy assassination, in a notably busy year.

Dan Rather caught the scent of behind-the-scenes hanky-panky while doing a report on the career of boxing entrepreneur Don King for CBS's "Who's Who." Suddenly the kingpins of TV sports, including ABC News president Roone Arledge, were down in Washington testifying before a congressional committee. Although no crime was

*See Appendix VIII for full text.

proven, all three networks experienced some embarrassing moments.

TV's responsibility in connection with the rising violence in America dominated the Senate Communications Subcommittee hearings on the broadcast industry.

In June, a survey of doctors released by the American Medical Association showed that 94 percent of those responding believed there was too much TV violence, and 14 percent said they had seen patients with behavioral or physical problems that might be related to television violence. Another 41 percent said they "suspected" that was the case.

The Ontario Royal Commission on Violence proposed barring violent U.S. TV series at the border.

The House Communications Subcommittee announced the prospective release of its report on TV violence. After six drafts the staff report containing significant modifications in favor of the networks was finally adopted in late September.

Elaborate tabulations of the incidence of violence were prepared by Dr. George Gerbner of the University of Pennsylvania, by the National Citizens Committee for Broadcasting, and by CBS. All agreed that there was a significant decrease in the incidence of violence in the 1977 summer entertainment schedules of all three networks, which seemed to indicate that if the networks would not acknowledge their culpability in the matter of violence, at least they were listening to those who saw a cause-effect relationship at work.

A federal district judge added to the confusion with a decision that the family hour—a voluntary restraint on TV violence by networks in their early evening schedules which had been challenged by Hollywood producers of TV series, among others—was unconstitutional.

The ultimate irony may have been the trial of Ronald Zamora for the murder of an elderly woman neighbor in Miami Beach. The core of Zamora's defense was that he was suffering from "subliminal TV intoxication," having spent at least five hours a day watching such crime programs as "Police Story," "Kojak," and "Helter Skelter."*

---

* The idea that even broadcast news had a contagious effect got some support from a study by two social psychologists, Stephen M. Holloway and Harvey A. Hornstein, whose conclusions were published in the December 1976 issue of *Psychology Today*. Describing the effects of broadcast news on various subjects, they found that "good news produces more favorable views of humanity's general moral disposition than bad news does—despite the fact that the news deals only with certain special cases and not at all with human nature on the grand scale.

"But something even more startling happens when people hear good or bad news. Not only do their beliefs change, so does their behavior. . . . Our findings are unmistakable and highly important, in our view. They suggest not only that the media influence our moral actions, but, more generally, that altruism in individuals probably rises or falls with the altruism, or lack of it, in social events that may not touch us directly."

The trial was significant not only for TV programmers but for TV journalists—as a news story, as a criticism of TV manners and mores, and as a journalistic breakthrough. A headline in *Editor and Publisher* announced: "Televised Murder Trial a Hit in Miami."

> The first televised murder trial in history became a hit show on a PBS station in Miami last week.
> Over a period of about twenty-five hours on eight nights, usually from 9 P.M. until 1 A.M., the daytime courtroom drama was replayed on TV in an experiment authorized by the Florida Supreme Court. Sets in more than 80,000 households were tuned in, according to preliminary estimates.

Demanding the right to cover courtroom proceedings, TV journalists had not only zeroed in on a fifteen-year-old murderer but on TV itself. Even though it was commercial TV which had fought and won the right to cover the trial,* it was public TV which took full advantage of it. While the network affiliates were unfolding their tales of make-believe, violence, and death, the local public TV station was running its tapes of the retribution (Zamora was found guilty) visited upon one addicted TV fan. The trial of Ronnie Zamora was a hall of mirrors, with TV caught in the multiple receding reflections.

Hyping the News

Sex, the handmaiden of violence in all discussions of undesirable commercial TV fare, had had an active year so far as news and public affairs were concerned. In the time period under consideration the ultimate taboo was overcome when NBC's "Weekend" devoted an entire ninety-minute segment to a midnight essay on incest. However upsetting the subject matter, the producer's prolonged look at a specialized clinic in San Jose, California, the seat of the richest county in the state, was hard to fault on grounds of taste or deliberate sensationalism. Similar care was invested by WPMB Minneapolis, which surveyed the same topic in its own community at somewhat shorter length.

Anal and oral sex were both mentioned explicitly, albeit in the least prurient of contexts. The same lack of sensationalism applied to some treatments of hetero- and homosexual rape, and of wife and child

---

* *Post/Newsweek's* two Florida stations, WPLG Miami and WJLB Jacksonville, had won a lawsuit in 1976 which resulted in the decision to grant TV a one-year courtroom test.

abuse. All too frequently, however, these subjects, along with adult and kiddie pornography and prostitution, were handled in a more cynical manner.

Exploitation of sex to increase news ratings characterized an increasing number of local stations, including those owned and operated by the networks. In such instances journalistic sex usually involved the doling out of deliberately titillating segments over a week's time. This careful rationing, soliciting the viewer (often with the help of massive ad and on-air promo campaigns) to return for each successive evening's offering, usually was scheduled during the quarterly rating sweeps so important to stations and advertisers in determining rates and profits.

Of the stations reporting to the survey, 50 percent admitted they took the month-long sweeps into account in programming their local newscasts. Some explained what they did to accommodate the raters and why:

> We schedule series to run during the rating periods—one a week. Series run during the remainder of the year on a sporadic basis.
> *Dallas, Tex.*

> We attempt a more planned and organized approach to selecting series, features, minidocs, so that a coordinated promotion campaign is possible.
> *Indianapolis, Ind.*

> Striving to build our audience, so our minidocs and specials will have greater impact . . . and to improve the overall profit potential for the station.
> *High Point, N.C.*

> Heavier promotion for individual stories, series and personalities.
> *Washington, D.C.*

> Intensified efforts subconsciously.
> *Jackson, Miss.*

> Not in programming—i.e., selection of stories—but in manner of presentation, we try to be interesting, visual and compelling television.
> *San Francisco, Calif.*

> We do not permit vacations during sweep periods.
> *Columbus, Ohio*

As for the importance of ratings, the news directors said:

> Slight dip in ratings has made position weaker in fight for increased station dollars. Direct effect on program content only gradually apparent, e.g. less investigative reporting, less film etc.
>
> *San Francisco, Calif.*

> Increase in ratings, 1976–77, created new interest from management.
>
> *Jackson, Miss.*

> The rating books show us audience flow, therefore we have an idea of where the most effective position in the show is for a particular feature or segment.
>
> *Portland, Oreg.*

> We study the effect of lead-in and lead-out programming with an eye toward making changes, where possible, when problems arise. Ratings also keep us informed about the strength of the competition, counter-programming, etc. They affect, to a certain degree, the amount budgeted for news. Lower ratings tend to produce higher budgets. But ideally, lower ratings produce market research which produces better newscasts which produce higher ratings.
>
> *Oklahoma City, Okla.*

Of the news directors reporting to the DuPont Survey 65 percent found that competitive pressures in their markets from other news operations had increased, 2 percent found they had decreased, and 33 percent thought they had remained the same—which in most instances meant intense. "It couldn't increase," wrote one news director in Pittsburgh. "It's fierce."

The excitement caused by the shift of a single rating point was indicated by the press release issued by WAGA-TV in Atlanta when its six o'clock news outrated archrival WSB-TV's 15 to 14.

> For the first time in more than twenty-five years, WAGA-TV, the Storer station in Atlanta, has captured the No. 1 spot at 6 P.M. with News Scene. In an unprecedented victory, WAGA-TV has beaten the long-time news leader, WSB-TV, in ratings, shares and women 18–49, according to the May, 1977 A.C. Nielsen reports.

The breakthrough was ascribed to the demotion of the "in-house Walter Cronkite" from the anchor position and his replacement by Jacque Maddox, a young newcomer. The next week WSB-TV was back in first place.

Major anchor shifts continued to characterize the cutthroat rating battles in San Francisco, Boston, Chicago, Cleveland, and Washington.

A half-million-dollar, five-year contract served to seduce anchor-man John Henning from WCVB to WNAC at the beginning of 1977, making him the highest-paid newsman in Boston history. This followed the unfortunate tenure of J. Hugh Sprott, an example of how far local stations could go in their search for anchor desk glamour. In an earlier bid to beat the news competition, Sprott, an earnest twenty-two-year-old Denver newsman out of Waco, Texas, had been spotted by the WNAC news director on the TV set in his motel room. Hired away at twice his Denver salary, he had been instructed to bleach his hair, wear contact lenses, and change his name to Jay Scott. Ten months later, when WNAC news ratings had not improved despite a massive build-up for Scott as the new sex symbol to replace Tom Ellis (gone to WABC in New York City), Scott-Sprott was unceremoniously fired.

In Chicago, where the 10:00 P.M. news was the real field of battle, an overall drop in news viewing from 85 percent to 70 percent of total audience, attributed to the arrival of "Mary Hartman, Mary Hartman" two seasons before, made the competition even more bitter. There were charges and countercharges of undue promotion during sweeps and of the monitoring of radio calls to cop the other station's stories.

Attempts to manipulate the ratings beyond the usual promotion hype were not unknown. Several instances of stations locating and tinkering with monitor diaries (going so far as to enter wall-to-wall viewing seven days a week for its own programming) had been reported in recent months, although the practice was deplored by all the reputable rating services.

The anxiety over ratings, particularly on the part of station managements, was explained by the fact that a newscast lead of one rating point over the competition could, in New York or Los Angeles, mean $1.2 to $1.6 million in income per year.

Ray Miller, vice-president for news and public affairs at KPRC Houston, said in a speech to a regional meeting of news directors:

> I am supposed to make a few remarks about television news competition in a major market and I guess I am qualified in one

sense, anyway. I have been working in television news in the major market in this state for way over twenty years. What I can say about competition in television news is that there is a lot of it. What I cannot say is that there is very much substance to it. Competition for television news ratings is what it mostly is. And it has more to do with hair styles and theme songs and microphone insignia than it has to do with covering the news.

And I am afraid that I think this is going to continue to be the case . . . and increasingly be the case . . . as television stations pass out of the hands of local interests and individuals and into the hands of carpetbaggers and conglomerates. Some people have blamed the news consultants for this state of affairs. But I do not think they are guilty of anything except supplying something that is wanted.

Some people believe that television news is news for people who will not or cannot read newspapers.

I believe that some people in the television business believe that television news is for people who don't want to be bothered with the news.

And this is what has created the demand for gimmicks and window dressing in our business. It is more important to have an audience for the news program than it is to have news in the news program. A Ph.D. named Mark Levy . . . has made a study of news audiences and he has concluded that most television viewers choose their TV news program because of the entertainment programs that come before or after the news. And the second biggest reason people he polled gave for choosing a particular station was because they liked that station's anchorman better than the others. In this study . . . only about ten percent of the people polled said that the quality of the news had anything to do with their decision about which station to watch.

I do not dispute his findings.

A side effect of these ratings wars, reminiscent of newspaper circulation wars earlier in the century, was an increase in news budgets, reported to the DuPont Survey by 85 percent of news directors. Seventy-five percent reported an increase in staff. Only 17 percent reported an increase in time allotments after several years of growth in length of local newscasts.

News consultants, once considered a mortal threat to broadcast news integrity, were more and more being taken for granted. In just one year the number of news directors who reported having used a consultant had jumped from 30 to 50 percent. Fifty-seven percent felt the consultants' influence had stabilized, 27 percent felt it was still increasing, and only 14 percent saw it as decreasing. Although the percentage of those who had once employed consultants and let them go had risen to 46 from 29 percent, it was still difficult to claim on the basis of these responses that the vogue for consultants had passed. However, the comments received by the Survey also indicated that the value of the consultants was still very much a question in the respondents' minds. Among the detractors:

> Consultants' influence being felt in a "sameness" or pattern in competition and an over-preoccupation with younger demographics and how "to get them" at whatever professional price. Most noticeable in resultant "surface" treatment of individual stories, perfunctory treatment of governmental matters and even a "puffy" trend in the choice of subject matter for minidocumentaries.
>
> *Milwaukee, Wis.*

> Their effects have been to dehumanize the news, monkeyize delivery, format and content. The reason for events has been missing in report formats. They're like rock & roll, MOR* or any other format—They're all the same!
>
> *Las Vegas, Nev.*

> Consultants present suggestions based on research. What they advise giving the audience is what they want, not necessarily what they need. Surely, a child will prefer candy to mashed potatoes; the question remains. What is best for him or her? In that sense, the consultants take the question of what to cover out of the news director's hands. They enjoy the advantage of guiding the news, without being bothered with the day to day problems.
>
> *Mobile, Ala.*

Among the enthusiasts:

> They are absolutely vital to the operation of a news department, and anyone who thinks they can do a good job of presenting the news without some input from a consultant (at least, from Magid —maybe not others) doesn't know what he is talking about and probably isn't doing a very good news program.
>
> *San Francisco, Calif.*

> In our instance, the consultant has been a direct help to us. His impact, for the most part, has led to improvements we needed . . . but were unable to swing through management. The big

*Middle of the road.

dollars paid a consultant made his opinion carry more weight
with management.

Redding, Calif.

I believe the consultant in this market (Magid) has generally
improved the competitive climate. . . . The consultants I've
worked with at other stations . . . can sometimes do wonders for
inexperienced reporters. They seem to fill a void that many journalism schools leave in broadcast journalism education . . . effective audio/visual presentation. . . . I believe consultants have
been unfairly maligned. Before their arrival . . . the majority of
TV news operations outside the top twenty-five markets were
pure crap . . . the consultants didn't introduce frivolity and
silliness to broadcast news. . . . It has been around for years. Case
in point: we have a weather woman in this market who was using
up to ten minutes of news time and acting perfectly idiotic
. . . and getting solid ratings . . . before Frank Magid was born
(the agency, not the man).

Evansville, Ind.

The majority still expressed some reservations:

We have had a news consultant for many years (Frank Magid
and Assoc.). We have also been #1 for many years, even before
the consultants. We have noticed, however, both our competitive
stations have added consultants to their staffs. As a news director, I feel consultants can be useful outside observers and critics
of your operations, but it requires a lot of effort to keep them
from running the news operations. First, by their own admission,
if there is a void in news leadership on the part of the news
director, they will . . . fill that void. It is also evident that station
management tends to rely on consultants and accept their advice
much more readily than that of their own news director. With
those reservations, I'm glad we've had a consultant.

Salt Lake City, Utah

There are few consultants concerned or qualified enough to determine content. We have had a content consultant, but even he
just suggests, and I glean what I deem valuable from his ideas.
We have had the "look" consultants too: Magid, in this and other
markets. I have found their advice to be strictly cosmetic . . . and
indicative of a sort of "knee-jerk reaction" to poor ratings. The
fault lies with stations which forfeit to consultants their duty to
give the local populace the important news.

Fort Wayne, Ind.

Many of the nation's news directors were accepting the central philosophy of news consulting, which, in the name of the public, relinquished to statistics the right to decide what kind of news it should have and at what length. The hallmarks of news consulting— young and beautiful anchor persons, matching blazers, designer hair- cuts, news desk badinage, socko short items, and seductively soft longer stories—had become predictable features of local news from coast to coast. There was also widespread evidence of a more serious intrusion, a gerrymandering of the news which left off the air those stories that were hard to explain or visualize—no matter how impor- tant. The excuse, once again, was that the public did not want it.

"The next evolutionary step will be substance in the news," said Mitch Ferris, former vice-president of Magid Associates, now news director of KRON-TV San Francisco.

The rapid growth of the minidocumentary at the expense of the more expensive, lower-rated, harder-to-assimilate thirty- to sixty- minute documentary could be traced to the influence, if not the spe- cific instructions, of the news consultants.

The percentage of minidocs submitted to the DuPont jurors had steadily increased. This year it stood at well over 50 percent of total programs. Four out of five of the news directors reported using the minidoc form regularly.

As minidocs increased in number so also did they improve in quality. The most conspicuous were often devoted to lurid and su- perficial treatments of promotable subjects. But there were many impressive exceptions. Among those viewed this year:

WBBM Chicago's merciless inquiry into slum landlords conducted by Susan Anderson and a series which documented in tragic human detail the story of the PBB feed-grain pollutions across the lake in Michigan.

WFAA Dallas's aforementioned pieces on the Teamsters and truckers, as well as a first-rate job on a series of little-known threats to the public health entitled "Clear and Present Danger."

KYW Philadelphia's week-long reexamination of the evidence against a West Philadelphia carpenter convicted for rape and robbery under questionable circumstances.

KSMP Minneapolis's series of heartbreaking vignettes on coma, a little-explored health problem.

WBAL Baltimore's series on the plight of one bedridden old man whose comfort and peace of mind were threatened by local bureau- crats and a first-rate local version of the great flu debate presented in balanced, well-informed segments.

KTVU Oakland's four-part series on illegal aliens, a familiar subject presented with sympathy and distinction.

KGO San Francisco's ten-part series, "The Aged: Where Did We Go Wrong?," a remarkable demonstration of how a station's full resources—their news team visited four European countries to do its research—can be employed in the miniseries form.

KMOX St. Louis's "An Uncommon Gift," a series about an eight-year-old girl on dialysis awaiting a kidney transplant which was transformed into an even more effective half-hour documentary.

KTVI St. Louis's "The Co-op Conspiracy—Pyramid of Shame," an old-fashioned investigative series which dug out the dirt on an alleged racket-connected farm cooperative and presented it to the viewer in terms hard to ignore.

WCCO Minneapolis's first-rate series on the controversial anti-cancer drug Laetrile, which had interesting local ramifications and took the researchers as far afield as Mexico.

The commitment to investigative reporting continued to grow, if the time to put it on the air didn't. All but 4 percent of the news directors heard from either had increased the amount of investigative reporting they undertook (47 percent), or held it at the same level (49 percent). However, by far the greatest number of them aired the results either in minidocs, single newscast items, or newscast series. In even the best of these investigative efforts there was an uncomfortable feeling that more time and fewer interruptions would better inform and serve the public.

The constant coming and going of news personnel who had no roots in the communities they passed through on their way to bigger ratings and salaries led to superficiality, a lack of understanding, and an indifference to important local concerns. For several years news directors in smaller markets have complained in the DuPont Survey of their inability to hang on to first-rate young reporters and anchor people who were changing jobs on the average of every two years. An RTNDA survey now indicated that a news director's average tenure had dropped to two and a half years per station.

Panicky managements who saw their news operations losing out even with the help of conventional news consultants were now invoking trendier and more occult presences. Entertainment Research Analysis (ERA) attached electrodes to the flesh of viewers to test the "galvanic skin responses" to the news and its purveyors. A growing body of suitably coiffed and blazered young newspersons could attribute their sudden fall from favor to this plugging in of the public. Ed Newman, balding, plump, and middle-aged, commented on the "Today" show:

According to *TV Guide,* stations in Los Angeles, Seattle, Minneapolis, Denver and St. Louis call in viewers to watch their newscasters and give the viewers skin tests while they watch.

Their hands are smeared with surgical jelly and attached to electrical sensors. If the viewers remain calm, their palms remain dry. But if the newscasts affect them somehow—scare them, please them, make them angry or guilty or arouse them sexually —their sweat glands open, the electrical sensors register that, and the next thing you know, some newscasters are on the junk heap where newscasters who leave palms dry deserve to be.

. . . it was never my ambition to make people perspire inordinately. Nor did I ever picture somebody applying for a television news job, being asked what his qualifications are, and replying "First, I arouse them sexually, then I tell them about plans to reorganize the Agriculture Department. It's sure fire!"

The tests *TV Guide* mentioned are designed also to show whether viewers regard the broadcasters as friendly, cold, warm, distant, shifty, believable, attractive, plain, familiar, dull. I find this highly flattering. Most of us have acting ability that, in the words of a famous review of Katherine Hepburn years ago, runs the gamut of emotions from A to B. We rarely change expression, and when we manage the faintest change in inflections, we think we deserve an award.

I know, of course, that it is different on some local stations, where what often counts is teeth and hairspray and breeziness. I don't understand how breeziness came to be left out of that list I spoke of earlier: warm, cold, shifty, believable, and so on. Those things don't matter. Is the broadcaster breezy? That is what counts.

By the way, one quality that might be asked about apparently isn't: Does the broadcaster know what he, or she, is talking about? Or is that a handicap?

Look, Ma, no sweaty palms.

ERA's spokesmen, in a recap of earlier protestations by the now quasi-respectable news consultants, complained that press coverage of their techniques was biased. "Journalists reject our research while management doesn't. That seems to be the division. We don't try to dictate stories. We just try to help news directors to communicate effectively. And sometimes, we find people who are better communicators."*

ERA's advice did not always reinforce that of the news consultants who generally preceded them. ERA tests proved that, at least in

*See Appendix VIII for a summary of ERA research techniques.

Chicago, rather than requiring a steady stream of thirty- to ninety-second stories, viewers could actually keep their attention on a single subject for as long as seven minutes.

Another resource of the desperate was the Athyn group, a consciousness-raising team which descended on TV stations in distress offering intensive care. This seven-man unit boasted a psychiatrist, a former minister, an advertising man, a lawyer, two university professors, and a specialist in group dynamics. Their effects were achieved through "psycho-educational processes." Formed in 1973, the firm by mid-1977 had administered its peculiar type of first aid to "more than five and less than fifty" stations coast to coast.

Both of these operations were described at considerable length in *The Newscasters,* Pulitzer Prize-winning critic Ron Powers's colorful account of "The News Business as Show Business," as he subtitled it, which was published in May 1977.

The most alarming symptom of a TV news establishment in upheaval was the shifting about that was taking place at the supposedly stable network news operations. In one eighteen-month period ABC had changed the man in charge of its network newscasts three times, ending where it had started out—with Av Westin. Two out of three networks had with very little ceremony or apology divested themselves of their news division presidents after tenures of five and three years respectively. Whatever the explanation, the reason was obvious. Ratings.

The changes that preceded or accompanied the arrival of new news executives at the networks were not all negative. NBC had initiated a new approach to the evening news which gave at least two opportunities per newscast for extended treatment of important subjects, an innovation which was having beneficial repercussions at the other commands.

ABC, out to catch up with the competition, resorted on occasion to sensationalism and softness, and wasn't above devoting its precious time to weather and the sports. But it was frequently going beyond NBC and CBS in its commitment of time and talent to important and difficult stories.

Still, neither NBC nor ABC was able to topple CBS from its preeminent position in the evening news nor dislodge anchor man Walter Cronkite from the affections of his bosses or the nation.

The year 1976–77 was the season of Paddy Chayevsky's Academy Award movie *Network,* according to some critics "a satire so broad as to be pointless," to others "a fiction that for all its apparent exaggeration came perilously close to actual fact." Chayevsky, a prominent victim of an earlier era of TV which eliminated the sort of serious drama he and his colleagues were writing in favor of assembly-line action adventures and westerns, portrayed in *Network* a similar blood bath. This time it was the news department, losing out in the ratings, which was turned over to a numbers-happy entertainment vice-president.

Pat Buchanan, Nixon's media gadfly, wrote in a *TV Guide* News Watch column that "It is an oft times brilliant, scathing satire, parodying the utter obscenity of values and baseness of motives that too often enter in network decision-making. It does for the networks what *Dr. Strangelove* did for the Strategic Air Command."

Two-thirds of the forty news directors responding to the DuPont Survey who had seen the film acknowledged the truth behind the exaggeration; one-third rejected it as inaccurate and unfair.

Even if it seemed farfetched, the behavior of broadcasters, in the months following the film's release, at both network and local level, caused critics to evoke Chayevsky's satiric fantasy with alarming frequency.

ENG

The use of electronic news-gathering gear continued to increase at an accelerating pace to the point where it was no longer an instrument for outflanking the competition. Still, it was enough of a novelty that NBC made much of putting on its first all-live minicam newscast, thirty minutes devoted to President Carter's energy proposals, involving the services of eight scattered NBC correspondents and seven minicam units. In the summer of 1977 CBS News announced its intention of eliminating film entirely and going all ENG by 1978. "There's not going to be any film within two years," said Group W's Pat Polillo, "anywhere."

Although 72 percent of the news directors reporting to the DuPont Survey this year indicated an increase in their investment in ENG, and a majority admitted that it had changed their style of news operation, not everyone was completely sold on the highly temperamental equipment. Most of the criticism seemed to be on technological grounds. Because of the relatively primitive state of the art, equipment not only was expensive, but quickly became obsolete. Also the cash investment required was large and frequently was held responsible for deflecting funds that might be better spent in improving the quality and extent of reporting. Some critics went so far as to claim that without ENG and its capability of being there and covering it live, the current epidemic of terrorism, hijacking, and hostage-taking would not have occurred.

There was no question that, particularly on an unfolding live story, the proper use of ENG required highly competent reportorial talent which the money spent for equipment frequently made it impossible to hire. Even an enthusiast like Polillo admitted the premium ENG put on intelligence, resourcefulness, and experience. "When you go live, you open the stations to destruction. . . . There are no erasers when you're doing live news."

An extended and vivid description of the worst possible impact ENG could have was contained in a full-page Cinema Products Corporation advertisement in *Television/Radio Age.*

Under the headline, "Whatever Happened to the Concept of TV News as an Important Public Service?" the ad read in part:

> A new mentality—a "minicam mentality"—seems to have invaded television news. A self-serving mentality that insists that all stations must go all-electronic regardless of news worthiness or cost effectiveness.
>
> Whatever happened to the concept of TV news as an important *public service*—which is what serious news programming is supposed to be all about?
>
> It is no secret that one of the first true casualties of this new "minicam mentality" is an O & O's* local evening news program in Los Angeles, for many years one of the most respected and admired news programs in the area.
>
> It is indeed a strange mentality that will not recognize that a "Top 20 News" approach has reduced this TV news program to a headline service at best.
>
> . . . a mentality that condescendingly presumes that the average viewer has an attention span of eight seconds, and an insatiable appetite for all the fires, accidents and murders that can possibly be covered—preferably live—during the scheduled news hour.
>
> . . . a mentality that deems it desirable to fire up to 50 percent of a station's veteran TV journalists, and by going fully electronic, to mechanize and computerize the news gathering process to where the reporter may become no more than a puppet at the end of a microphone!
>
> It is a vacuous "minicam mentality" that would judge a newscaster's performance by measuring (through some dubious "skin test" response) an audience's reaction to his TV screen personal-

*Owned and operated.

ity, rather than evaluate his effectiveness as a journalist performing an important public service.

As if the name of the game in television news is purely show biz and higher ratings! (Interestingly enough, this O & O's evening news program is still very much behind in the daily ratings!)

And yet, all the hoopla and ballyhoo in support of going all ENG continues unabated. For the "minicam mentality" refuses to recognize that the recording and transmitting paraphernalia of ENG still make it far less portable and versatile than a newsfilm camera, and would have us believe that merely speeding up the news is in the public interest.

What it really aims to do is provide us with an electronic brand of "instant news"—cosmetic, pretty packaging (with blood and gore, to be sure), but without any substance.

Needless to say, this is patent nonsense. Any real newsman knows it! And so do serious station owners and managers who won't let themselves be sold a bill of goods and be made suckers for a fad!

Some of Cinema Products' points were reiterated, although in a calmer tone, in the same magazine by the new president of NBC News, Lester Crystal.

Money is a factor that will always be present in determining the limits of what can be done. As technology has advanced, it has tended—overall—to raise costs, not reduce them. This, coupled with inflation and our ever-improving living standard, has put a very high price on each electronic breakthrough. The technological horizons are expanded faster than the financial capacity to keep up with them. The cost-benefit ratio may not be a pleasant equation for a broadcast journalist to wrestle with, but it is taking on a growing importance.

Most of the recent changes in reporting the news have taken place at the local level. The changes which have been solely cosmetic—and there have been plenty of these—have not constituted an improvement in how the news is reported. The "package" may look different, but the information is not being presented in a better way. These changes have not brought added clarity or understanding to television reporting.

The local response to the minicam has been mixed. The clutter of supered promotion each time the electronic camera is used, in the hopes of creating a false sense of excitement, is silly at best. At worst, it substitutes show business for information.

Probably the most beneficial change has been the expansion of local news. This has led to the reporting of a broader range of information—much of it quite useful to the audience. It has widened the definition of what is news. It has increased the opportunity for investigative reporting, for examining and discussing critical community issues and for looking at important areas beyond the usual staples of crime, disasters, politics and government, areas such as business, consumer issues, medicine and the arts. Not all stations have taken full advantage of these opportunities, but the trend is decidedly in that direction.

Crystal's predecessor, Richard Wald, saw the minicam as the threshold into a whole brave new world of TV news.

Live television can be cheaper than any other kind. There may or may not be live drama in prime time in our future, but it seems to me that as the price of film or tape *reruns* approaches the size of the national debt, news as an economic means of programming becomes more attractive. If the cost of doing a news program is half the cost of doing an entertainment feature, but the revenue runs to three-quarters the revenue of an entertainment feature, there becomes a business rationale for looking toward more news. . . .

What I think will happen to networks is that their main *daily* product will be news, and networks will remain the main purveyors of national and international news because it is hard to pull together alternative manpower organizations. But . . . the networks will be supplying news both as complete programs and as pieces to insert into local station programs, roughly as they do now. But they will supply a much greater volume of such material. . . .

There will be time on the air for whole court cases and big chunks of medical information or debates or county fairs. We will probably expand the universe of specialists. . . . What will happen, I think, is that news will move out of the domain of being a program and will become a service in a far more constant way.

Most local news directors were equally enthusiastic:

When we shot film only, we normally would not process for a noon or five P.M. news interview show. . . . With ENG we are able to use visuals that are topical on all newscasts. . . .

We are now in the process of "selling" the local district court judges on the idea of attempting ENG coverage of a trial.

ENG has also allowed us to use live-micro-waved reports. This is a daily item while the state legislature is in session. Our deadline time is restricted only by editing time.

Topeka, Kans.

It has made us more aggressive and has permitted us to expand our news gathering ability up until the time we leave the air. It has added credibility to our news because we are able to take people to the scene of events as they happen and let them see for themselves. We lose some production merit with one camera live remotes, but the public finds them more believable.

Columbus, Ohio

We are able consistently to get late stories on the air. The use of minicams and tape is revolutionizing news coverage. We can put stories on the air live or within minutes after the event occurs. The quality of our stories is vastly improved. No dirty film, no mylar splices jumping in the projector gate, no film breaks, no slow film rolls. I would compare our production values with any station in the country, and we can do a story many times faster than film.

Dallas, Tex.

TV Magazines

The network magazine show was at least as old as the experimental ninety-minute Public Broadcasting Laboratory of the late 1960s, which was generally credited with setting the example for such early commercial network versions as "First Tuesday" and "Sixty Minutes."

Now it was "Sixty Minutes," with its high ratings and relatively low costs, which was serving as the pattern for a new generation of hopeful network shows. Nearly a dozen network and syndicated magazines had been announced in recent months with three, including CBS's own ill-fated "Who's Who," actually getting on the air. The others were "Now," a trendy hour of offbeat subjects which NBC put on during the summer doldrums in 1977 to deserved critical blasts; and "People," an attempt at a syndicated TV magazine fashioned on the highly successful Time, Incorporated, product of the same name which was presented in two pilot versions.

Solidly established monthly magazines were NBC's late night ninety-minute "Weekend" and CBS's "Magazine," a high-quality daytime show which had finally been assigned a regular slot at 10:00 A.M. the first Thursday of every month.

If an eagerness to emulate the success of "Sixty Minutes" was apparent on the network level, it was even more prevalent among local stations. The magazine vogue, in addition to being ascribed to "Sixty

Minutes," was also blamed on the increased cost of syndicated programming and network reruns.

Almost half the news directors reporting to the Survey had a magazine on the air at least once a month, variously labeled "Thirty Minutes," "Indiana Illustrated," "Saturday Magazine," "Eyewitness Magazine," "Montage." There was even a short-lived TV magazine called "Tabloid," aimed by its proprietor, Metromedia, at the blue-collar market.

The most ambitious and expertly produced of these local magazines was probably KPIX's "Evening," which boasted sophisticated camera work and literate scripts. Broadcast every weekday during prime access time on Westinghouse's San Francisco outlet, its format had, by the fall of 1977, been adopted by the four other major market Westinghouse stations. In each case it was a distinct improvement over the usual fare offered by local stations in the prime time access slot. It was also a belated demonstration by Don McGannon, the man who dreamed up the access concept in the first place, of how this half hour returned to local major market affiliates might be put to creative use.

However, Group W purposefully avoided investigative and documentary features in favor of useful information and human interest. Permissible subjects included life styles, leisure time, pop culture, famous people, fascinating places, consumer tips, and modern city living.

"28 Tonight" on KCET, the public TV station in Los Angeles, was more catholic in its fare. Five nights a week it offered a mixed menu of imported features and hardnosed investigative reporting on sensitive and seldom-covered subjects including industrial lead poisoning, out-of-control police, the Bureau of Land Management's regulation of miners, the foibles of local bureaucrats, guardians, conservators, and tax assessors. It also turned over its time to documentaries such as Lynne Littman's "Number Our Days," an alternately joyous and touching portrait of a community of elderly Jews in Venice, California.

KCET's magazine was one of the few which on occasion gave all its time to a single story. Indeed, the principal concern among broadcast documentarians was that the growth of the magazine show on both network and local levels, when joined to the thrust toward minidocumentaries and fragmented newscast series, would further diminish the opportunity for more extended reports, not just by using up precious time and money, but by cannibalizing the subjects which could have justified more sustained treatment.

Documentaries

The growing popularity of minidocumentaries and magazine shows, if it had already affected the number of documentaries produced, had not had an adverse affect on the quality of those that did get on the air. Some of the most impressive material viewed by the DuPont jurors this year fell within this increasingly neglected category.

Group W, since the closing down of its Urban America Unit in 1971, had steered clear of a regular group commitment to the documentary form. It returned with an impressive series, "Six American Families." Cosponsored and funded by the United Church of Christ and the United Methodist Church, it went on the air over 222 public TV stations as well as Group W's own five outlets, conceived and executed by Paul Wilkes and Lisa Director, it employed the talents of half a dozen gifted directors, including Arthur Barron and the Maysles brothers. The resulting family portraits managed to touch on most of the concerns, aspirations, and tribulations of a majority of Americans, urban and rural, rich and poor, fortunate and not so fortunate.

The process of Americanization which was taken for granted in Westinghouse's series was the principal theme of the Downtown Community TV Center's highly authentic picture of Chinatown. Produced in conjunction with the TV Lab at WNET/13, it eschewed the quaint and exotic in favor of a sequence of sharply observed vignettes that underlined the universality of the lot of immigrants—particularly those who have, wave upon wave, settled in urban ghettos.

Religion played a central part in at least two of the outstanding documentaries of the year, one network, the other local. ABC's "Close-Up on New Religions—Holiness or Heresy," applied hard-nosed investigative methods to two highly successful modern sects. L. Ron Hubbard's Scientology and the Reverend Sun Myung Moon's Unification Church. There were some disquieting results for both religionists and viewers. WBBM's "Once a Priest" was perhaps even more startling, since it dealt with the turmoil, not in a small fanatical sect, but the Roman Catholic Church. Taking the class of 1957 at Illinois's Mundelein Seminary, producer Scott Craig selected ten representative members and told what had happened to their faith and their vocations in the two decades since graduation. Considerable tension was created in covering what on the surface might have seemed a bland subject, and the reflection of America in two of its most tormented decades was sharply focused. As in all first-class mysteries, it was impossible for the viewer to guess who would stay the course and who drop by the wayside, until the documentary chose to reveal it.

The commitment of large blocks of time to a single subject was less rare on local TV than on the networks. Among the outstanding programs which involved more than the canonical thirty to sixty minutes was WFAA's two-hour essay "The Energy Crisis," a well-organized, expertly reported treatment of the year's most unmanageable subject which took the station's news crews and viewers across the country into a cold home in New Jersey to show what the crisis was like outside of Texas. The same station's two-hour exploration of the black-white-Chicano situation in Dallas was filled with sharp and humane insights and encouraging surprises, another example of the station's willingness to spend an appropriately large amount of time and effort on a large subject.

The longest local documentary of the year was WTMJ Milwaukee's "A Human Relations Test," a three-hour essay which gave the definitive statement on race relations in the Wisconsin city, keyed to the imminent desegregation of the local schools. Put on the air from 7:00 to 10:00 P.M. on a Thursday evening in early September 1976, it was the latest and perhaps most impressive example of what a conscientious, community-oriented TV station can do in explicating a complex and, to some, threatening human situation.

Producer Michael Hirsh at WTTW Chicago produced a brace of programs on two of the most troubling moral questions of our time, premarital sex and abortion. Beginning with the staggering statistics that 1 out of every 10 teenage American girls will become pregnant in the next twelve months and that 600,000 will give birth, "Guess Who's Pregnant?" gave the subject a frank and unsensational treatment, handling firmly and fairly such touchy issues as sex education and contraception for the young and unmarried. The same meticulously objective treatment was characteristic of "The Politics of Abortion," which took on this incendiary issue in a courageous and honest manner which was likely to be unpleasing to extremists on both sides.

Another pressing community issue was handled with admirable finesse and thoroughness in KGW-TV Portland's "The Timber Farmers." Fifteen special reports which culminated in a sixty-minute documentary, the series dealt with one of the most important questions before the nation's Northwest: how best to handle its great stands of timber. News analyst Floyd McCay and cameraman Doug Vernon put together a package which was not only top-quality reporting, but managed to satisfy the general viewer as well as the often unreconcilable experts in governmental, environmental, and industry organizations.

The hardest subject of all, nuclear power, was undertaken by WGBH Boston on its distinguished "Nova" series. "An Incident at Brown's Ferry" was fascinating and informative television, again not satisfying the extremists, but leaving the viewer with the sensation of having been instructed in the worst that might happen and then brought back to a reasonable middle ground.

Actually, reasonableness was more characteristic of the year's documentary fare, local and national, than controversy and experimentation. Frederick Wiseman, noted for taking chances in subject matter and approach, was represented by "Meat," a two-hour tour of a cattle and sheep slaughtering facility which was frequently visually stunning, but ultimately seemed as cold as the lockers in which the dead animals finally were hung. Another group of young experimenters, the West Coast-based TVTV, was also heard from. Its big effort of the season was devoted to one of the nation's favorite TV institutions, the Academy Awards. Sometimes hovering along the sidelines and then slashing in for a devastating behind-the-scenes look, the irreverent young documentarians succeeded as they had with "Lord of the Universe," the Democratic national convention, and Gerald Ford's Washington in holding up pretensions and illusions to the slightly wavering and jaundiced eye of the hand-held camera.

A genuine experiment was undertaken by all four *Post/Newsweek* stations when they went on the air with evening-long programs designed to give their viewers an extended say about how the station was spending its time and how it might do better. A new way to fulfill the FCC's demand for public ascertainment, it also made interesting viewing and commanded respectable audiences.

Opening up the air to viewers was also a regular function of KYW Philadelphia's "Meeting House," a regular monthly feature which during the year was able to explore such pressing local questions as "How to Survive a Transit Strike" and "How to Survive a Newspaper Strike."

Public Broadcasting's exemplary "MacNeil/Lehrer Report," an experiment of three years back which was steadily building audience and expertise, was now visible in 242 markets across the nation. Augmenting its two-city in-studio discussions with out-of-studio coverage of such subjects as energy, labor disputes, and the national park services, it had also added a woman, Charlayne Hunter-Gault, to its pair of male interrogators—another indication that it had no intention of resting on its already substantial laurels.

Broadcasting and Government

The complexity of broadcasting's relationships with the nation's legislators and administrators had seldom been so clearly revealed as during the appearance of veteran CBS Washington correspondent Daniel Schorr before the House Committee on Standards of Official Conduct in September 1976.

Like Barbara Walters, Schorr had found himself in that uneasy territory between reporting the news and making it, but with strikingly different results. By slipping the Pike report of the House Intelligence Committee to the *Village Voice*, Schorr had made himself the subject not only of headlines but of disciplinary action by his own network and congressional criticism and subpoena. Viewers who knew Schorr principally as a reporter feisty and adventurous enough to get himself on Nixon's enemies list were treated to a long list of rumors to explain his sudden suspension from all broadcast activities. He had alienated his top boss William Paley by revealing certain past connections with the CIA; he had upset his colleagues by criticizing in public their handling of Nixon's resignation; he had made enemies of several more by his unprofessional behavior in allowing the shadow of suspicion to fall on a colleague in order to protect his source; CBS Radio affiliates had demanded that he be taken off the air. Whatever the true reason or combination of reasons for Schorr's enforced absence, after an eloquent defense of the First Amendment* before his congressional interrogators and a final appearance on "Sixty Minutes" with Mike Wallace, he announced his resignation.

CBS News president Richard Salant was gracious in his letter of response. "I say once again," he wrote, "that, in your appearance before the Ethics Committee, you did a superb and eloquent service to all of us in journalism and, above all, to the principles of the First Amendment and the public's right to know."†

Schorr's own feelings were indicated in his announcement that he didn't intend to continue working in commercial TV news. "I don't think I'd find at another network what I didn't find at CBS News." Later he added, "It's not going to be a big encouragement for a twenty-year-old starting out in the profession. A guy stuck his neck out, and it wasn't Congress that silenced him, but his employer."

Advertising Age, in an editorial applauding the network's and Mr. Schorr's dignified handling of a treacherous situation, had said:

*See Appendix X.
†According to a later account, contained in Schorr's book *Clearing the Air,* Schorr's departure had been agreed upon long before his congressional appearance. Salant relented, but Schorr, warned by his lawyer that he might be dumped later with a less advantageous settlement, resigned anyway.

If there is anything the ad business doesn't need now it's a public fuss which furnishes ammunition to those who say an advertiser-supported medium has no place for individuals who stand their ground on controversial issues of high principles.

Our nation needs TV news organizations that aggressively engage in the kind of investigative reporting Mr. Schorr represents, and this cannot happen unless news personnel can count on support from top management when they incur the wrath of the politically powerful.

Considering the final outcome, it was a double-edged compliment.

"If all there was at CBS was a news division without a corporate structure around it and affiliate pressures," Schorr told *Broadcasting* magazine following his resignation, "I don't know of any problem we had that couldn't have been resolved. . . . I'm a maverick. I don't function in normal ways. I have my own ideas about how to get news and how to handle it. . . . I think eventually I was indigestible."

According to Schorr, an important part of his problem was that he had involved television in an argument with Congress when Congress was looking balefully at the broadcast industry anyway. "And I had flaunted the idea of press disclosure when disclosure was retreating before a secrecy backlash, and the press was fretting about public hostility to the news media."

Washington had indeed developed a rather baleful countenance toward broadcasting—or so it seemed to the more paranoid segments of the industry. Richard E. Wiley, chairman of the FCC, in his valedictory to the National Association of Broadcasters at their convention in March 1977, delivered some ambiguous and vaguely threatening words:

. . . Broadcasting is a great industry which has well served the citizens of this country. What I am suggesting today is that it can be yet a greater medium. With very fundamental questions concerning the future of broadcasting now being raised on Capitol Hill and elsewhere, I believe that the time has come for members of the industry to focus on this potential. There is—and there must be—more to broadcasting than simply spinning the latest record or taking the available network feed (however much this programming may satisfy some members of the public). If not, then the whole concept of local, public trustee broadcasting—on which the Commission has placed such emphasis in structuring your industry—must be called into serious question.

One of the biggest questions in Washington was the rewriting of the 1934 Communications Act. Despite the fact that it had been passed long before the arrival of television and the vast expansion of the industry that followed, broadcasters contended that the act had served them well and they saw no reason for altering it. Any change had to be, so far as they were concerned, a change for the worse. However, they seemed unable to deflect Congressman Lionel Van Deerlin, a former broadcaster himself, from continuing with his extensive hearings in connection with the project. Legislative proposals, if not a total rewrite, were scheduled for early in 1978.

Another threat to the broadcasting status quo lay in the promise of newly appointed FCC chairman Charles Ferris to reactivate the network inquiry petitioned for by Group W president Don McGannon. There was also under way an FCC inquiry into the economic relationship between cable and conventional broadcasting which implied that the commission's traditional bias in favor of over-the-air broadcasting might be moderating. Indications of a friendlier attitude toward cable on the part of the administration and its appointees were equally distressing. (For a report on cable see page 168.)

Further, an out-of-court settlement by NBC had done nothing to deter the Justice Department in its suit charging TV networks with monopoly programming practices.

Overt government actions which might be considered friendly to the broadcast establishment included the modification of the House report on TV violence, which weakened its criticism of the networks; the delay in the ban on saccharine; proposed legislation extending the license period for broadcasters; and the shelving of the bill to establish the Agency for Consumer Protection.

Characteristic of Washington's ambivalent view of the networks were four paragraphs buried in the appendix of "The Second Report with Recommendations of the Temporary Select Committee to Study the Senate Committee System." Flattering in that it concluded network TV news and public affairs had an important effect on federal legislative policy and congressional relationships with the White House, it was devastating in its chronicle of how over the years the networks had used that power:

> Congressional committees have been the subject of television network news reports since the late 1940s. In March 1951, live coverage of hearings of the Senate Select Crime Investigating Committee, chaired by Senator Estes Kefauver, was broadcast regionally along the eastern seaboard and in the Midwest, reach-

ing an estimated 20 to 30 million viewers. Three years later, the major television networks televised extended news coverage of the Senate Army-McCarthy hearings nationwide, heralding a form of coast-to-coast special television network coverage which, when repeated in the decades to follow, would profoundly influence the development and resolution of tense conflicts between the White House and Congress.

In the mid-1960s, two of the three commercial networks—CBS and NBC—provided television viewers periodically with special coverage of Senate committee proceedings. Such coverage, however, fell off sharply in the late 1960s and ushered in a trend of negligible special news coverage of Senate and House committees which lasted into the 1970s. The pattern of negligible special news coverage of congressional committees by the three commercial networks was broken abruptly in 1973 by their more than 100 hours of coverage of the Senate Watergate Committee hearings.

This was followed in 1974 by extended live coverage, rotated among the three networks, of the impeachment proceedings of the House Judiciary Committee. The following report suggests, however, that the commercial networks' coverage of Watergate were in response to extraordinary news events and were deviations from apparent trends to which the networks subsequently returned. Indeed, in 1975 and 1976, the ABC, CBS and NBC networks preempted no regular programming to cover either Senate or House committee proceedings, despite major committee inquiries into the policies of the government's intelligence agencies and into various facets of national energy policy.

From 1971 to the present, the Public Broadcasting Service, which distributes programming to the nation's public television stations, has been the chief vehicle for bringing Senate and House committee proceedings to television viewers in the form of extended special news coverage. As such coverage by the commercial networks has dropped off, the amount of special news coverage of committees presented over PBS has grown.

The report concluded that there was one preeminent reason for this apparent decline of network interest in matters of government—the enormous increase in network earnings and the huge loss of profits that would result from any preemptions.

Once again broadcasting's prosperity had militated against fuller performance of those news and public affairs functions which at an earlier stage of its development it understood as a public duty.*

The growth of the Public Broadcasting Service and its commit-

*Another index of network television's declining commitment to such public service was the coverage of the U.N. See page 93, note.

ment, so far as its limited resources allowed, to such coverage had served to take some of the heat off the networks. There was more and more serious talk of turning over to the public broadcasters the commercial networks' traditional coverage of the political conventions. The networks could then do "selective coverage" and use the time cleared for more profitable programs.

Public Broadcasting

Whether or not they were going to take over one of the most conspicuous public service functions of network TV, things might be looking up for public television's news and public affairs. After the bleak Nixon years there were some encouraging signs from the Carter White House. First, the president had sent to Congress a bill which proposed long-term financing at a substantially increased rate ($1 billion for five years) designed to insulate public broadcasting from congressional intrusion. It would also give public broadcasters the right to editorialize if they so chose. A much higher percentage of the money, 25 percent, would be earmarked for national programming. The president's motives were "to encourage public broadcasters at all levels to engage in active news reporting and public affairs." Nor would he and his administration "try to dictate what issues public broadcasting should cover, or how it should cover them."

Additional encouragement came from his choice of Frank Lloyd to block out the administration policy on public TV. Lloyd had been general counsel for the National Public Affairs Center for Television (NPACT), the unit, defunct since 1974, that was responsible for the Watergate coverage. He was quoted as saying, "We're not afraid of a public system that does aggressive journalism and will get an audience."

Broadcasting magazine was less optimistic, stating editorially that it was

> unrealistic to suppose that the noncommercial system can go deeply into venturesome journalism or expression of opinion on political issues or events without encountering persistent political reprisal that can strike at the source of its funds.

The *Wall Street Journal* commented:

> . . . it is a little bit unrealistic to believe that as federal funding increases, public broadcasting will have more insulation from political interference. There will still be the possibility of future

Presidents vetoing an appropriations bill, as President Nixon once did, out of pique over "ideological plugola."

We would urge public television to try to make the most of the increased federal money. But we would urge them also to keep plugging for other sources of funding if they want to protect the measure of independence they now have.

Despite such forecasts of trouble ahead, administration support seemed unequivocal.

One detracting factor which had nothing to do with outside resistance was the continuing struggle for power between the Corporation for Public Broadcasting, which had the responsibility for allotting federal funds, and the Public Broadcasting Service, which had been created by CPB to distribute programming. In February 1977, Representative Van Deerlin told the PBS convention in Atlanta that he intended "to take the most exhaustive look at public broadcasting since its start in 1967" and that an examination of the jurisdictional disputes between CPB and PBS was high on his list of priorities. Although a truce had been declared between Henry Loomis, head of CPB,* and Lawrence Grossman, president of PBS, duplication of staffs, high expenses, conflicting authority, and the lack of funds for national programming ($13 million out of a total of $103 million) continued to rankle supporters of public television.

One hopeful sign was the formation of a new Carnegie Commission on the Future of Public Broadcasting under the leadership of Columbia University President William McGill. The commission, with a budget of a million dollars and a board of twenty distinguished Americans, was intended to update and correct the sightings made by the original commission, which had drawn the blueprints for public television in 1967.

One ticklish question so far as public TV news and public affairs was concerned was the growing importance of corporate underwriters. Four out of five programs put on the national interconnection were beholden, at least in part, to the generosity of big business. Citizen groups in San Francisco, filing with the FCC against the renewal of the Bay Area public television and radio stations licenses, claimed that they had forfeited their public broadcasting status by "operating commercially on a number of fronts," and that, in their eagerness to develop their "national production center," they ran what amounted to an "advertising agency for hire."

Although public broadcasting exerted every effort to prevent intru-

*In December 1977 Loomis announced his resignation as of September 1978 or sooner.

sion into its program decisions and frequently rejected corporate proposals, corporate support had become as important to public as to commercial TV. Considering that they were attempting to produce higher-quality programming than the commercial networks with five percent of their program budget, the help of big business was even more urgent. For similar reasons there was an increased interest in public television ratings, which for the first time in history were registering on the charts with some frequency.*

Measured by the ratings, the principal triumphs of the PBS year remained in the entertainment sector, including broadcasting's best dramatic and musical fare. Public television's documentaries, although frequently of superior quality, still steered clear of the controversial. The Station Program Cooperative, set up to facilitate program production and distribution among individual stations of the public system, bought the first documentary series in its four-year history, eight one-hour programs to be produced by WTTW Chicago.† The Ford Foundation and the National Endowment for the Arts set up a $500,000 fund to encourage the production of documentaries for public TV. The Corporation for Public Broadcasting had also set up a $1 million revolving fund for documentaries chosen for production by local public TV stations. The first project to be completed, Don Widener's "Plutonium: An Element of Risk," toward which CPB had contributed $125,000, was rejected by PBS because it "does not conform to the PBS document of journalism standards and guidelines." Nevertheless, a half dozen West Coast stations chose to run it.

Another discouraging note was struck when, after eight years on the air, KQED San Francisco's "Newsroom," which had set the pattern for public newscasts across the country, went off the air for lack of adequate funds.

Money remained public television's most pressing problem. If public TV was going to continue to be the chosen instrument for quality entertainment, as commercial TV's programming policies and pronouncements seemed to demand it should be, the system would need more and more production money. If, in addition, it was going to have increased responsibility for live coverage of important national and international events and reassume its early role as the pacesetter in

---

*The elitist, anti-minority image of public TV seemed to be cracking a bit. Nielsen figures for October 1976 showed a dramatic increase in nonwhite viewing (up 47.5 percent over the previous year) and the Black Opinion Poll in Chicago, asking viewers which local channel they would choose if they could watch only one, were told most frequently the public TV station WTTW.

†However, a bid by WETA Washington for $1 million to defray expenses in covering governmental events for the public system was cut back to $300,000.

serious and controversial news and public affairs, the funding had to be not only generous but insulated.

So far no one had found a satisfactory solution to these chronic problems.

The Future

In the summations of a large number of the DuPont correspondents this year, there was a sense of a crossroads at hand. They reported an increasing professionalism in news and public affairs in their respective communities, more money, bigger staffs, and a substantial allotment of time. But there was ambivalence still about how this impressive commitment might best be used—to serve the community, or to make more money?

The quality of broadcast journalism has improved in terms of scope of coverage. However, both radio and television stations continue their pronounced drift away from information and toward more entertainment in their news programs. All three television stations have now retained consultants who recommend elements of entertainment (Magid, McHugh-Hoffman, Al Primo). One news director, disenchanted with the trend, resigned last month and joined Associated Press at almost half the salary.

An all-news radio station affiliated with NBC's NIS is drifting into a talk-show format now that NIS is dead. Another radio station active in news is adopting a news format that conveys information in the form of banter between DJ and newscaster. The only other station active in news, KSL-AM, has doubled its staff for news in the last year and is actively seeking remote live coverage of events. It is the one exception to the drift to entertainment.

The amount of time television stations devote to news has diminished. KUTV, which had expanded its early news to a full hour in 1974, found itself languishing third in ratings and cut back to a half hour in January. It also abandoned some vigorous investigative reporting it had been doing for the last two years. All the stations rely heavily on cosmetics now to attract the desired audiences.

The public television stations program no news, and most of their public affairs programs are interview programs.

The public radio stations, KUER-FM and KBYU-FM, both program news, but news programs are produced and voiced by students in broadcast journalism training programs . . . good for the students, but not good for journalistic programming.

Salt Lake City, Utah

This market has long been dominated by one TV station—KTBC. . . . This domination of the ratings has allowed KTBC to be very complacent in its news programming. Now, however, KTBC is beginning to feel a real challenge to its high profits from the other stations, and thus changes have begun.

KTVV began it by hiring a new station manager, news director, and anchorman, and pouring dollars into a publicity campaign for its news shows. This got KTBC scared—KTVV hired away some of KTBC's people and started paying higher salaries. Then KTBC's national "rep," the national sales agent in New York, said though the total ratings were high, only the 18 to 49 year olds mattered, and KTBC did not have enough of them.

Result? KTVV did not greatly improve its ratings, or the quality of its news, but it got KTBC's attention. Changes in news may be starting at KTBC, but it will be next year before we know whether they are for the better or the worse as far as quality journalism goes. Suffice it to say that the only real motivation for change of news quality, content, or format in this market has been inter-competition between stations for profits, and an outside New York sales organization saying change was needed in order to sell more ads. The desire is not to have quality journalism, but news that sells. The journalists working in the stations hope it is good journalism that ultimately will sell the best.

Austin, Tex.

Over at least six years, news broadcasts on radio have dwindled in number and quality. Radio news staffs have decreased for most AM stations, though FM stations have begun to broadcast news and, therefore, to increase news staffing.

Radio stations have tended to be dominated by formula programming—with top 40 formats and brief newscasts—and by special interests (country-and-western, religion, hard rock and "easy listening.")

TV is best characterized by dependence on ratings. In that respect, it is not unlike national television. When a station sees its ratings falling, it jumps into whatever format another station has used successfully. We still have considerable emphasis on the happy talk and banter among on-the-air newscasters.

WSPD TV (Ch. 13) is now embarked on a complete change in emphasis. Young on-the-air people—male and female, black and white—dominate on TV newscasts. Females—black and white—now either co-anchor newscasts or serve as special reporters. There appears to me to be a dreary sameness to what is promoted as change and diversity.

In the Toledo area, I believe that there will be a continued emphasis on male-female anchorpersons on news broadcasts, with at least one black or ethnic minority on the air. The situation, I propose, is largely the result, in my opinion, of consultants and others placing the news programs in the form they feel is most attractive to a majority of viewers. Some examples of the promotional announcements for WSPD TV's latest changes in format:

1. One promo presents a new symbol ("13 Strong"), followed by —depending on the promo—a female, a male, a black, or a Mexican American, each of which gives a trite reason for the importance of the station's new efforts in news.

2. In some promos, the tag is a shot of the "weather lady" turning quickly to face the camera and saying, "You better believe it."

3. There is a weekly editorial, presented by a high school student, and the editorials are changed from school to school in the area each week.

4. There is a sports quiz in five parts—one for each night of the week—for which viewers send in their answers to all five questions and have a chance to win a black and white TV.

5. A "bowler of the week" feature, in which the male and female bowlers picked by the station receive trophies. They're presented on the sports news.

I'm sure there are other promos that follow the same general pattern.

I don't believe that such changes have anything to do with the quality of the news people. My feeling from my dealings with many of them—at all stations—is that they're well educated, experienced and interested in doing a good job within the limits placed on them.

Perhaps my observations are best expressed by stating that news staffs on local television are hampered in their work by outside interference. In part, I think, Toledo is slowly following the lead of the networks, both of which have been pressured to employ women and minorities.

In this area, I think that the most improvement in news and public affairs has been in radio, and more in FM than in AM.

Toledo, Ohio

I have a feeling what's ailing broadcast journalism in this community is no more and no less than what is ailing all journalism (in this and probably most other communities): a battle weariness by both journalists and the public as far as the great public issues of the day are concerned, an increased interest in the little, manageable details of everyday personal lives and of the immediate surroundings. People seem to prefer to focus on how not to serve water in restaurants than on the ramifications of dam-building in relation to California's drought; on how to shop for bargains or health foods rather than for honest, intelligent public officials; on how to examine themselves for cancer rather than the body politic for non-democratic practices. I think broadcast journalism plays up to these inclinations, but no more so than the newspapers with their magazine-type supplements on "where to get the 10 best ice cream sodas in California" etc. etc. In the absence of a public hunger for hard news, and a commitment to broadcasting as such, I think you get all the phenomena of "happy news," glamor-girl reporters, too many specialists, etc. etc. Some of these specialists are excellent in their field—e.g. Dr. Art Ulene on KNBC on health. It's the generalists that don't have a chance to enlighten the public.

Finally, I would just like to make a rather obvious point: that Southern California is a vast territory with a lot happening in broadcast journalism, both good and bad, and often sadly evanescent so that it does not get reported on. (There is a definite dearth of print media reporting on broadcast journalism—much more coverage is extended to broadcast entertainment!) And, in the final analysis, broadcast journalism does depend a great deal on the state of the art elsewhere, although there are certain regional quirks to be noted, which provide ongoing change.

Los Angeles, Calif.

News directors' view of the future tended to be somewhat narrower in focus, and frequently even harsher in tone.

As has been the case for twenty-five years, it still is in a state of major change from a technological standpoint. These electronic advancements permit us to bring more complete coverage of events and will continue to do so but with increasing problems. Example . . . live reports with attendant dangers. More and more information to relay to the public, but the same amount of time in which to package it. News will need more time locally to meet its responsibilities of properly informing the public. The question may be: will the public sit through more than thirty minutes as coverage increases?

Lincoln, Nebr.

Local broadcast journalism has been going through a maturing process during the past decade. I think we are going to see a quickening of the pace toward two essential goals, one being the defining of the local television news role, and secondarily, an increased independence on the part of local news managers to institute special services to their community.

In the past, we have often spent too much time trying to define ourselves in relation to either the networks or large newspapers. It should now be obvious to everyone in local television that our role will never be defined unless we begin thinking in terms of our service as a unique and special part of the information combine available to the American people. With our roles defined, we can then gain a new confidence and begin searching for those many particular services which local television news can provide, such as strong local polling of audience attitudes, strong local live coverage of major events, and endless amounts of nonrepetitive, original reporting of items uniquely suited to television. All of this, however, is only possible when local broadcast managers spend less time worrying about old traditions and become more involved with trying to formulate new standards. The modern broadcast news manager is one of the most important individuals in the community, and his/her potential is only realized when he/she shows an active concern for the totality of his/her product, the lasting impact of the product, and the societal role which his/her product can and should play in the coming years.

Boston, Mass.

I think broadcast journalism has become a major influence in our lives, and it is extremely important how that influence is used in coming years. Broadcast journalism has a potential greater than any other medium: the ability to bring film of war and riots into our homes: the capability of showing emotions and confrontations.

I think we are seeing and will continue to see a trend away from spot news coverage (accidents and shootings, etc.) and instead, a trend toward more in-depth reporting [of] economic, political and social issues.

Miami, Fla.

The present state is good. More and more network news is doing gutsy stories.

While there are too many young people coming into the field, the ones that do make it are highly skilled and have great promise. This augurs well for the future.

Seattle, Wash.

. . . Unless we get our heads together on a national level and fight against government interference, maintain our First Amendment rights and keep the quality of our product high, we're in trouble. If integrity instead of ratings were the prime factor in broadcast journalism, we'd be okay, but as long as ratings and profits control the future of news on television, it's going to be a constant struggle between journalists and profiteers.

Charleston, W.V.

I think broadcast journalism is in kind of a holding pattern. The new ENG technology and its implementation has preoccupied many news directors and news departments, leaving less time and thought for the journalistic side of the business. Despite that, generally, I think television news is doing a better job of covering the day's news, day in and day out. A more thorough job. But, we are still finding too little time for the news that doesn't come out and poke you in the nose. We're covering the predictable, the dependable. But we're reacting more than we're acting; there still is far too little truly enterprise reporting, too few stories that really have an impact on people's lives. Often, there just isn't enough time in the day.

I think we're already seeing an increase in the immediacy of television news, thanks to ENG. And the future will hold more of the same. Television news, I believe, will be less and less confined to certain newscasts at certain times. Like radio, television news will be on more frequently, reporting *when* and *as* the news is happening.

Minneapolis, Minn.

Overemphasis on production and style to detriment of content. Trend toward frivolous news—no time or interest in "heavy" news. The "look-alike" trend.

Kansas City, Mo.

Too much emphasis on form and not enough on content. May die down as ENG "fever" subsides and medium accepts it merely as another way to cover stories.

Los Angeles, Calif.

Broadcast journalism is confused. It's undergoing a kind of institutional identity crisis. It's sort of like a small town beauty queen suddenly thrust into the spotlight . . . making lots of money, recognized and responded to by millions, being pampered and messed and fussed with by consultants, managers, powerful corporate executives . . . under constant pressure to keep up an audience-gathering image. An image arrived at in large part by accident and a little trial and error . . . and, therefore, not precisely definable. The result is a mild to severe neurosis. Since we want to be . . . indeed, *have to be* loved or at least liked a lot in order to survive the ratings competition . . . we have, in far too many cases, taken to acting quite ridiculous, indulging in outrageous, attention getting pranks. We put on airs of warmth and personability . . . anything to be admired, adored because it means a 30 share in the Nielsens or Arbitron.

Evansville, Ind.

Going through a tough period of transition. The sixties and seventies suddenly thrust TV into the lead as America's major news source—and that was followed closely by technological advances (ENG). I think TV suddenly got drunk on its own power. Now it's time to pull back—get back to the basics of solid journalism and stop looking for another Watergate or SLA shootout. Let's uncover the things people are most concerned about.

Binghamton, N.Y.

Shaky. The few people with strong convictions are outnumbered by audience manipulators and image analyzers and technical wizards. I look for more gimmicks and less news.

Houston, Tex.

Going down hill—will get worse, largely because industry is not policing its own ranks. If we don't weed out the sloppy reporters, government will be doing it for us.

Cadillac, Mich.

I am disturbed by the continued buffoonery which can be seen on the news each night and the continued success of "happy talk" and "action news" formats. It is deplorable that recent technological advances (Electronic News Gathering) have resulted in increased gimmickry and an actual decrease in content. So called "live" coverage in most newscasts boils down to a reporter manufacturing a story for the mere effect of using a live camera. Hopefully, increased sophistication on the part of the audience will eventually bring a decline in this kind of foolishness. The increase in viewership of alternative programming during the evening news period may be the beginning of a serious and welcome public disgust. . . .

Boston, Mass.

Growing; finding its role. It has finally discovered it is not a newspaper and not a radio station. But it has not really discovered with any consensus *what it is solely!*

Will become more informational and not trapped in the thirty minute box. Will spread over the broadcast day with higher interrupt rate. Exciting future.

Will continue to be most responsive medium to stories that strongly relate to largest number of persons.

Champaign, Ill.

Security of job for news director and personnel getting more shaky . . . consultants still having adverse influence. On-air people fired by consultant recommendation are in "blacklist" position many times . . . other stations afraid to hire "deadwood" by consultant definition. Mobility of job movements and short tenure enjoyed by newsmen cause news rooms to be staffed by people out of touch with the community and area they are reporting on. This gives rise to superficial and skimming the top news reporting, which further deprives the news consumer of getting what he should be told about. Sales-oriented station managers still keep a steady stare at the profit ledger and an occasional blink at the news operation unless they feel a shakeup might enhance income via ratings or demographics changes. Broadcasting is still a needlessly difficult arena for the professional journalist who, while professing news does not have to be dull . . . still wants to be left alone to do his job.

Miami, Fla.

In my humble opinion, the future of television news depends on an end to governmental regulation. We need to operate on thought and principle, not middle-ground caution.

When that happens, the ratings and economics will take care of the rest. The irresponsible will be found out, the journalists will rise above the rest on the merits of their stories.

General managers of television stations are a much more refined breed than ten years ago. There is more awareness of principle, of independence. There is a long way to go, though.

One great help may be the move of news directors to the general manager position. All news directors aren't principled, but they'll at least feel some guilt if they sell out.

Atlanta, Ga.

We still manage to scratch only the surface and are apparently becoming more and more of a headline service. Content is being lost along the way. Perhaps consultant firms have helped lead us down the path where news is truly where the cameras are instead of the cameras being where the news is.

Sacramento, Calif.

Dismayed over management desire to be competitive without providing the tools (and money); dismayed over programming judgment consistently winning out over news judgment.

Springfield, Mass.

Broadcast journalism is active and moving . . . but not necessarily well. Most broadcast news operations are undermanned. Most are not properly staffed. Most do not practice good journalism. Management interferes in news in too many stations. Sales affects broadcast journalism in too many stations. In looking at the news programs and reports cited for national awards this year, I could not help but wonder whether they were deserved. This was not the year for the investigative report. Most stations lack courage. They are unwilling to buck the establishment . . . to challenge through investigative reporting . . . to fight the FCC . . . to fight for First Amendment rights for broadcast journalists . . . to encourage independent journalistic thought in the news operations . . . to wage the war against unscrupulous attorneys who threaten libel and slander actions . . . to accept responsibility for the journalistic side of their operations. Thankfully, my station does.

Miami, Fla.

Broadcast journalism is to some extent resting on its limited laurels from the Watergate era. The accolades from that period have allowed news managers to compromise more than they should have on the question of substantive coverage versus coverage designed to increase the appeal of the particular local news operation. Broadcast journalists (again, myself included) must fight hard to retain substantive coverage of local news, the primary motivating factor in local newsroom budgets.

Rockford, Ill.

I think it still has a long way to go and, perhaps because TV is a commercial medium, it is unsuitable for serious journalism.

The chief deterrent, it seems to me, is a lack of real conviction on the part of many station managers that news is important. They've put up with it because of government and group pressures and because it has become profitable, but in too many cases it is simply considered another show.

Its future depends on the quality of persons involved both on the operating level and management level. I am hopeful. Not optimistic.

Portland, Ore.

I hope news directors are learning that instead of investing so much time in the development of ENG units they should have spent time retraining reporters to work better under pressure, ad lib situations. How many times have we seen an ENG unit working perfectly from a technical standpoint and a reporter delivering a report that was wordy, clumsy and possibly even inaccurate? ENG could be a real plus in covering events once we stop treating it as a gimmick and realize its full potential.

Miami, Fla.

We must be doing a lot of things right. The polls tell us more people get their news from TV than from any other source. Our local news ratings are the showcase of the station.

But I'm concerned about the direction the industry seems to be headed. The emphasis seems to be edging more and more toward show biz.

The new people I see in the network news departments are all attractive and young. There's certainly nothing wrong with being young and attractive. But I don't see the nets hiring news people like Alexander Kendrick or Edwin Newman, people who made it on their ability as journalists, not because of the way they looked and sounded. Can looking and sounding good be taking the place of ability?

I'm also worried about the star image projected by Barbara Walters on ABC, our network. When she goes to London and appears on the nightly news, as she did the other night for the Silver Jubilee, and talks about what "I did today" and where "I was today," I feel a bit uncomfortable. Does it really matter what she does or where she did it? I thought the important thing was what the other people did, the people she was there to report on. It was a small thing on Barbara's part—a short segment at the end of the cast—but I wonder if it were another indication of the direction even the networks are headed.

Certainly a lot of local markets already are there. "Reporter involvement" has been taken to ridiculous extremes—even on hard news stories. But I've yet to see proof that this kind of reporting, of itself, helps ratings.

I'm also concerned about the impact of technology on broadcast journalism. In our area we see examples of major markets structuring their whole operation around the "Live Eye," or "Action News" concept. Airplanes, helicopters, mobile studio vans, new sets . . . at a cost of maybe hundreds of thousands of dollars.

These simply become new toys in the rating battle; rather than hiring better people, buy the latest equipment. It seems we're losing sight of the fact television remains a medium for people who can write, report, and edit. All this equipment doesn't mean much if you don't have people who have the basic skills of journalism. But I don't think the basic skills mean as much today as they did a few years ago, at least not to station management. *Ratings* are in; journalism is out.

I think what's needed is for someone in a major market like

New York or L. A. to dominate with an operation that's based on solid journalism. Maybe that would start a new trend—away from show biz and back to journalism. Local television news has been around now for about thirty years. It's time we matured.

Meantime, down here in Jonesboro, we feel we'd have it made —if we just could get a new sound camera.

Jonesboro, Ark.

Women in Broadcasting

De Jure, De Facto

by Barbara Murray Eddings

> There can be no doubt our nation has a long and unfortunate history
> of sex discrimination. Traditionally, such discrimination was rational-
> ized by an attitude of romantic paternalism which, in practical effect,
> put women not on a pedestal but in a cage. . . .
>
> William J. Brennan, Jr.
> *Frontiero* v. *Richardson* 1971
> U.S. Supreme Court

"BABY" HAS indeed come a long way since 1972, when the DuPont-
Columbia Survey of Broadcast Journalism called station WSNS Chicago to task for having newscaster Linda Fuoco deliver the evening
news from her sponsor's heart-shaped bed. "Baby" may no longer be
in the bedroom, but neither is she in the boardroom, although she has
ceased to be a curiosity in the newsroom.

While women are entering the job market in ever-increasing numbers,* of the 449,000 Americans earning more than $25,000 annually,
only 2.4 percent are women. When *Broadcasting* magazine in June
1977 published top-level salaries of sixteen corporate directors and
officers in communications, only one woman, Katherine Graham of
the Washington Post Company, was on this very exclusive list.

Six years have passed since the FCC, responding in 1971 to the
repeated petitions of the National Organization for Women and the
United Church of Christ, decided to include women in its affirmative
action program for broadcasting. In those six years the biggest proportionate gains for any job category have been recorded by women
newscasters, with television's commitment exceeding that of radio.
Almost 90 percent of the TV stations and 72 percent of the radio
stations reporting to the DuPont Survey in 1977 said they employed
women newscasters. More than half of the TV stations and one-third

---

*U.S. Bureau of Labor statistics report that women, 53 percent of the population, hold
41 percent of the jobs, a doubling over the last twenty-five years.

of the radio stations had women producers. Yet while women are making gains on the air and in the credits, the DuPont-Columbia correspondents, our cross-country network of local monitors, estimate only one of five on-air reporters and producers are women.* Pam Hill, ABC producer, told the survey: "Throughout the news division as a whole, the problem of having women in the highly visible jobs, on camera, but not in the real decision-making, producer and executive level jobs, continues."

In top management the Survey figures mirror this concern. Only 3 percent of the television stations and 2 percent of the radio stations reporting to the survey had women as station or general managers. In 1975 and 1976 5 percent of TV and radio stations had women news directors. In 1977 the figures remained unchanged in TV, although radio stations reported a 4 percent increase over the previous year.

Writing in the Radio Television News Directors' Association's *Communicator* in March 1977, Ted Landphair, manager of news and public affairs at WMAL Radio in Washington, D.C., said:

> Great actresses and newswomen have emerged. Just enough to serve as carrots to the generation of idealistic young women who follow. Not until these women have tested the "real world" do they feel the stick. Someone else, maybe committees of someone elses—usually male—manipulates their professional lives.

Richard Wagner, WCHS-TV news director in Charleston, West Virginia, reported:

> I feel that at present there is still an atmosphere of discrimination against women in the media from men in the media who see them getting in easier than they did, from viewers who think all they are is a pretty face, and from management who look at them only as a statistic that needs to be filled in on an EEO form.

The 1976 annual reports of the commercial and public networks are evidence of the dearth of women on the corporate level as well. ABC reported only one woman on its sixteen-member board, none on its executive committee, and only one in a list of twenty-four officers. On the CBS seventeen-member board, one is a woman; of twenty-two officers, one is a woman; and there are no women officers in the five-member CBS Broadcast Group listing. NBC, with thirteen mem-

*In network TV, *Time* magazine in March 1977 reported women constitute 13 percent of all on-camera news gatherers.

bers on its board of directors, had one woman; of ninety-seven officers, six are women. The Corporation for Public Broadcasting reported four women on its fifteen-member board,* and one of six executive officers is a woman. Of the Public Broadcasting Service board of thirty-three lay directors, six are women. There is one woman on its fifteen-member board of professionals, and neither of two management directors is a woman.

The Radio Television News Directors' Association for 1977 has no women officers, and of the fourteen regional directors none is a woman.†

Further, broadcasting's "big brother," the Federal Communications Commission, has had only three women commissioners since its inception in 1934. The two seats vacated in the fall of 1977 were both filled by men.

Commenting on the asymmetrical state of the industry, Marlene Sanders, former vice-president for ABC News and director of documentaries, told the Survey:

> I am the first woman in any network to be a VP in news, so while I'm doing all right, lots of others aren't. . . . The net looks for experienced people in the first place and they have to get that experience out of New York, or at local stations. Women are hired in few numbers in those jobs and so there are too few qualified for middle management and above.

Summer of 1977 found the industry in a defensive posture with the publication of the United States Civil Rights Commission report "Window Dressing on the Set," which charged that women and members of minority groups were almost totally excluded from decision-making positions in TV and that their actual employment status was misrepresented by the local stations. The news segment of the study covering commercial and public TV stations in the top forty markets during 1974–75 found that white males made 88.6 percent of the monitored appearances of TV correspondents during that period and that most important stories were reported by men.

The first network to issue a denial was NBC, which charged that

*Since its inception in 1968, of the thirty-six board members, eight have been women. In October 1977 President Carter appointed two women, Sharon Percy Rockefeller and Gillian Sorensen, to succeed in seats vacated on the CPB board by two men, Thomas W. Moore and Robert Benjamin.

†At the 1977 RTNDA convention in San Francisco women members, piqued at being ignored by their male counterparts (no women on convention dais and no newswomen on panels), called a special study group to ensure representation at the 1978 convention.

"some of the commission's broad-brush charges appear to be based on out-of-date data and are not in accord with the facts, at least as they might concern NBC."* Yet the network's news personnel listing, dated 1976 and updated in August 1977 for the Survey, lists only two women out of sixty-two managerial positions.

A former NBC woman producer of documentaries told the Survey: "There is some visible progress in the lower ranks, minimal in the middle ranks, significant progress in on-the-air reporters, and none in management." In the last year, she said, NBC has lost every senior newswoman—Barbara Walters, Lucy Jarvis, Christy Basham, and Joan Konner.

Executives at ABC responded to the Civil Rights Commission report by expressing confidence in their own organizational policies and claimed their practices "are in full compliance with applicable federal laws and regulations." Midge Kovacs, former ABC senior promotion writer, commented to the Survey: "Each department is run by a man and each department has a few women with dead-ended positions. . . . The ABC experience has made me a corporate drop-out permanently."

Bill Leonard, CBS vice-president for Washington, D.C., said that equality of opportunity is "the very linchpin of CBS policy" and that 46 percent of CBS employees are women. Leonard did not break down these figures according to importance of positions.† Ellen Erhlich, director of information services at CBS, told the Survey:

> As I go around the country, I see many more women in anchor positions and as reporters of hard news. I think the main area where we have not done as well is in top and middle management where the decisions are being made. We need more Marlene Sanderses.

Broadcasters have, nevertheless, been pointing with pride to their top-level women. Pauline Frederick, prize-winning veteran broad-

---

*Any change in the NBC track record, far from expressing independent action on the part of the net, was the result of a February 1977 $2 million out-of-court settlement of a sex-bias suit brought by women employees in December 1975. Under this agreement NBC was required to make "good faith efforts" to promote women to a wide range of professional, managerial and official positions. Spelled out, the settlement called for a specific goal to include 15 percent of the top NBC positions below the rank of vice-president as well as specific goals for hiring women to fill vacancies in technical jobs and news positions during the next five years.

†On November 8, 1977, Richard S. Salant, CBS News president, went on record to advocate preferential promotional treatment of blacks and women newscasters at his net "until we get a better balance," in a speech made to the North Carolina Associated Press Broadcasters Association annual meeting.

caster,* and Barbara Walters moderated two of the three presidential debates in the fall of 1976. Walters's appointment to an ABC anchor position caused a media uproar in April 1976. Less heralded, but tradition-breaking, was Lynn Scherr's appointment in the summer of 1976 as the first woman to serve as an anchor of a regularly scheduled prime time TV network news series.†

As early as 1974 ABC broke tradition by naming Ann Compton to be the first woman full-time network White House correspondent. Two years later NBC named Marilyn Berger as its White House correspondent.‡ Joining Compton and Berger and moving into areas once considered all-male domains were Cassie Mackin (in 1972 she became the first woman network TV floor reporter at a national political convention), Connie Chung, and Enid Roth (who directed NBC's TV floor coverage during the convention), all prominent figures at the 1976 political conventions. In September 1977 CBS promoted newswoman Lesley Stahl to a Washington co-anchor spot on its "Morning News," replacing Bruce Morton. And in October 1977 Charlayne Hunter-Gault, metropolitan reporter for the *New York Times,* joined the MacNeil/Lehrer Report.

In management Marion Stephenson had become the first woman vice-president and general manager in radio history with her appointment at NBC in May 1975. ABC promoted Marlene Sanders in January 1976 to be the first woman network vice-president for TV news. In September 1976 Susan Harmon was elected chairperson of the National Public Radio board of directors. In January 1977 Ann Berk became the first woman station manager for a network-owned station with her promotion at NBC's flagship station, WNBC-TV New York. In June 1977 Jo Moring became the director of news for NBC Radio.

Yet, despite this, Anita Miller, presiding over the California Commission on the Status of Women, charged the broadcast industry with tokenism: "We've got to have more than Barbara Walters. . . . We do not feel that when a single woman is promoted to co-anchor person of a news program that it qualifies as an overall effort to really address the problem." Walters herself told the Survey:

*Frederick, who for over twenty years served as U.N. correspondent, won a DuPont Award in 1953.
†Walters did not take over her spot until October 1976; Scherr began her public broadcasting job the summer before.
‡Connie Chung had been second-string White House correspondent for CBS until she became news anchor for KNXT-TV in Los Angeles, a CBS-owned and -operated station.

I don't see the day we'll have a woman anchor alone. If Harry Reasoner were to leave, there would be no question about me doing it alone. They would bring in a man. At NBC they made the decision to take off Jim Hart, but they made Tom Brokaw co-host. But [after I left] they made Tom Brokaw the host and put the woman [Jane Pauley] in a subsidiary position. . . . They will not accept a woman as the head of the program. I can't imagine two females doing the news, as Chancellor and Brinkley. Of course they allow a woman alone on Sundays, but that's throwaway time.*

Lynn Scherr in a *Time* magazine interview in March 1977 reinforced Walters's view. "Think of the possibility of two women anchors on a network news broadcast," she said, "and you'll understand we're still in the Ice Age."†

The small percentage of women who achieve management status in the industry rarely attain parity with men in authority or pay. One young woman, a multiple award winner in the nation's top radio market who asked to remain anonymous, was promoted to management when her male predecessor resigned. She kept her street reporting assignment along with her new responsibilities and was given a $20 a week raise for doing both jobs. (The station saved over $18,000 a year on the deal.) "I would have advanced farther economically," she said, "had I been a man. Because I am young and female my compensation for being the head of a department is abysmally low. A lot of blood is squeezed out of the female turnips at this station." The summer of 1977 was a busy one for a reporter-producer, she said, referring to the metropolitan area blackout and the Son of Sam murders. She was told, nevertheless, that she would be paid for an eight-hour day only. (Her male predecessor had been paid overtime.) She accepts the dual responsibilities and long hours without fair compensation as "a fact of life for most women who want to succeed in a man's world."

Summing up the true status of women in the industry, Patricia Reed Scott, a former government press officer and now producer of the 1977 Emmy Award-winning series "Getting On," told the Survey:

I was always aware that, excepting on-air reporters, hardly any women were visible in news assignment, line production, or any

*Cassie Mackin was an anchor person on NBC Sunday Night News until she moved to ABC. Jessica Savitch, former reporter and co-anchor of KYW-TV Philadelphia, is now in the "throwaway time" at NBC.
†Scherr has also gone to greener pastures at ABC.

key policy positions. I still see too many women who work in broadcasting getting no further than production assistant, researcher, assistant-to, and producer of no-budget, ghetto-time public affairs.

Perhaps one of the most scathing criticisms of the industry and the FCC came from the United Church of Christ in January 1977 in its annual report, "Television Stations Employment Practices, 1976: The Status of Minorities and Women." Although the UCC found a slight improvement for women in TV broadcasting, it remained skeptical. Dr. Ralph Jennings, associate director of the UCC's Office of Communications, in a report written with Allan T. Walters of Temple University, said he doubted his own job analysis. While overall employment of women in TV had risen since 1971, the year of the first study,* Jennings was concerned about the Federal Communications Commission reporting form (Form 395), which gave vague job titles subject to free interpretation, as well as manipulation by the licensees. Jennings said the job classifications "do not fit the positions that exist in stations" and, as a result, "can easily be distorted." He claimed the FCC has "ignored the need for tightening up its categories and has watered down its rules." The report charged the industry with a continuing policy since 1971 of making "paper promotions" to satisfy FCC equal employment opportunity requirements. Since 1971, according to the report, stations created 6,122 upper-level jobs, while 3,024 lower-level (clerical and service) posts have disappeared. Between 1975 and 1976 alone, upper-four jobs increased by 705 and lower-five jobs declined by 291 until today there are more than three upper-level employees in TV for every support member.

This increase in the number of higher-paying positions was also reported in the third annual FCC report released in the spring of 1977. According to the FCC, of 34,324 women employed full-time in 1976, 15,067 (or 44 percent) held upper-four-category positions (or 17.7 percent of these positions), an increase of 9.1 percent over 1975.

"It seems improbable," said Jennings, "that this greatly increased corps of management personnel can function with reduced clerical support." Jennings's boss, Dr. Everett C. Parker, director of the UCC, added that, while there are many honest broadcasters striving to raise

---

*The report showed an increase from 19 percent in 1971 to 42 percent in 1976 for women in the upper four job categories (officials and managers, professionals, technicians, sales workers) while women in clerical posts dropped 22 percent in this same period, from 77 percent to 55 percent of full-time women employees. (Clerical posts are in the lower five job categories, which also includes craftsmen, operatives, laborers, and service workers.)

the status of women and minorities, "the fact that 78 percent of all jobs are now reported to be in the upper level, higher-paying decision-making categories is proof that others are making paper promotions, taking advantage of FCC indifference to make industry employment practices look better than they are."

The murkiness of Form 395 made such deception easy.*

Reflecting this view, Professor John Abel and Judith Saxton of the University of Michigan, as a result of their own study of Form 395, filed a petition for rule making at the FCC with a proposal for standardized industry-related employment categories. They contended, "Women do not hold executive level positions in the broadcasting industry. They are excluded from the decision-making process and, therefore, have no real influence on station policy."

In their brief to the FCC, Abel and Saxton said that the broadcast industry is a powerful image creator and, thus, an important socializing force:

> It can be assumed that whoever occupies the executive level position at television stations across the country wields great power in influencing this socialization process. If a majority of these positions are held by only one segment of society, the ideas presented on television will reflect only the ideas of that one segment. If women are excluded from these positions, the picture being presented will be male oriented.

Abel and Saxton were reiterating the concerns of women and minority advocates and broadcast reformers. Any trend showing gains for women in broadcasting became suspect as early as 1970 when the FCC adopted Form 395. A holdover required by the Equal Employment Opportunity Commission of all federal contractors, the FCC admitted in its report and order requiring the annual report, "The appropriate job categories present a difficult problem . . . are generalized and not particularly suited to the broadcast industry."

Nevertheless, the commission adopted the form, justifying its use on the grounds that "it would allow inter-industry comparisons and would simplify the reporting for all stations."

At an NBC-owned and -operated station, a producer charged:

*The U.S. Civil Rights Commission study also condemns Form 395: "The FCC Form 395 allows licensees to imply erroneously that women and minorities are moving into decision-making positions when their job titles and salaries suggest that they perform primarily clerical and routine administrative tasks." In April 1977 the House of Representatives Subcommittee on Communications called for a review of Form 395 in its Report of Findings and Recommendations of the Enforcement of Equal Opportunity and Antidiscrimination Laws in Public Broadcasting.

The 395 Form that each station must file with the FCC giving EEO information lists many more women in the "Officials and Managers" category than can be found actually operating on that level. Many "Supervisors" and "Administrators" who are women are included in that category, no doubt.

A news reporter in Houston said:

> . . . As I understand it, one woman now categorized as office manager was before the EEO reports just a secretary, and the traffic director was also considered simply a clerk. We also have one woman who doubles as a receptionist-secretary and a reporter. I would not be surprised to see her listed under "professional" rather than "clerical."

A reporter in Oklahoma City said:

> Being a producer (at this station), while it certainly is good for overall experience, is close to being a secretary. The title producer sounds big, but it involves no decisions regarding news format. . . . The producer more or less retypes scripts . . . types up rundowns, picks up slides for news stories.

A reporter in St. Louis charged: "I was given a phony title when hired, Director of Community Involvement Programs. . . . I was directing no one, not even myself."

Yet, under chairman Richard Wiley, the FCC refused to change its monitoring form. Further, the commission announced in mid-1976 a rule change which would eliminate some 6,000 stations from the monitoring process despite the April 1977 House Subcommittee on Communications recommendations to the contrary. The agency proposed that only those stations with more than ten employees be required to file an EEO report. It also exempted from filing a job title analysis (vital because Form 395 was not descriptive of the industry's jobs) those stations with less than fifty full-time employees. This new ruling would have exempted 88 percent of the noncommercial TV and 100 percent of the noncommercial radio stations. Richard Wiley defended the ruling as still covering 85 percent of broadcast employees, or 92,000 jobs, and said it would provide for more realistic monitoring by reducing paperwork. Wiley also promised that the commission would utilize the time, energy, and resources saved in doing more on-site investigations. Jennings responded by calling the FCC "the handmaiden of the industry it regulates," and charged that, by exempting some two-thirds of the industry from filing, the FCC would be closing job entry and training doors for women and minorities.

However, in August 1977, in response to citizen groups,* the U.S. Court of Appeals for the Second Circuit, New York, unanimously struck down the new rules as "arbitrary and capricious" and ordered the commission to return to its former practice. The appeals court ruling represented the first major victory for citizen groups since 1971, when the FCC adopted rules prohibiting broadcasters from discriminating in employment because of sex.†

To date no license has been revoked on sex discrimination grounds. Moreover, by April 1977 only five hearings on EEO grounds had been held by the FCC.‡ This contradicts a promise made by Commissioner Wiley in August 1975 in an address to the Community Film Workshop Council in New York: "Where it appears that the broadcaster has followed discriminatory employment practices, I can assure you that the commission will not hesitate to order a hearing to resolve any substantial and material questions of fact."

Despite such protestations, a study by Citizens Communication Center (a public interest law firm in Washington, D.C.) showed substantial gaps in FCC enforcement of its EEO policies and charged that the FCC standards fall short of those applied by the courts in judging discrimination in employment. The Citizens Communication Center condemned the commission for allowing a licensee to upgrade its employment following a license challenge and, thus, avoid a renewal hearing.§ This particular practice was a

---

*UCC, National Urban League, National Association for the Advancement of Colored People, Communications Commission of the National Council of Churches of Christ, and UNDA-USA (the national Catholic communications association).

†In 1972 the Office of Communication of UCC began its own annual analysis of all Form 395s as the result not only of the FCC's failure to include the category for gender reporting on its standard renewal application forms, but also its failure to implement an effective compliance program once this omission was corrected. The forms finally returned by the stations were actually filed away by the FCC without action because, they said, they lacked the personnel and funds for analysis.

‡In April 1977, however, the U.S. Court of Appeals for the District of Columbia reversed the FCC license renewals of three broadcast stations without an FCC hearing; this decision would indicate that from now on the FCC will be required to stage more hearings on EEO issues.

§This practice was notable in the case of WRC-TV Washington, D.C., in May 1972 when, over the opposition of NOW and the CCC, the FCC accepted updated employment statistics. Four years later, in February 1976, the FCC rejected EEOC's finding of discrimination and ruled WRC-TV's employment practices satisfied the public interest standards. Benjamin Hooks, then FCC EEO commissioner, while voting with the commission for renewal of the WRC-TV license, nevertheless questioned the process which denied a hearing and said, "The commission must do more than summarily dismiss a petition to deny." In April 1977 the

major sore point in the U.S. Civil Rights Commission report, which read that the FCC

> is not interested in eliminating discrimination by its licensees. Instead, it is interested only in learning that licensees intend to make "good faith effort" to provide equal employment opportunity.

The commercial broadcast industry was not the only recalcitrant employer. The primary EEO battleground this year was waged in public broadcasting.

In April 1977 the Congress threatened to withhold federal funds unless public broadcasters came up with some hard facts, figures, and recommendations to implement findings of the 1975 Report of the Task Force on Women in Public Broadcasting.* The report charged "pervasive under-representation of women in employment," citing the fact that white males held 97 percent and 98 percent of the two top management positions in public TV stations (general manager and station manager).†

Furthermore, data submitted by the Corporation for Public Broadcasting in April 1977 to the Senate Appropriations Committee's Subcommittee on Labor, Health, Education and Welfare‡ showed an actual decline of 1 percent in the proportion of women in the upper management levels in public television between January 1, 1976, and January 1, 1977.

Middle-management women in public broadcasting complained to the Survey of job titles with no authority or responsibility, and a reluctance on the part of management to promote qualified women. Two of the women who have since left public broadcasting said:

> All decision-making positions are filled by men. The only exception is executive producer and production teams for women's programs where the teams report to two male program execu-

---

U.S. Court of Appeals affirmed the FCC's renewal of the license and said the FCC may consider post-license term employment data in determining whether or not a broadcaster has complied with the EEOC's standards.

*The task force was established in November 1974 with the blessings of the CPB; the report was published and unanimously accepted by the CPB board in 1975.

†The UCC annual report in January 1977, analyzing FCC Form 395 employment figures, found that 80 percent of upper-four-category jobs in public television (officials and managers, professionals, and technicians) are held by men at the 143 stations monitored.

‡An EEO update required quarterly by a Senate report attached to public broadcasting's 1977 appropriations bill passed in 1976.

tives. Virtually all assignments relating to the station's image are male.

And: "Management in public TV is white and male almost exclusively. . . . Departments often reject qualified women candidates who are brought to their attention."

The DuPont correspondent in Memphis said: "Public TV here is so short on women in key positions, they list the station manager's secretary on the masthead of the monthly program guide to add another female name."

Lionel Van Deerlin (D-Cal.), chairman of the House Subcommittee on Communications, in the Oversight Report on EEO Compliance condemned the Public Broadcasting Service's lack of improvement as "bordering on negligence" and said "CPB's continuing reluctance to impose tougher restrictions on its community service grants appears to stem as much from a fear of political reprisal by the stations as from a commitment to preserve its insulation from government interference."

His statement reiterated earlier congressional threats. Representative Louis Stokes (D-Ohio), member of the Labor/HEW Appropriations Committee, had warned eight months earlier that, unless action is taken, "Congress will be in the untenable position of unconstitutionally providing financial assistance to aid prohibited discriminatory conduct." And, in February 1977, when Henry Loomis, president of the Corporation for Public Broadcasting, applied to Congress for an increase in funds for 1980, Senator Edward Brooke (R., Mass.) insisted that CPB show improvement in its female and minority record before he could comfortably approve new-appropriations, and said he hoped employment problems could be solved without "tacking an amendment on the appropriations bill."

The major roadblock clearly centered around enforcement.

At the House Subcommittee on Communications hearings in August 1976, Loomis agreed that, while CPB is subject to Title VI and VII of the Civil Rights Act of 1964 and Title IX of the Education Amendments of 1972, once federal funds leave the CPB they are no longer considered to be federal funds in order to insulate receiving stations from the federal government influence on programming. Further, according to Loomis, compliance can be enforced only when a court or competent government agency, not the CPB, determines a station is in violation. This enforcement circle includes a catchall of federal agencies, each with its own regulations and authority: Justice

Department, FCC, Department of Health, Education and Welfare, and the Equal Employment Opportunity Commission.*

Two months before these hearings the FCC, despite its plenary enforcement authority, had announced the changing of its monitoring rules over the objection of the public broadcasters, and also refused to consider their recommendation that Form 395 be made more relevant to broadcasting. Both actions on the part of the FCC would clearly hamstring any good intentions the public broadcasters might have had. Further, at the August hearings, FCC Chairman Wiley actually chided the public broadcasters for their EEO record and charged them with having a higher duty in this regard than do commercial broadcasters, since they operate partially on federal funds.

EEO enforcement in public broadcasting was a "Catch 22" situation, prompting the Citizens Communication Center to ask, "Where does the buck stop?" Every agency was caught in the enforcement bureaucracy, but each clung to its own territorial confines.

Thus, in April 1977, when the House subcommittee's report showed that Congress, too, was confused on enforcement, an interagency task force to include *all* the agencies was established to look into the problem. Chairman Van Deerlin's committee report stated:

> [Admitting that] existing antidiscrimination laws appear to apply to stations, there are significant gaps in enforcement authority to render their application more apparent than real. . . . as a result of gaps in the law, inadequate personnel, and an overall lack of commitment, the federal agencies which share responsibility are doing a poor job of enforcement. There is little or no coordination of effort on the federal level.†

Particularly called to task was the FCC: "Unfortunately, the record of the FCC on EEO matters has been singularly disappointing. . . . The commission has shown an obvious reluctance to assert itself in handling EEO complaints."

The report recommended to the FCC short-term license renewals

*Title VI, administered by HEW, prohibits discrimination in a federally assisted program; Title VII, administered by the EEOC and the Justice Department, prohibits discrimination in all industries affecting interstate commerce; Title IX, administered by HEW, prohibits discrimination in education programs or activities receiving federal financial assistance; the FCC, due to the confining of EEOC jurisdiction to those employers with fifteen employees or over, is the only federal agency with plenary authority.

†House Subcommittee on Communications of the Committee on Interstate and Foreign Commerce, "Report of Findings and Recommendations of the Enforcement of Equal Opportunity and Antidiscrimination Laws in Public Broadcasting," April 1977.

for those stations not in compliance with EEO, a revision of the much criticized Form 395, an increase in the FCC's EEO personnel (presently there are just six people monitoring the employment records of 9,224 TV and radio stations), and the development of a formal working arrangement with the EEOC to facilitate the exchange of information.

Enforcement proceedings were delayed for a few more months while still another committee looked into the matter. But the public broadcasters got their money and no amendment was attached to their appropriation.

In October 1977 President Jimmy Carter proposed a $1 billion package to aid the public broadcasters, this time with presidential strings attached. "The Corporation, its grantees, subgrantees, contractors, and subcontractors shall be subject to the requirements of Title VI of the Civil Rights Act of 1964 and Title IX of the Education Amendments of 1972."* Barry Jagoda, assistant to President Carter for media and public affairs, told the Survey:

> The bill makes it clear for the first time that the employment discrimination laws apply to stations and other producers that receive federal funds. . . . CPB will be under intense congressional scrutiny in this area.

Frank Lloyd, White House Office of Telecommunications Policy, and one of the drafters of the bill, said:

> It now spells out that any recipients of funds are now subject to Titles VI and IX. This has never been clear before. It is the first time any President has addressed the issue as it applies to women in public broadcasting.

While it is true that no president has addressed this particular issue with regard to women before, public broadcasting *has* been under intense congressional scrutiny in this area for over four years. Both the Justice Department and the Congress have held that public broadcasting is subject to Titles VI and IX.

Neither the House nor the Senate was pleased with the entire bill. Carolyn Sachs, staff assistant to Van Deerlin, said:

> Someone is going to have to bite the bullet. We were hoping to get the White House view [on the enforcement agency]. They

*Public Broadcasting Financing Act of 1978.

did not make the hard decisions. It's a political involvement, trying to please too many people. The bill is too weak. By applying the provisions of Titles VI and IX to the CPB grants, the bill really does nothing more than confirm the findings of the subcommittee and sheds no additional light as to where EEO responsibility for enforcement lies.

As for the FCC being the agency of enforcement:

> Their record is not good and there must be some attention paid to clarifying their EEO response before we simply reaffirm their responsibility to public broadcasting EEO. The bottom line is there will be no further authorization until this is cleared up.

The concern now is over a possible challenge to enforcement recommendations and even to the president's bill as it concerns them.* Lawyers differ on the interpretation of Titles VI and IX as they apply to public broadcasting. Originally the purpose of insulating public stations from government interference was to protect their rights on programming. Now it has become a political issue with the Congress, advocacy groups, and the White House on one side and the public broadcasting stations, fearful of infringement of their "First Amendment" rights, on the other.

There are other important decisions to be made within the next year which may affect equal employment opportunity.

Two bills now before the Congress would give reimbursement to citizen groups to provide financial assistance for participation in agency proceedings.† FCC Commissioner Joseph Fogarty endorses financing (as did former commissioner Benjamin Hooks). Former FCC chief Wiley maintained that the leadership in public financing must come from the Congress and he did not, therefore, support any FCC rule making in favor of it.

The broadcasting industry is opposed to such financing. *Broadcasting* magazine, in an editorial in August 1977, charged that such funding "would only enlarge the body of lawyers now mostly funded by foundations and specializing in attacking regulated businesses. . . . Public interest lawyers would begin recruiting litigants and magnifying or inventing grievances."

This charge came on the heels of the Senate Government Affairs

---

*In mid-October Frank Lloyd told Congress that the administration plans to submit an amendment in January 1978 providing for an EEO enforcement mechanism.
†The Kennedy-Mathias bill (S. 270) and H.R. 3361, introduced by Rep. Peter Rodino (D-N.J.)

Committee report made earlier in the month which endorsed financing on the grounds that the public interest groups have a very small voice in agency proceedings while the regulated industries dominate. The report also said that public interest groups are hampered in proceedings because of lack of money. The report particularly singled out the poor record of the FCC in citizen participation proceedings.

In October 1977 FCC Commissioner Margita White said she expects a notice of proposed rule making soon calling for revision of the much maligned Form 395. Support by fellow commissioner Fogarty, the new chairman Charles Ferris, and the recently appointed commissioner Tyrone Brown is expected.

The public broadcasters announced in October 1977 a $190,000 commitment to help improve their job picture. People and Careers in Telecommunications is a nationwide job-matching system for women and minorities. Administered by the National Association of Educational Broadcasters, PACT will operate a job bank and placement service. Joseph Schubert, acting director of PACT, said, "We are ready to become the headhunters for the industry."

Thus, proposed legislation for financing indigent advocacy groups; new faces at the FCC; the return to the old FCC monitoring rules and the more than likely revision of Form 395; the congressional muscle that has brought some resolutions from the public broadcasters; the study of public broadcasting by the Carnegie Commission; the rewrite of the 1934 Communications Act; and the new Carter bill for public broadcasting, with the promise of an amendment for enforcement, could all bode well for women.

Nevertheless, present signs—such as consideration by the FCC of long-term license renewals for the industry as a whole and the reluctance of the FCC to hold hearings on challenged licenses—could offset any future gains for women in broadcasting. An immediate step by the Congress in the form of a realistic financial appropriation to the understaffed FCC EEO unit, along with legislation granting authority to the commission to levy fines on those stations not in compliance (monies to be used for training grants for women and minorities) would do much to further the cause.

Women are emerging from journalism schools in ever-increasing numbers. This year the graduate division of the Department of Journalism and Mass Communications at New York University enrolled forty-one men and eighty-three women. Professor David Rubin, chairman of the department, commenting on the preponderance of women, said, "We have no quotas. It is simply a matter of accepting the best people, and two-thirds of the best people in this class happen to be women."

The enrollment of women at the Columbia Graduate School of Journalism rose from twenty-seven in a class of sixty-three in 1967 to seventy-nine in a class of 147 in 1977. Elie Abel, dean of the school, said, "The significant change is that women are now going after the management jobs, on the news desks, as editors, and in broadcasting as producers."

Carolyn Wean, news director at KDKA-TV in Pittsburgh, told the Survey:

> The long-range test of how the changing role of women in society will affect the role of women in broadcasting is yet to be seen. The clues to any results will only be seen in the next five to ten years when and if the pool of women now in broadcasting share a larger portion of the middle and top level management positions.

In the years to come it would be a sad commentary if women were to reiterate Professor Kenneth B. Clark's warning to the Kerner Commission on Civil Disorders in 1967: "It is . . . a kind of Alice in Wonderland . . . with the same moving picture shown over and over again . . . and the same inaction."

Cable Television

A New Chance or More of the Same?

by Ann Rauma

"IT IS TIME," FCC chairman Richard Wiley told the National Cable Television Association in April 1977, "to recall that our regulatory purpose has never been—and never should be—to protect broadcast revenues, as such, but only to guard against a possible loss of service to the community."

He chose his words carefully to please the cable industry, long aggrieved over the preferential treatment accorded over-the-air broadcasters. He continued:

> It is time to determine whether the potential danger of widespread audience diversion, or "fragmentation," through cable's offerings of nonlocal signals is correct in theory and demonstrable in fact. It is time to utilize the considerable data and experience that have been accumulating over the past five or six years for a basic evaluation of the relationship between television station audiences and television station revenue. . . .
>
> Recalling that the twin goals of our cable regulatory program include not only the maintenance of local over-the-air broadcast service, but also the promotion of diversity and new video and nonvideo service through cable's multiple channel capacity, we need to address ourselves intently to the factors—regulatory and nonregulatory in nature—which are now inhibiting or may later restrain the expansion of broadband capacity. . . .

Wiley received only perfunctory applause, and *Variety* observed: "Two or three years ago, that same speech would have been greeted with astonishment and thunderous ovation. Now with . . . several seasons of success under their belt, cable operators are wondering where Wiley was when they most needed him—a view they made known by their silent reception of his speech."

They had most recently needed him in the Home Box Office battle between cable and broadcast interests. The FCC sided with the National Association of Broadcasters, arguing that its restrictions on the movies and sports that could be available to pay cable were necessary. Without these restrictions, it said, audience fragmentation would hurt broadcasters and ultimately public service. But in March 1977, the Washington, D.C., Court of Appeals overturned the FCC's pay cable restrictions. The cable industry had won despite FCC opposition.

The cable industry would have appreciated more support from the FCC at any time in its twenty-seven-year history. Seeking to protect commercial broadcasting, the FCC extensively regulated the cable industry—from the number of signals it could import into a market, to which programs it could play, to what rates it could charge.

In June 1977, Anthony Oettinger, chairman of the Community Antenna Television Commission of Massachusetts, testified before the Senate Communications Subcommittee hearings on cable that the cable industry was "straining at the straightjacket." He said that the FCC had "mistakenly" identified cable "solely with retransmission services ancillary to broadcasting. All this was done in so fanciful a climate that cable had the misfortune of becoming regulated even before it was born."

Irving B. Kahn, communications consultant and former head of Teleprompter, bluntly echoed many in the cable industry when he addressed the Federal Communications Bar Association. He denounced the FCC as "the single most effective negative force in the communications industry," and communications attorneys as its "handmaidens" in protecting the status quo.

Wiley's speech, however coolly received, was one of several indications that the climate for cable, both in the market place and in government, had dramatically improved. The cable industry was increasingly optimistic about its future when it tallied its earnings, the HBO victory, and a series of pro-cable FCC actions.

The industry was growing at an average rate of 12 percent a year. As of September 1, 1976, there were 3,715 cable systems in the United States, serving 12.5 million subscribers—about 17 percent of all 72 million U.S. television homes. The previous year, 3,366 systems served about 9.8 million subscribers. Revenues for the twelve-month period ending October 1976 exceeded $895 million, an increase of almost 50 percent in two years.

Teleprompter, the country's largest cable operation, reported that net profits for the first quarter of 1977 exceeded its total profits for all of 1976. Net income was $1.2 million for the quarter, a 151 percent increase over its 1976 total income of $445,000. Home Box Office, controlling 80 percent of the pay cable industry, announced in its third-quarter report for 1977 that it was making its first profit in nearly five years of operation.

As the climate for the cable industry improved in the mid-seventies, it was hoped that cable would at last fulfill its long-time promise of increased diversity and its potential for special-interest, nonentertainment programming. Although cable and diverse programming had long been uttered in the same breath, there was reason to doubt that increased prosperity would in fact result in more and different kinds of news and public affairs programming. Bold experiments in news and nonentertainment programming remained the exception. Not required by the FCC to provide public interest programming, many systems abandoned news shows and discouraged public access programming, a relatively inexpensive means by which volunteers from the community could cover neighborhood issues and events.

In 1969 the FCC had ruled that every system with more than 3,500 subscribers was required to originate local programming. It abandoned those rules in 1974, requiring only that each system provide four access channels—for educational, governmental, public, and leased access.

The National Cable Television Association reported that 22 percent fewer systems originated local programming in 1975 than in 1974—dropping from 589 of 3,158 systems in 1974 to 484 of 3,366 systems in 1975. The report cautioned that "there is not enough evidence to link the drop in local origination to the elimination of the mandatory requirement," but it observed that the cutback occurred during an inflationary period, and that "local origination—never a money maker—was the first to feel the effects of this retrenchment."

In April 1976 the FCC eased its requirements still further. Instead of four access channels, a system with over 3,500 subscribers need have only one shared access channel—and then only if the station had the channel capacity.

Less channel space did not disturb the independent programmers working to boost community affairs programming. David Hoke, advocacy committee chairman for the National Federation of Local Cable Programmers, called it "acceptable. . . . There is no point in having four blank channels," he said. "If we have all four on one channel, great. Let the operator make some money. If the cable system isn't viable, there is no place to put our programs. No cable—no us."

Though not required to provide news and public affairs, a few cable systems have combined technical skill with social concern to provide in-depth news coverage to special interest audiences. In October 1977

Showtime, the pay cable subsidiary of Viacom, announced that it would begin programming independently produced documentaries "on a fairly regular basis."

Possibly the most spectacular project was launched in December 1977 in Columbus, Ohio, by Warner Cable Corporation. Parceled out among the thirty channels of programming—ten pay channels and twenty "free" channels—was "Columbus Alive," ten to twelve hours a day of locally produced programming concentrating on community events and "life style" features that related to Columbus. The format was modeled after NBC's "Today" show. The brainchild of Michael Dann, former vice-president of CBS programming, it included on-the-street and studio interviews and coverage of local events, with at least two minicam units continually on the street.

"Columbus Alive" distinguished itself from broadcast television by setting a precedent in the amount of time devoted to local programming, and by featuring the technical capacity for the home audience to participate in the program. Viewers, pressing buttons on their consoles, were able to respond to guests on the program, vote yea or nay on issues, and even suggest subjects they would like to hear discussed. The *Wall Street Journal* quoted an "industry observer" who said she was "looking forward to the time when a reporter will be interviewing a controversial local official on the air, and then will be able to turn to viewers and ask, 'Well, do you believe him?' "

Gustave M. Hauser, chairman and chief executive officer of Warner Cable Corporation, said before the experiment started: "We are entering the era of participatory, as opposed to passive, television. This is a serious effort that will tell us a great deal about whether cable television can do more than it does today. It will teach us whether there's a market and how people will use two-way television."

A more limited experiment in two-way cable television had already achieved tremendous success in Reading, Pennsylvania. That project was started in 1975 by the New York-based Alternate Media Center, with a grant from the National Science Foundation to explore new ways of delivering social services. By 1977 it was independent of the center, with over eighty-five hours a week of locally produced programming. Cable penetration was relatively high in Reading, at 60 percent. Considering that the community already received Philadelphia stations without cable, some attributed the high penetration to the menu of local programming.

Unlike the Columbus experiment, much of the Reading fare was produced by the residents themselves—from concept, to production, to participation in two-way programming.

Until the project was off the ground, Red Burns, co-founder and director of the center, worked exclusively with senior citizens to initiate programming. She described the Reading system:

> The basic thrust . . . was to create a technological system that would allow people access to it, and more importantly, where they would decide what they wanted to see—as opposed to a group of programming people sitting around saying, "Old people are going to like this and we're going to do the program." And that's essentially the difference between the broadcast approach and the access approach.
>
> How do you find out what people want? With endless questionnaires and surveys. But if you ask what people want, they are really loath to tell you. They're likely to tell you they don't like what they see, but they're not likely to give some notion about what they would like to see. What we really did in Reading was to provide a framework, rather than programming.

Two-way "communications centers" were set up in the lobby of a senior citizens' high-rise apartment, in the recreational room of a garden apartment complex, and in a senior citizens' social center. Remote origination sites rotated from city hall, to the Social Security office, to the county courthouse, to the high schools.

The senior citizens initiated such programs as "The Generation Gap," an ongoing dialogue between the elderly and high school students, and "Inside City Hall," where the elderly asked questions of the mayor and city council members.

"The questions are not the studied questions of the press," said Burns. "They are the questions of the people who live in the community and require services." She described how one woman had been assigned to report on action at city council meetings from a senior citizen's perspective. The mayor complained to Burns that the woman was confusing the issues rather than explaining them. But Burns maintained that as long as the mayor had time to clarify and correct issues immediately afterward, the people were being informed.

Burns quoted one of the senior citizens:

> I don't know what this television is doing, but it must be stimulating my brain or something, because now I'm reading the newspaper. Now I really understand much better what's going on in Reading, because if I have to go to these meetings, I have to know what I'm talking about.

According to Burns, the programs have given the elderly a sense of purpose and community, as well as access to public services.

The largest community access system in the country is Manhattan Cable, with 120 hours of programming a week. In April 1974, its access budget was $80,000 and its staff was two full-time employees and one part-time assistant. By spring 1976, it had grown to a budget of $300,000 in operating expenses, $177,000 in capital investment, and a staff of twelve full-time and two part-time employees, plus thirty-five "interns" recruited from colleges.

Squeezed between cable call-in quiz shows and sex therapy rap sessions were community news and public affairs programs. The weekly "Chinese Cable Television Program," produced by about thirty volunteers, reported news of Chinatown in Cantonese and featured special reports on health, housing, and employment. The "Irish Freedom Show" covered Irish events and personalities, and "Harlem, Here It Is" devoted itself to the concerns of Manhattan's black community. On "Manhattan-at-Large," councilmen-at-large Henry Stern and Robert Wagner, Jr., held weekly office hours on the screen. Assemblymen Mark Alan Siegel and Pete Granis reported on state assembly activities of interest to East Siders on "East Side Report." "Global Issues and New Dimensions" featured interviews exploring programs at the United Nations.

The public access channel in York, Pennsylvania, is much smaller than those of Columbus, Reading, or Manhattan, with twenty hours of local programming, but it has experimented with special-interest documentaries and found that they generated dialogue between community parties and solved problems. David Hoke, access coordinator for the York system, cited an emotional confrontation between teenagers who were dissatisfied with the city's recreational facilities and the officials of their housing project. The youths were unable to negotiate with either the police or the housing authority. A neutral party filmed a conversation with the teenagers, which clarified their complaints. The film was taken to the police. Another film was made of police response, proposing concessions. Both of the tapes were taken to the housing authorities, who agreed to some of the concessions and explained why they could not make others. The entire hour-and-a-half program was aired on cable.

"A local commercial broadcaster can't afford to cater to a small group," Hoke said. "At most, they'd spend two to three minutes on it—and that would sensationalize it rather than solve the problem."

Exciting as the experiments in Columbus, Reading, Manhattan, and York are, they remain exceptions. As of January 1977, only 117 of the 3,715 cable systems operating nationwide had public access channels—and many of them were unused. One hundred eighty-one systems had a school channel and 682 had any local live programming, either station or community originated.

The cable industry and independent programmers doubt that localized, special-interest news and public affairs will become widespread —regardless of how healthy the industry becomes. Daniel Aaron, chairman of the NCTA, said:

> The greatest demand for public access, both on the part of the audience and on the part of the participants, lies in the urban markets. It does not lie in small communities, which cable primarily serves. Not until the major markets are fully wired will the large demand open up. . . . In the smaller communities there is no demand for it.

Walter Kinash, general manager of Teleprompter in Johnstown, Pennsylvania, is one operator who has tried public access and now wishes it would die a quiet death. "Public access has very little viewership for two reasons—content and the production quality," he said. "If it's bad quality, it's not going to be watched." He listed technical problems with lighting, camera shots, black spots in the tape, poor audio, and poor production. He complained there were times that scheduled programs were not ready on time. "And the operator gets the calls." He said further:

> Their attitude has been, "We're amateurs, so we don't have to have the quality of broadcast television,"—which I think is wrong. Public access is a novelty to them. They want to get their fingers on the camera until they get tired of it. Their interest doesn't lie in good production.

When asked about cable's long-standing refrain that it can provide programming that has only small audience appeal, he said:

> The programs we put on, we think, will have the greatest number of viewers. We don't necessarily select for maximum viewership, but we want to put programs on that will be viewed. If we can get the required monthly service charge fee to do this kind of thing, great. But it's got to be subsidized. How far can the operator go?

Ted Carpenter, executive director of the National Citizens' Committee for Broadcasting, conceded that there is limited demand for public access. "No one is beating cable's door down saying, 'We want news and public affairs.' But you can't ask for what you don't know about," he said.

Pointing out that there is interest in places such as Reading, where there was an effective outreach program, he said that most cable operators are not supporting public access. Many have no outreach program to stimulate community interest, or staff to instruct volunteers how to use the equipment. Some have discouraged what interest does exist. They have scheduled access production at inconvenient hours and made the service too expensive for most groups by requiring union cameramen or by charging for playback of independently produced tapes—a service that should be provided free, according to the FCC.

Micky Brandt, project adviser for the Public Access Production Corporation, agreed with Carpenter. He put the responsibility on industry leaders:

> Public service use of their channels by third parties is resisted and derailed. There is no cooperation. There are too many problems to make you think it's anything other than a lot of lip service and public relations. The leadership of the cable industry has not shown enough positive movement toward public service.

The National Federation of Local Cable Programmers as of late 1977 had begun to document the "surprisingly high" number of cases where potential cable programmers were stifled or refused access to cable channels.

But why would cable operators be reluctant to cooperate with eager volunteers willing to contribute to the diversity and special interest fare that cable had promised?

David Osler, of the Community Media Center in San Jose, where the number of programming hours had been cut from over 100 to 20, had his own observations. "It's a pain in the neck for them," he said. "They have to deal with the public and they don't want to do that. Any little aggravation they'd rather do without."

Carpenter, of the NCCB, pointed out: "There is no economic, institutional, regulatory, corporate incentive to do specialized programming—no dollars, no good marks."

Many cable operators who could not afford a professional news program or public access relied on the wire services to provide their system with a news service. Out of the 3,715 cable systems operating nationwide, 2,224 systems had time and weather data, 513 had a news ticker, 237 a stock ticker, and 162 a sports ticker. UPI, the leader in cable news, serving 305 systems, provided two cable services—the national and international wire and the state report, which covered local events. The coverage included business news, stock quotations, and weather. The reports were timed in fifteen-minute packages, every hour, twenty-four hours a day.

The wire services were developing in different directions. UPI was developing news pictures with audio, while Associated Press, which served nearly 200 systems, was looking ahead to twenty-four-hour live video news. Reuters, distributing news to more than 200 systems, was planning to provide a "cheap" home terminal by the early 1980s that would decode videotext news and information broadcast over the air or over cable and allow the viewer to summon the story he wanted without having to wait for it to appear in the cycle, according to Michael Blair, manager of media services for Reuters. The first IDR terminal was already in use by 350 businesses hooked up to Manhattan Cable.

Teletext is in limited operation in England, provided by the British systems, CEEFAX and ORACLE. In June 1978, the British Post Office will begin a trial of VIEWDATA, which has a much larger capacity for information than its competitors—70,000 pages of news, travel timetables, and tax information—and which cuts in half the amount of page transmission time, from eighteen seconds to nine seconds.

Kenneth Edwards, associate professor at the University of Alabama School of Communications, studied the English systems and contends that teletext has a bright future in the United States. Addressing the INFCO convention in October 1977, he said:

> Teletext has provided a potential for replacing much of our newsprint, and maybe, in time, all our delivery people as well. If we think of newspapers as being the printed object that is delivered to our homes, we may be talking about replacing newspapers with electronic signals. But if we think of newspapers instead as organizations which disseminate news and information by the most efficient methods available, then we are thinking in terms of applying new technology to an existing institution.

Edward Ney, chairman of Young and Rubicam, speculated that by the end of 1981, 30 percent of all U.S. homes will be cable subscribers, and that newspapers may begin to be interested in entering the teletext business. He observed:

Any newspaper owning a TV station or cable system could enter the teletext business, provided the Federal Communications Commission approved. Any publisher of a newspaper could enter the business with an investment of a few hundred thousand and approval by the FCC. That agency's attitude and how long it takes for manufacturers to agree on equipment specifications for broadcast and decoding, are the two questions that will determine how fast teletext develops in the United States.

The cable industry was racing the telephone company to establish domain over two-way data retrieval. In an effort to preempt cable's development in this field, AT&T introduced legislation—the so-called Bell bill—in both the House and Senate. But as of September 1977, *Broadcasting* magazine reported it was "barely breathing." The legislation had taken a back seat to the House Communications Subcommittee's primary concern—the rewrite of the 1934 Communications Act.

The rewrite of the Communications Act, which controls broadcasting, telephone, and telegraph transmission through the FCC, could have major impact on the future of the cable industry. The subcommittee staff released its 664-page, generally pro-cable options paper in April. Hearings began in May. The subcommittee was scheduled to have its bill drafted and ready for committee consideration in January.

Among the many issues it will consider will be the extent to which cable should be allowed to compete with broadcast television. Commercial broadcasters have long contended that cable's prosperity will cut into their revenues and this in turn will affect their budgets for news and public affairs. Small stations will fold, and there will be no local source for local broadcast news, the broadcasters say. Herman Land, executive director of the Association of Independent Television Stations and author of *Television and the Wired City,* explained the position of many in the broadcasting industry:

You need an institution that can underwrite costs and losses and follow through. There is some kind of strange wisdom which lodges responsibility with broadcast institutions for these things. . . . This is one of the things I object to in a completely unfettered cable system. You'll drive it all out. Once the box office is all, then you wind up with a variation of what you have in the theater business. You don't have any institutionalized responsibility.

Never one to argue for excessive profits, I do think that it is necessary to reach a certain level of profitability before you can do worthwhile things on a sustained basis. There is merit to the argument that perhaps you need economies of scale—represented by the networks and O & O's and big stations—to do socially valuable things you might not be able to do otherwise. They take a long time, they're difficult to do.

To achieve some of those things, we may as a society have to pay certain costs, and one of them is to maintain a profitable broadcast system. And I don't find anything wrong in that.

Ted Carpenter of the NCCB called that argument "subterfuge. . . . It's a threat without teeth. Besides, news is profitable. Who are they trying to kid? It has been for some time. It's a childish characterization on the part of the broadcasters—'We'll take away something you like, if you do that to us.'

Walter Breede, public relations director of Teleprompter, also challenged the broadcasters' argument. "Take a look at their 1977 earnings figures—they're higher than ever before," he said. "If they're endangered, it will be a long, long time before they experience any possible harm."

A January 1976 report for the Subcommittee on Communications of the House Committee on Interstate and Foreign Commerce also questioned the broadcasters' case:

> Broadcasters have no guaranteed right under the public interest standard to the very high level of profits now earned by so many of them. If cable diminished those profits by alleviating the present artificial scarcity of television channels, it would not follow automatically that the public interest would suffer. If, as we believe would be the case, broadcasters generally maintained an economic base sufficient to permit discharge of their obligation to act as a fiduciary to present local or informational programs on "matters of great public concern," there would be no detriment to the public interest, but only benefits from the added diversity supplied by cable. . . .
>
> News programming represents the great bulk of the local or informational programming produced by broadcasters, and it is profitable for most stations in the major markets. Indeed, because it is so important a "lead-in" to the rest of the schedule, there is fierce competition in this area. Public affairs programming is generally not profitable and is supported by the rest of the entertainment/sports/news schedule . . . but public affairs represents a minute fraction of a broadcaster's time and expense. A serious question is raised whether cable's development should be held back because of claimed risks to such small efforts.
>
> Stated differently, assuming for the sake of argument that what

is endangered by cable is not broadcast service as such, but rather the unprofitable public service efforts, it would seem incumbent upon the [Federal Communications] Commission to balance that loss against the gain in diversity and new services from cable's operation, and then make a judgment as to where the public interest lies. This the Commission has never done.

The FCC notice of inquiry, initiated in June 1977, would accumulate data on the cable industry's economic impact on over-the-air broadcast revenues.

The cable industry welcomed the FCC survey and the rewrite of the Communications Act. Confident that the data would support its arguments, the NCTA felt that the rewrite could only result in improvements in cable regulation.

Preliminary research by the FCC's Cable Television Bureau had shown that lifting signal-carrier restrictions on most cable systems would have only slight impact on local stations—less than 1 percent of television homes. John Whetzell, chief economist for the FCC's cable bureau, reported that though "each market reacts to audience diversion differently . . . in almost every case, cable television bolsters the audience of UHF stations, rather than diverts any audience away."

The NCTA was also optimistic because of a series of regulatory victories that suggested a more receptive attitude in Washington toward cable television.

Beginning in the fall of 1976, the first revision of the copyright law since 1909 established that for the first time cable operators (and public broadcasters) would have to pay copyright royalties—1.1 percent of their revenues—into a pool for copyright owners.

Broadcasters were disgruntled. They claimed that the cable fee was only a token payment, and that it gave cable unfair advantage over broadcasting. It costs television stations 25 to 30 percent of their revenues for programming.

Robert Schmidt, president of the NCTA, pointed out that in fighting relaxation of cable rules, the networks had argued that cable doesn't pay for any of the programming it charges subscribers to watch. "Now we're paying," he said. "That's an argument I think they wish they still had around."

In December 1976, the FCC cleared the way for small-dish earth stations, reducing the acceptable diameter from 9 meters to 4.5 meters. This reduced the cost by about two-thirds—from between $75,000 and $100,000 for a 9-meter dish in 1976, to between $25,000 and $30,000 for a 4.5-meter dish. And this made it technically possible for the smallest cable operator to import programming from across the continent, distributed by satellite. The ruling made the networks uneasy, because satellite transmission may enable independents and cable operations to offer advertisers the same national audience the networks do.

Cable won another skirmish in March 1977. The FCC redefined cable television, deregulating operations with less than 500 subscribers, but leaving open the possibility of later deregulating operations up to 1,000 subscribers. It deleted any reference to the community served and to the specific technology of cable and wire. The impact was more symbolic than substantial. Though cable systems with less than 1,000 subscribers constituted 42 percent of all cable systems, they served only 6 percent of all subscribers.

The most notable legal victory was the HBO ruling in March 1977 by the U.S. Court of Appeals, Washington, D.C. The decision overruled the FCC's anti-siphoning rules for movies and sports on pay cable on jurisdictional and First Amendment grounds, but reaffirmed rules as applied to pay TV. The FCC pay cable rules had prohibited the showing of movies between three and ten years old. The court said there was no proof that cable would siphon off top attractions and weaken programming of broadcast television.

The broadcast industry was stunned. One NAB attorney told *Variety:* "I didn't think we would win the pay cable case, but I didn't think we would lose this bad either."

Within weeks the NAB announced it would appeal all aspects of the ruling. The FCC said it would appeal only the section regarding sports and unlawful extracurricular communications and accept the ruling on movies. In early October the Supreme Court, refusing to review the lower court's decision, left it standing.

Bolstered by its recent successes and faced with the possibility of sweeping changes in telecommunications policy, the NCTA used the opportunity to call for the complete removal of all government restrictions on distant signal carriage. According to their proposal, broadcasters could seek individual relief, a year after the deregulation program began, but the burden would be on them to provide financial data to prove their claim. The FCC would establish standards of audience loss warranting relief in advance. The House subcommittee staff report also offered the "deregulation" option—letting market forces work to "allow cable to offer all the services it is technically capable of providing" without hindrance from the FCC.

The possibility of deregulation worries not only broadcasters, but groups concerned with local community access and public affairs programming. Micky Brandt, project adviser for the Public Access Production Corporation and programmer for the cable channel in Vineland, New Jersey, said that there should be some legal provision for access programming:

> As the new services begin to flow from the cable wires, someone had better make sure that not just the most profitable services go on the available channels. Support for nonprofit uses and the absolute reservation of channel space for local use must be guaranteed by law, because so far the industry has a dismal record on encouraging this on its own.

John Whetzell, economist for the FCC's cable bureau, intimated that, left to market forces alone, the outlook for news and public affairs programming would be bleak:

> It would appear that local origination of news and public affairs programming will remain unprofitable on cable systems. The possibility of documentaries on a pay program basis would depend on the demand for such programming. News programming is very expensive and has to be supported either by large audience contributions or advertisers. We do not see these contributions coming in the near future.

Ted Carpenter of the NCCB doubted that even a thriving cable industry would provide news and public affairs programming without being required to by the FCC:

> I don't see it happening. If there is no regulatory or corporate incentive, there won't be service. There isn't anything to indicate feeling that, "If it works in Reading, we'll have to try it in Santa Rosa." They're not talking that way.

And he was not optimistic that either the FCC or Congress would reinstitute requirements for public interest programming:

> I thought the early FCC requirements requiring mandatory public access, local origination, franchise negotiations, were a really good guarantee of public interest in exchange for a monopoly—a license to print money.
> The constituency that would make that demand has been decimated by the pullback by the FCC and individual franchises. There really isn't any constituency. I don't see a strong movement happening, demanding public service.
> I'm not hopeful at all.

It appears unlikely that the FCC will revise its public interest programming requirements, given its uncertain authority while Congress wrestles with the Communications Act. Considering the strength of the opposition, even if Congress does move to require news and public affairs on cable systems, it could take years to become law.

It seemed that Wiley's pledge to the NCTA to "guard against possible loss of service to the community" and to "address ourselves intently to the factors . . . which are now inhibiting or may later restrain the expansion of broadband capacity" would be met. Whether electronic news and public affairs would be damaged or benefited by such an expansion seemed to depend on the disposition of Congress and the ingenuity and good will of an increasingly prosperous cable industry.

Appendix I

Remarks by Walter Cronkite at
CBS Affiliates Conference,
Century Plaza Hotel,
Los Angeles, California

Wednesday, May 5, 1976

I REGRET that my schedule did not permit me to be present this morning to hear the News Division presentation. I've been wondering what's going on there. I also had a question or two I would have liked to raise with the News Division management. Such as: "Mr. Salant, did you mean it when you said I was worth 16 million dollars?"

Of course, I know he meant it when he said he was locking his door.

This Barbara Walters thing can make a fellow paranoid. Last week I was the recipient of some rather meaningless award in New York, and there were a couple of pickets outside the hotel draped with hand-painted sandwich boards proclaiming that I was biased and unfair to someone or other. I have gotten used to that sort of thing —or I thought I had. But I found as I sat on that dais that I was thinking of those pickets. And do you know what I was thinking? I was thinking: "Just two little shriveled-up pickets out there. Two of them! I wonder how many pickets Barbara Walters would have?"

Well, a person can't permit himself to think like that—even if others around him seem to lose their heads. My hairdresser, for instance. He was on the phone when the big news came last week. He wanted to know when our contract was up for renewal.

And my agent is working up a co-production package in which I'll host four prime time specials each year, on the entertainment side, of course. One, I think, has real possibilities to display my singing and dancing talents. We want to cash in on the award theme rage. We're thinking of calling it "Heterosexual of the Year." It will be sort of a minority showcase.

The Barbara Walters news did shake me up at first, as it did us all. There was a first wave of nausea, the sickening sensation that we were going under, that all of our efforts to hold network television news aloof from show business had failed. But after sleeping on the matter, with more sober, less hysterical reflection, I came to a far less gloomy view of the matter.

For one thing, Miss Walters' qualifications as a journalist are not all that lacking. It is not as if ABC had hired a singer, dancer, or ventriloquist to share the Evening News duties with Harry. Barbara started out as a writer—even worked for CBS Morning News once. She is an aggressive, hard-hitting interviewer. She does her home-work. Her background is not what I would call well rounded—news-papers, press services, the police, county courts, statehouse beats—but who is to say that there is only one route to a career in journalism?

It is not very productive, either, to talk about whether she is worth one million dollars. Compared to what? Compared to a good teacher? Probably not. Compared to any rock singer? Almost certainly yes. It *is* a marketplace situation. If she can get a million bucks from ABC, presumably she is worth a million. That's what we like to think of as the American way.

The problem really is not in what *is,* but what the public perceives it to be. And I'm not really certain what the public does perceive here. In our self-consciousness, I think that we believe that the public looks with distaste, even revulsion, on such ridiculously high salaries. We've heard that ball players have lost some of their aura as hero figures because of their huge contracts, and this may be so. But the bleachers and the two-dollar seats—if you can find them—are still filled with fans, and we're led to believe that they are there to see the stars.

What counts is the quality of the play. For their million-dollar contracts they had better play the game better than anyone else—and if they don't, then the fans will let them know that they don't believe they are earning their expensive keep. In accepting that big pay check, Barbara Walters also is taking on a big responsibility to deliver. The proof of her value will be in the pudding.

And on those sober, second-day thoughts, I came to feel, too, that some of us might be indulging in just a bit of hypocrisy when we accused ABC of plunging our profession into show business with the Walters contract. My friends, if salaries *alone* are the criterion, we in television news have been in show business a long time, and the difference between Barbara Walters' new remuneration and that of the rest of us on-air news people is but a matter of degree.

And that is not a fact of recent days: it goes back to Ed Murrow and beyond. Using the only available comparison, newspaper work, print journalism, we in broadcast news have been getting show business salaries since the beginning.

But that is not a really valid comparison, either. What we on-air broadcasters do comprises a dimension beyond the skills required by the newspaper reporter, writer, and editor. If we do our jobs well, we do those things—reporting, writing, editing—as well or better than the print journalist, but beyond that we have to have the special skills —talents, if you please—to present our material through the spoken word and in a visual medium, frequently to think on our feet, and to be right the first time with no editor imposed as a protective buffer between us and the public. We must be able without reference to written works to pull from our heads the background of a given story, complete with the historical reference when relevant. We have to balance the moral and the immoral, the appropriate and the grossly inappropriate, the acceptable and the offensive, the right and the wrong even as facts are tumbling in upon us, and there are no second guesses. With a certain degree of immodesty, I suggest that those of us who can do that are worth a little more than the print journalist —or, perhaps, a lot more.

What I do have some problem understanding is why an anchor person who does not have those qualifications still draws down such large compensation. In fact, I wonder if those stations that hire the young and beautiful but inexperienced and callous to front their news broadcasts are not getting ripped off.

I echo Charlie Kuralt's famous speech to the Radio-Television News Directors last fall: It seems to me as I travel about the country that all it takes today to be an anchor person is to be under twenty-five, fair of face and figure, dulcet of tone, and well coiffed. And that is just for the men! That and to be able to fit into the blazer with the patch on the pocket.

This doesn't make a journalist, and I think the public may be more aware of that than the stations which cling to their belief, or the persuasion of an out-of-town consultant, that the anchor man or woman's personality, rather than his or her news ability, is the key factor in building an audience.

Let me say right here, that I am not one who decries ratings. Those among us in the news end of the broadcasting business who do are simply naïve. Of course ratings are important and no one, newsman, program manager, salesman, or general manager, need hang his head in shame because that is the fact. We've been cowed in to that position by a bunch of newspaper critics who conveniently forget their own history when they harp on our ratings battles.

How short is their memory or venal their intent when they fail to recall, as they criticize us, the great circulation wars of the past, when newspapers stooped to every dirty trick in the book, not halting before murder, to sell a few extra papers.

The best newspaper in the world isn't worth very much if nobody reads it—or if not enough read it to keep it in business. The same is true of broadcasting, so let us put to rest any moral arguments about ratings.

But it is *how* we get those ratings, what we do to make us competitive, that bothers me, for just as it is no good to put out a superior product if you can't sell it, it is far worse to peddle an inferior product solely through the razzle-dazzle of a promotion campaign.

And aren't we guilty of that when we put the emphasis in our news broadcasts on performance and performers rather than content? Isn't that really what we are looking for when we examine ourselves to see whether we are indulging in show business rather than journalism?

There is no newsman worth his salt who does not know that advisers who dictate that no item should run more than forty-five seconds, that there must be a film story within the first thirty seconds of the newscast and that it must have action in it (a barn burning or a jackknifed tractor-trailer truck will do), that calls a ninety-second film piece a "minidocumentary," that advises against covering city hall because it is dull, that says the anchor man or woman must do all voice-overs for "identity"—any real newsman knows that sort of stuff is balderdash. It's cosmetic, pretty packaging—not substance.

And I suspect that most station operators know that too. But I think they've been sold a bill of goods, that they've been made suckers for a fad: editing by consultancy. Yes, suckers, because there is no evidence that this formula news broadcasting—the top twenty hit news items—works.

It may—*may*—produce a temporary one- or two-point rating advantage, or an interesting set of demographics. But the evidence that it does not work is in the startling turnover of anchor people and news directors in our affiliated stations. Inexact but indicatively approximate figures show that 50 percent or so of these people change jobs every two years, and for many stations the rollover is quicker than that.

Now, that's no way to build a reliable, dependable news staff. For one thing, these fly-by-nights don't know the territory. They don't have the credibility of long-time residents, nor, what is worse, do they have any long-term interests in the community, and the unsettling fact must be that the would-be viewers are impressed unfavorably by these frequent comings and goings. These transient performers are simply using the broadcast manager as a stone in the quicksand to hold them up long enough to jump to the next rock.

Let me play consultant for a moment. Permit me, if you will, to talk directly to those of you whose stations may have been caught up in this formula news presentation.

The reason you are being taken is that the answer to your news problem probably is right under your nose. In the first place, why buy somebody else's idea of an ideal anchor person or news editor for your market? Your anchor person is the most intimate contact you have with your community. Don't you know what sort of person your neighbors like? Don't *you* know better than any outsider the tastes of your friends and acquaintances? If not, I suggest that maybe *you* ought to be the one to move along.

Second, isn't a hometowner, or a long-time resident, or at least a young man or woman who has chosen your community and wants to make a career there—isn't he or she likely to give a great deal more in enthusiasm and dedication and interest—qualities, I might point out, that are easily detected across the airwaves—than the wanderer looking for the next big break in the next biggest town? So why don't you try building a staff of such people, and then promote from desk writer to street reporter to anchor person —from within?

And if you don't have those people immediately available, have you thought about raiding your local newspaper? For what you pay those inexperienced announcers, you could hire the best—the best newspaperman in your town—as on-air broadcaster or news director, or possibly both: a fellow or gal who knows the city like a book, likes the city, warts and all, and plans to raise a family there.

He very possibly has a little gray in his hair, may be bald, may wear horn-rimmed bifocals, likely his collar is somewhat crumpled and his tie is done in an old-fashioned four-in-hand instead of a properly bulbous Windsor. But I'll guarantee you this: he knows more about your town and what makes it tick than will ever be learned by that young fellow from 500 or 1,000 or 2,000 miles away that some consultant tells you got a good rating there. And you know what? That slightly tousled codger is going to exude more authority and reliability and believability and integrity from the nail on the little finger of his left hand than that pompadoured, pampered announcer is ever going to muster. And isn't that really what our news departments are all about—isn't that really what you want to sell: authority, believability, credibility, integrity?

Who has said that won't work? Some market analyst who has no concern for news integrity but is looking only at the numbers? You really don't mind abdicating your responsibility to him?

And listen, what about this question of age, anyway? I admit I speak on this issue with a certain passion of special interest, but what about it? Why do you necessarily believe the demographic demons who think it takes a kid to appeal to kids? Let me just mildly and as modestly as possible note that the hottest tickets on the college lecture circuits, packing them in wherever they go, are some newsmen with a little gray at the temples and a crinkle or two around the eyes, perhaps even a dewlap under the chin: Dan Schorr, Dan Rather, Eric Sevareid—and I'll even mention yours truly.

Since I've stumbled onto my favorite subject, let me dwell—lovingly—there for a moment. I've gained a certain prominence in this business. There are those polls that show I'm the most trusted American—my, God, what shape the country's in! There is the new *U.S. News & World Report* survey that purports to show that I'm the sixth most powerful man in America, a perfectly ridiculous assessment, of course.

But what is important about all this is that I have become a sort of symbol of television journalism, a generic face of television news, spoken of as an authority figure—and occasionally asked by our critics to shoulder the blame for all our sins as well.

Why this exalted position? Longevity. I'd like to think I've done a good job, but it goes deeper than that. I've been tolerated for a long time as the front man for a solid, consistently good news organization that through the years has never wavered in its total dedication to the principles of ethical journalism. Doesn't that say something to all of us?

What people are really recognizing in honoring me is this steadfastness of CBS News as represented by this long-time association. The two things cannot be separated.

While I certainly do not recommend that you try to pattern your news organizations after ours, it seems to me that at least in this matter of building some seniority into your staffs, off- and on-air, you would not only be better serving your community, but you would not be suffering in the ratings battles—and, over the long run, you might even win a few.

I think that with few exceptions—heck, I know that with very few exceptions—you are anxious to make your news operations the very best you can, that you won't sell out cheap, that you don't want to pander to show business values in an area of the business where that is a fatal flaw.

So don't let someone else who claims to know better than you what your community news needs are, dictate your news operation.

You have in your command such vast power, such great potential for leadership in your community, such an overwhelming responsibility, that it is nothing short of sinful if you turn your backs and fail to play the role that has been presented to you.

This world of ours is in a pretty frightful mess. There are decisions on the cosmic scale that must be made in the next decade that will determine, literally, whether we live or die. We cannot long tolerate delay in reaching solutions for such problems as population, pollution, depletion of natural resources (including food), and nuclear proliferation.

Not one of these problems can be solved in Washington or New York without contribution of ideas and support from the population at large. Our strength comes not from Washington, but from Houston and Wichita and Salem and Missoula and Charleston. And the leadership begins there, too. And *you* are the leaders.

Your responsibility to your stockholders is great, and must be considered prime—for, as I have said earlier, if you don't stay in business you can't very well discharge the other responsibilities that station ownership and management have visited upon you.

But this does not give you license to ignore those other responsibilities, and I'd like to suggest that in the discharge of those other responsibilities you may well find the greatest satisfaction for yourselves, for your communities, and thus, as day follows the night, for your stockholders.

Broadcasting can be responsible in the news areas, and simultaneously successful. And I invite you to look again at the networks—at CBS and, yes, NBC too. The managements of our networks have built vast show business empires. Never in the history of man have there been such impresarios as our network executives; never has there been such a sales medium; and never, of course, has there been anything like that combination.

But at the same time, never has there been such a news medium as television news. And yet those same men who built those great blocks of entertainment in a competitive environment with more dollars at stake than many of us can even dream of, who never lost sight of the sales potential in every tough decision—those men have been so perceptive that they have seen, too, that news is something vastly different, and they have fought to protect the news teams they chose from the pressures of the marketplace and the political forums.

We of the news departments made—still make—impossible demands upon them. We ask them to appeal to public acceptance for sixteen or seventeen hours of the broadcast day, and then for an hour or two, turn their backs on public favor and permit us to broadcast that which has to be said, pleasant or unpleasant, bland or highly controversial.

They have been forced to stand against the most horrible political pressure. They have valiantly protected news integrity against commercial demands. It has taken extraordinary courage, but the Paleys and Stantons and Taylors and Schneiders have done it, and are doing it.

And, the network that has the highest confidence of the people, as shown in the news ratings, also happens to be the biggest money maker. Playing it honest, playing it for integrity, hasn't seemed to hurt. I suggest it probably has helped.

You at the local level, just as we at the national, are a vital force in the free flow of information without which democracy cannot survive. I envy you and your opportunities to play that lofty role in your communities, from which the strength must flow for the challenging battles ahead.

Thank you.

Appendix II

Remarks by Walter Cronkite at the RTNDA Conference, Miami Beach, Florida

Monday, December 13, 1976

GOOD MORNING.

If we this morning were operating under the same strictures which bind you and me in doing our daily jobs, I now would have finished my speech—eleven seconds after starting it.

Whatever I am about to say would have to be compressed into that length of time to make it on an evening half-hour newscast.

I don't know that what I have to say is very profound, but I know darned well that whatever it is cannot be synthesized into that small a capsule.

The best that could be hoped for—if this were to be reported as a "tell" story—would be the presentation of one single idea, or one claim, or one denunciation, and that without any, *any,* of the qualifications, reasons, or background that led me to make that assertion.

Matters would be no better—in fact, very well could be worse—if our medium chose to report my speech with a filmed or taped excerpt, for this, too, would be shortened to only a sentence or two, and, while no more complete than a "tell" item, would, by presenting me in person, place the stamp of authenticity on my words.

You will recognize in what I am saying an indictment of what you and I are doing every blessed day of our lives.

Nor is the sin ours alone. Our print brothers and sisters, with far greater space than have we, still are limited in what they can say— they cannot write on endlessly, of course. And they, too, commit the error of inadequate quotation and/or explanation.

I, unfortunately, am in a peculiarly advantageous position from which to observe this phenomenon at work. By the strange laws that govern such things, I and my colleague anchor persons have become stars, celebrities, authorities, news sources. And when we speak out, we get quoted. We are in this uncomfortable posture of being both newspersons and newsmakers. We are subjected to the same treatment we give to others. We can see what it is like. And, believe me, the view of us journalists from the other side of the mirror is not a very handsome one.

It is not just a question of the inadequate quote, the overcompression of news, but not infrequently the totally phony quote. Just last week the *National Enquirer* bannered a story claiming that I believe in flying saucers. The full-page story by one Robin Leach was a total lie from beginning to end. He did *not* interview me as he said, the incidents he quoted me—directly quoted me—as reciting were totally unknown to me, and the conclusion that I believe in flying saucers was, itself, erroneous.

Mr. Leach's defense was that a *third party,* whom he trusted, told him that I had said and believed these things on which he directly quoted me.

But don't hold the illusion that such practices are prevalent or permitted only in publications such as the *National Enquirer.* Some of the journals which supposedly monitor the performance of the news media are also guilty of reaching for the sensational with little regard for, what at least used to be, basic standards of journalism.

Virtually the same practice of unchecked alleged third-party information is tolerated by *More* magazine. One Philip Nobile cited me as having said something I never even thought, let alone said. I complained in a letter to the editor. I noted that Mr. Nobile had never attempted to check the matter with me. But in his printed answer Mr. Nobile ducked that rather basic allegation and simply said that he stood by his trusted sources.

What kind of journalism have we come to? And that in a journal that presumes to monitor *our* performance.

(Incidentally, half of the other communications by the offended in that same Letters column in *More* also complained of quotes that allegedly were never rendered, and of failure to check the original source—one of them from Jimmy Breslin, like me not exactly unreachable by our colleagues of the press.)

But these are the *extremes* of bad journalism. Let me cite a couple of examples of the more frequent transgression, the one that I am afraid we all commit with regularity:

In a speech to our CBS affiliates last May I said that when I first heard the news that ABC had hired Barbara Walters, I was "sickened" because I felt that our efforts to hold the line at the networks against show business encroachment in the news area had been lost. But I said in the next sentence that, on reflection, I had *changed* my views and I gave the reasons why.

Well, what got into the papers and even onto some newscasts was only the first sentence, and, as is true of all such errors, the misrepresentation has a life of its own. Just a couple of issues ago, *Time* reprinted only the statement that I was "sickened" by Barbara's appointment. Untrue in its essence, and unfair to Barbara and to me.

And in that same speech to the affiliates—the far more *important* part of the speech, I think—I decried the hiring of anchor people solely for their looks and their ability to perform.

That, too, was widely quoted, but far less often did the reports go on to make it clear that I was citing this only as symptomatic of a greater problem—local management abdication of responsibility to consultants in the drive for ratings.

This led to unfortunate misinterpretation by a lot of our colleagues, by possibly some of you, who did not have easy access to my entire speech.

And just for the record, since we are on that subject, let me cite some of that speech to you. I said:

> I wonder if those stations that hire the young and beautiful but inexperienced and callous to front their news broadcasts are not getting ripped off.
>
> I echo Charlie Kuralt's famous speech to the Radio-Television News Directors last fall: It seems to me as I travel about the country that all it takes today to be an anchor person is to be under twenty-five, fair of face and figure, dulcet of tone, and well coiffed. And that is just for the men! That and to be able to fit into the blazer with the patch on the pocket.
>
> This doesn't make a journalist, and I think the public may be more aware of that than the stations which cling to their belief, or the persuasion of an out-of-town consultant, that the anchor man, or woman's, personality, rather than his or her news ability, is the key factor in building an audience.

I go on to say that I don't underrate ratings.

> But it is how we get those ratings, what we do to make us competitive, that bothers me, for just as it is no good to put out a superior product if you can't sell it, it is far worse to peddle an inferior product solely through the razzle-dazzle of a promotion campaign.
>
> And aren't we guilty of that when we put the emphasis in our

news broadcasts on performance and performers rather than content? Isn't that really what we are looking for when we examine ourselves to see whether we are indulging in show business rather than journalism?

There is no newsman worth his salt who does not know that advisers who dictate that no item should run more than forty-five seconds, that there must be a film story within the first thirty seconds of the newscast and that it must have action in it (a barn burning or a jacknifed tractor-trailer truck will do), that calls a ninety-second film piece a "minidocumentary," that advises against covering city hall because it is dull, that says the anchor man or woman must do all voice-overs for "identity"—any real newsman or woman knows that sort of stuff is balderdash. It's cosmetic, pretty packaging—not substance.

And I went on to say:

And I suspect that most station operators know that too. But I think they've been sold a bill of goods; that they've been made suckers for a fad: editing by consultancy. Yes, suckers, because there is no evidence that this formula news broadcasting—the twenty hit news items—works.

It may—*may*—produce a temporary one-or two-point rating advantage, or an interesting set of demographics. But the evidence that it does not work is in the startling turnover of anchor people and news directors in our affiliated stations.

Inexact but indicatively approximate figures show that 50 percent or so of these people change jobs every two years, and for many stations the rollover is quicker than that.

Now, that's no way to build a reliable, dependable news staff.

"Let me play consultant for a moment," I said.

Permit me, if you will, to talk directly to those of you whose stations may have been caught up in this formula news presentation.

The reason you are being taken is that the answer to your news problem probably is right under your nose. In the first place, why buy somebody else's idea of an ideal anchor person or news editor for your market? Your anchor person is the most intimate contact you have with your community.

Don't you know what sort of person your neighbors like? Don't you know better than any outsider the tastes of your friends and acquaintances? If not, I suggest that maybe you ought to be the one to move along.

Second, isn't a hometowner, or a long-time resident, or at least a young man or woman who has chosen your community and wants to make a career there—isn't he or she likely to give a great deal more in enthusiasm and dedication and interest—qualities, I might point out, that are easily detected across the airwaves—than the wanderer looking for the next big break in the next biggest town? So why don't you try building a staff of such people, and then promote from desk writer to street reporter to anchorperson—from within?

I noted the longevity of most of us in network news and went on:

While I certainly do not recommend that you try to pattern your news organizations after ours, it seems to me that at least in this matter of building some seniority into your staffs, off- and on-air, you would not only be better serving your community, but you would not be suffering in the ratings battles—and, over the long run, you might even win a few.

Now that is what the speech to our affiliates was all about. Yet what you read and perhaps heard was only that I was sickened by Barbara Walters' hiring and criticized pampered and pompadoured news readers.

These examples of my own that I cite are not important in themselves, and I do not mean to exalt them by this lengthy explanation. But I hope they are illustrative of our problem—the inadvertent and perhaps inevitable *distortion* that results through the hypercompression we all are forced to exert to fit one hundred pounds of news into the one-pound sack that we are given to fill each night.

In World War II, a sack overstuffed to that degree was called a "blivet." We are hitting our public with a series of blivets every night.

The cumulative effect is devastating, eating away at our credibility. Perhaps it will take a while for the masses to catch on—they usually are the last to know the truth. But among the informed, the opinion leaders, those whose views eventually will *influence* the masses, the awareness is spreading—the awareness that our abbreviated versions of the news are suspect. They or their friends and associates have been victimized by our truncated reports, and they spread the word.

The *single* episode in itself is serious enough. Misrepresented views can embarrass at the least, can destroy a carefully built reputation for expertise at the worst.

And to compound the difficulty for the offended newsmaker, he or she cannot make the claim of simpler days that he or she was misquoted, for that is not what has happened.

It is not the misquote today, but the *malquote*, that is doing the damage. With the print reporters' increasing use of tape recorders, and our own broadcast equipment, rarely is the quotation itself wrong. It is the lifting of it out of context and our failure to include the explanations and qualifications which accompany it.

This, to my mind, is the most serious aspect of our time limitation because it does encroach on an individual's rights to be fairly presented. But we are indulging in similar, again inadvertent, distortion in most of the items we tell.

We attempt to include all the pertinent sides to a story, particularly a controversial one, for we are professional journalists, but not infrequently we find we must dismiss one argument or the other with barely a parenthetical phrase.

When the question of fairness arises, we can search back through the scripts and prove our effort at objectivity. And, indeed, if the report had been in printed form for easy reference in the first place, questions probably never would have been raised. But what our average listener actually heard, or what he thought he heard, or the impression he gained, may have been something vastly different than that which we intended.

We *do* try to guard against that, but in the compression process forced upon us by the severe limitations of time, the job is incredibly, almost impossibly, difficult. I'm afraid that we compress so well as to almost defy the viewer and listener to *understand* what we say. And when that becomes the fact, we cease to be communicators.

And if we fail at that task we have assumed, this republic is in dire straits. We have *now* a communications problem of immense dimensions, partly of our own making. Many of our newspapers, partly because most of them are monopolies, are not doing as thorough a job as they should in covering the news, trying instead to emulate television by entertaining the reader instead of informing him.

Meanwhile, according to the polls, 60 or 70 or even a greater percentage of our people now are getting most of their news from television, and an increasing percentage of them are getting *all* their news from us.

Those figures do not show what percentage of viewers were exposed to *no* news before the advent of television—those who cannot or do not read their daily newspapers. For them we clearly offer a vast improvement over their previous state. For those who *do* read their newspapers, our ability to present the people who make their news and show the places where the news is made adds a depth of understanding impossible through any other medium.

But we fall far short of presenting all, or even a goodly part, of the news each day that a citizen would need to intelligently exercise his franchise in this democracy. So as he *depends* more and more on us, presumably the depth of knowledge of the average man diminishes. This clearly can lead to disaster in a democracy.

There are some remedies available to us. Of course, we could quit entirely. Simply admit erroneously that we cannot do an adequate daily news broadcast, turn the time back to the quiz shows and the situation comedies, and force the people seeking news back to their newspapers, also too frequently inadequate.

Or we could stop somewhat short of suicide and drop the pretense of the daily news summary by substituting a daily magazine format —one or two minidocumentaries in the fashion that "Sixty Minutes" does so well, backgrounders and special take-outs on past or future stories.

But both of these solutions are a denial of the great potential of television as a *daily* news medium and hence an abdication of the responsibility of those of us lucky enough to be in the business. They would represent an artificial blackout imposed by those of us journalists too honest to go on as we have, and on the other hand, too gutless to fight for and help engineer the one viable solution.

That solution quite simply is, for the network newscasts, more time, and for the local newscasts with enough time, a better utilization of it. In the latter case, in many of *your* cases, I think that comprises doing what you, as experienced news directors, would like to be doing rather than what consultants or non-news-oriented station managers believe you should be doing. In other words, it means covering the meaningful, the genuinely important, relevant, and significant news of your communities—city hall, county courts, the state house— whether there is a picture story there or not, whether the resulting story can be told in twenty seconds or not.

For the networks it means primarily: give us at least a two-pound sack for our hundred pounds of news each night. Now *that* will not be enough. There is no way we can ask the public to sit still in front of the box long enough to get *all* the news it needs. We always will be a complementary medium to print for those who would be fully informed.

But with another half hour, by doubling our time, we could take a long stride toward eliminating *distortion* through overcompression. We would not have many more items, would not present features and extraneous interviews, but we would take a little more time with *each* item—enough extra time for the explanatory phrase, the "why" and the "how" as well as the "who," "what," "when," and "where."

We in the network news departments have been discouraged this fall by the failure of our companies to move ahead immediately with expanded evening news periods. But we must not let the discouragement turn to defeatism.

We must redouble our efforts to convince all those concerned that the republic, that the people, need this hour not just so we can do a different job, but so that we can do a better, more *honest* job of carrying this tremendous responsibility that rests on our shoulders.

You on the local level can be of help. You can help educate your owners to the need for the expanded network news and help clear away the principal impediment to its realization.

I know that there are men and women at both network and local management levels who are as sincere about discharging their public responsibilities as are any of us newspeople. Their failure to give top priority to making whatever arrangements, network and local, are necessary to offer the public the full hour news, is our failure in convincing them of the need. If we are to be honest with the public and with ourselves, then perhaps we must be even more honest with them—and courageous in continuing to demand the tools to do the job we know must be done.

Meanwhile I suggest that each of us redouble the effort we already are exerting to eliminate as nearly as is possible distortion through compression.

We are good—you are good. Top professionals all. Nothing I have said here should be taken as any denial of that.

We can hold our heads high in that regard with any form of journalism anywhere. What I have said here this morning is in the spirit of candid self-criticism and as a keynote suggestion of a problem we should be attacking to improve and perfect an already excellent product.

Thank you all and have a great convention.

Appendix III

"The Cronkite Hour"

Variety, August 11, 1976

HERE'S A RUNDOWN on CBS News' first hour news test, with the approximate times:

9:45 P.M.—Walter Cronkite lead for national unemployment story by Neil Strawser.

9:48 P.M.—Unemployment sidebar by Ray Brady (with statistics from a CBS-N.Y. Times poll).

9:50 P.M.—Cronkite previews the coming news.

(Dead air for first of nine commercial inserts.)

9:55 P.M.—Cronkite to Marya McLaughlin for story on tax reform bill, featuring quickie interviews with a couple of solons and a brief conversation featuring some "of course, Walters" from McLaughlin.

(Blurb insert.)

9:55 P.M.—Film story from Lebanon by Doug Tinnel.

9:58 P.M.—Cronkite debriefing of Mike Lee on Lebanon from London by satellite.

10:01 P.M.—Cronkite "tell-story" (straight reading) on rioting South African students.

(Blurb insert.)

10:03 P.M.—Legion disease story with President Ford statement and correspondent Jim Kilpatrick.

(Blurb insert.)

10:08 P.M.—Cronkite lead-in to genetic engineering series. First part of series by Don Kladstrup.

10:14 P.M.—Cronkite tell-story on cholesterol.

(Blurb insert.)

10:17 P.M.—Cronkite tell-story with stills on Chicago plane crash.

10:18 P.M.—Cronkite tell-story on Viking One, followed by Hal Walker report on Washington hearings on Teton Dam collapse.

10:20 P.M.—Cronkite stock report, followed by items on the wildcat coal strike and Russell Means' murder trial (he was freed).

10:21 P.M.—Cronkite tell-story, with credit to the Omaha World, on whistling evangelist George Madrigal, who said the Lord would take care of his hotel bill (he was evicted).

(Blurb insert.)

10:23 P.M.—Phil Jones report from Washington on Ford's checks on veepee candidates.

10:25 P.M.—Terry Drinkwater from Philadelphia on the Reagan campaign.

10:27 P.M.—Bob Schieffer with campaign report from the White House (live in the darkness).

10:29 P.M.—Drinkwater in Philadelphia debriefed by Cronkite.

10:31 P.M.—Cronkite tell-story on politician killed in plane crash and trouble between Kenya and Uganda.

(Blurb insert.)

10:34 P.M.—Musical interlude in piece produced some time ago by Richard Threlkeld on new Bach manuscripts featuring Bach scholar on harpsichord (Cronkite in intro pronounces Bach's first name with a hard "J"—"Johann").

(Blurb insert.)

10:38 P.M.—Cronkite news briefs.

10:39 P.M.—Charles Kuralt with feature from Madison, Wis.

(Blurb insert.)

10:44 P.M.—Cronkite recap.

Appendix IV

Report on Complaints Received by the National News Council About NBC's "Danger! Radioactive Waste"

Aired January 26, 1977

Complaints No. 10–77, 17–77, 17B–77
24–77, 40–77, and 83–77 (Filed February 23, 1977)

Cohen, et al.
v.
NBC News

Nature of complaint: On January 26, 1977, a one-hour documentary on the subject of nuclear waste was broadcast by NBC News. The documentary, entitled "Danger! Radioactive Waste," was followed by a wave of protests from the nuclear industry. Complaints were received by The Council from:

1. Dr. Bernard L. Cohen, a professor of physics at the University of Pittsburgh.
2. John R. Hoffman, a registered professional engineer, of Sturbridge, Massachusetts.
3. Carl Walske, president of Atomic Industrial Forum, Inc.
4. IEEE Power Engineering Society.
5. American Nuclear Society.
6. J. Stewart Corbett, of Chem-Nuclear Systems Inc.

Complainants charged, individually or in concert, that the program lacked balance and was replete with major factual errors and misrepresentations, and that the producer omitted significant material which would have given the viewers perspective, and "resorted to emotionalism, show-biz gimmicks and heavy-handed editing to create a classic propaganda piece in the guise of news."

As to the complainants' charge of *lack of balance,* it was asserted that:

—Significant points which one would expect in an objective report were omitted and those which were referred to in the program, but which were not antinuclear, were not done justice; "they were not given the prominence of the 'bad points.' There were no production tricks used to make them stand out for the viewer's attention."

—"NBC had full and complete cooperation by the nuclear industry in the preparation of this program," but only a relatively small portion of the total interviews with experts was used.

—The producer was antagonistic in conducting interviews with industry and government representatives and in one instance the "portion used was focused to embarrass without enlightening."

As to the complainants' charge of *factual errors and misrepresentations,* it was asserted that:

—A number of purportedly factual statements made in the program have no scientific support. (*E.g.,* that uranium will run out by the year 2000; that wastes dumped in the ocean will remain deadly for hundreds of thousands of years.)

—A number of hypotheticals were "far-fetched and misleading."

—Several mathematical calculations were incorrect.

—Allegations in the program to the effect that present technology is inadequate to assure the safe disposal and responsible handling of nuclear waste are incorrect. "There is no new technology required to implement a safe radioactive waste disposal program."

—There is no evidence to support certain implications of hazards to the environment. (E.g., that the water and cattle near Maxey Flats were tainted by radiation.)

—The theories of one scientist-interviewee given prominent coverage in the program "have been substantially refuted by responsible authorities."

As to the complainants' charge of *lack of perspective,* it was asserted that:

—"The program was presented in a contextual vacuum." Of particular note was the absence of any discussion of the seriousness of the energy crisis and the increasing reliance on electricity. The benefit of nuclear power was not balanced against the impact. No quantitative estimates of effects were given.

—The comparative safety of fossil fuels; chemical wastes (hydrocarbons and heavy metals) was not examined.

—Sources of radiation other than nuclear waste were neglected. "[M]an has always been bombarded by radiation from above (cosmic rays), from below (uranium and radium in the earth), from all sides (same in building materials), from within his own body (potassium, a naturally radioactive material, is vital to life), and from the air he breathes (radon gas); *each* of these sources gives him at least a hundred times more radiation exposure than *anyone* expects him to get from radioactive wastes even if all our power were nuclear. Moreover, medical and dental x-rays give him several hundred times as much."

—The handling of radioactive wastes from commercial nuclear power plants (1 percent of total) was given disproportionate significance as against the weapons program. Disposal practices of universities and hospitals were ignored completely.

As to the complainants' charge of *production tricks,* it was asserted that the program used (quoting the complaint):

—Manipulative background sound effects, including dirge music, "Taps" and the score of "The Sorcerer's Apprentice," as well as the repetitive use of the click of a geiger counter even where it had no relationship to the content of the show.

—Electronic visual tricks, to make nuclear plants seem to give off colored rays and to make radiation symbols waver as if emitting a gas.

—A propagandistic script. The narrator constantly used such phrases as "cemeteries without headstones," "colossal graves," "technology's mummies" and "ghosts that haunt the atomic graveyard." Waste materials were described as a "radioactive monster with no cage to keep it in."

—Emotional scenes that have no connection with nuclear power or waste. Some of these included an apparently dead fish, the "largest sponge in the world" and "strange milky material" in a stream near a nuclear facility. . . . None of these have been shown to have any connection with radiation, yet they were used melodramatically throughout the program. The most offensive example was the heartless exploitation of a former nuclear worker who has two sons born with genetic disease. . . . (End of quote.)

In summary, complainants contend that the viewing public was ill served by this documentary, calling it a program designed "to exploit the viewer's fears and uncertainties," "to scare them—not to inform them" at a time when information on this subject may be of key importance as the nation prepares to make possibly crucial choices.

Response of news organization: Richard Wald, then-president of NBC News, provided The Council with both the transcript and a videotape of the documentary. In view of the possibility that a third party (not complaining to The Council) might complain formally before the Federal Communications Commission, NBC declined to participate in the investigation. However, copies of the specific responses to various complainants were provided to The Council by NBC or by the complainants themselves. The producer, director and writer, Joan Konner, who is not associated with NBC at this time, first referred the staff to NBC's two outside consultants who had approved the final transcript and later spoke with staff by telephone concerning two aspects of the program discussed in the conclusion.

Responding to complainants' assertions regarding *lack of balance,* NBC declared:

> We are aware that there are differing points of view on this subject, and that it is one of many interrelated energy and environmental issues and questions. This program was only one part of our ongoing coverage of all facets of the energy problem in various NBC News programs.

Responding to the assertions of *factual errors and misrepresentations,* NBC declared:

> The facts in the program were compiled over many months by several people, and all have been documented. It was produced in consultation with scientists highly respected in the scientific community.

The responses went on to give specific rebuttals to most of the assertions of scientific and mathematical error made by complainants. In essence, NBC stood behind the facts as it had presented them, citing scientific authority where appropriate and challenging the calculations and statements of complainants.

Responding to the assertion that the program *lacked perspective,*
NBC declared:

> In the program, we were not discussing nuclear power as an
> energy alternative, we were examining one problem with nuclear
> energy. We in no way advocated the abandonment of nuclear
> power, only the need to find a satisfactory solution to a problem
> that has been growing for thirty years and will, unless solved,
> continue to grow as the nuclear power industry expands. Our
> report did state that 99 percent of today's existing waste was from
> the nuclear weapons program. However, as we pointed out at the
> beginning of the report, the government feels the United States
> will need 500 nuclear power plants by the year 2000—a huge
> increase over the present number.

Further, as to the omission of material complainants believe was
particularly significant and necessary for perspective, NBC said:

> We do not think that the existence of dangers in other forms of
> energy or in other toxic elements negates the dangers of radioac-
> tive waste, although those dangers are frequently cited to mini-
> mize the danger by special interest parties.
>
> There have been many studies documenting the danger of
> radiation. There is a certain amount of radiation over which we
> have no control. We do have some control over how much addi-
> tional radiation we permit.

In concluding, NBC gave the following response to the charge of
gimmickry and emotionalism as *production tricks:*

> As for production techniques, these are a matter of opinion, and
> the fact is that there has been at least as much praise as criticism
> for the production.

The [National News Council] staff consulted outside experts and
persons interviewed on the program. These included:

> Dr. Robert Singer, director of the State of Kentucky Animal
> Disease Diagnostic Laboratory
> Dave Clark, supervisor of the Environmental Surveillance Sec-
> tion of the Radiation Control Branch of the State of Kentucky
> Dr. Robert Miller, chief of Clinical Epidemiology at the National
> Cancer Institute
> Dr. Merril Eisenbud, director of the Laboratory for Environmen-

tal Medicine of the New York University Medical Center
James Neel (interviewed on the program), president of Nuclear
Engineering Company (Kentucky)
Dr. Irwin Bross (interviewed on the program), director of biostatistics at the Roswell Park Memorial Institute
Frank Baranowski (interviewed on the program), formerly with
the Energy Research and Development Administration
(ERDA)
G. A. Franz III (interviewed on the program), Senior Health
Physicist (Colorado)
Kenneth R. Chapman (interviewed on the program), formerly
with the Nuclear Regulatory Commission
Lauriston S. Taylor (interviewed on the program), formerly president of the National Council on Radiation Protection
Ralph W. Deuster (interviewed on the program), president of
Nuclear Fuel Services (New York)
George Burton, Jr. (interviewed on the program), formerly president of Atlantic Richfield Hanford Company

Other persons interviewed on the program could not be reached.

Dr. John Gofman, identified only as M.D., Ph.D.; and
Dr. Robert Seamans, formerly with ERDA.

The staff was unable to interview or to obtain substantive responses
from NBC's consultants:

Dr. Harry Woolf, director of the Institute of Advanced Studies
at Princeton University
Dr. Howard Seliger of Johns Hopkins University.

Conclusion of The Council: The debate concerning nuclear waste is
undoubtedly of public importance and efforts by documentarians to
illuminate that debate for the average viewer are to be supported.
Before considering the specific charges of the complainants we would
like the record to indicate that we applaud NBC for bringing this
substantial controversy to the attention of its viewers. The blandness
of television programming troubles us; provocative discussion must be
sought after and encouraged.

We turn then to the allegations of lack of balance. Often we are
confronted by complaints alleging bias in the presentation of a documentary. In this instance, complainants have charged that the "Danger! Radioactive Waste" documentary was "quite deliberately biased
in an anti-nuclear manner." What is essential in a documentary is that

its conclusions be based on verifiable information—that is, on documentation—and not that it be fully objective. A major function of journalism is responsible interpretation.

Whether this Council or the complainant agrees or disagrees with the conclusions of a particular news report is not relevant. Provided that the news organization has first presented enough basic material on which the public can reach its own conclusion, then the news organization is free to indicate its own thrust. The issue for us, therefore, is whether there was in the documentary a fair reflection of the major viewpoints, scientific as well as factual. We believe that there was.

This is not a case in which a report ignored the views of those who felt that there was no danger, or little danger, or even those who felt that the energy needs were so great that the risks were outweighed by the social needs. On the contrary, the views of the supporters of nuclear energy and of the notion that there are no real dangers, or that the risks are outweighed by the benefits, *were* presented. A particularly apt response was made by NBC to the criticism of its choice of a scientist-interviewee whose theories have been substantially rebutted:

> Debate in the scientific community is commonplace. . . . It is not unknown that a single scientist considered by a majority to be wrong in his time, later turns out to be correct. *In any case our purpose was to present the debate, not to make a judgment as to who is correct.* (Emphasis added.)

It then becomes a matter of emphasis and we do not think that the Council should substitute its judgment for that of NBC. The complainants' charge of lack of balance is accordingly found unwarranted.

Similarly, we find the complainants' charge of lack of perspective also unwarranted. Not only are we persuaded on this issue by the response of NBC and by our examination of the transcript, but we must note the thrust of the documentary. Indeed, an integral part of the documentary, what it was all about, was whether the energy shortage warranted the risks—and hence the "need" for nuclear power.

As to the complainants' allegation of factual errors and misrepresentation, we note first many of the so-called errors cited by complainants are, in truth, matters of opinion, interpretation and emphasis. There are few absolutes and indisputable facts on this subject; scientists rarely agree. By and large, we believe that the documentary gave reasonable journalistic interpretations of scientific opinions, evidence and studies. The responses of NBC and of independent experts interviewed by the Council's staff would seem to us to indicate that sufficient support exists for most of the assertions in the program.

However, on examination of the charges, together with study of the transcript and viewing of the tape, we believe that the program was seriously flawed in several respects and with that in mind, we cannot say that the complaints are without merit.

Several allegations of factual errors and misrepresentations concern us: most notably the coverage of the "problems" at Maxey Flats, Kentucky, site of a nuclear waste storage facility; and the coverage at a New York state nuclear facility of a transient worker's possible genetic damage. Following are excerpts from the transcript, the precise charges of complainants and the NBC responses. We quote at length because we believe that the editing, juxtapositioning of verifiable statements with conjecture, and choice of words are important elements and cause for concern.

Maxey Flats

NARRATION: In 1975, the Environmental Protection Agency, the EPA, reported that radioactive material had moved off-site. . . . The EPA said there was no immediate danger to the public, but people who live in the area were alarmed. Many of them are farmers and some are having unexplained problems with their animals. Most of the concerned people live along the banks of a creek which at times has been filled with a strange milky material that has come from the Maxey Flats site. The cattle on the Hall farm drink from this stream.

MRS. HALL: Our biggest concern is the fact that in the report released concerning this, that it had been leaking for approximately four years and we weren't told until about a year ago that it was leaking, and that neighborhood children have always swam in the creek, played in the water, and we begin to notice changes in the creek water at times, not all the time, but at times, the creek water would be like a light gray water full of a different type soil than we had here.

NARRATION: Oscar Hurst's cattle have been sick. About a dozen cattle have died in the past few years. He is worried about the radiation.

MR. HURST: Hair's been turning gray, grittin' their teeth and they're a-dying, going up and down in milk. I talked to the local veterinarian and he says he didn't know, and Doctor Singer says it is copper. I tried to talk to some of the fellows taking samples from the nuclear plant and find out the symptoms of it, and they said they talked like I was crazy thinking about this thing.

MRS. HALL: Just like they might come today and check the water and some of that might seep in tomorrow somewhere, and we're afraid of what we don't know; we don't know if there's a danger from it or not.

NARRATION: The cattle have been tested by the local veterinarian and the state. The results, obtained with some difficulty by the people, give no evidence to link the illness of the animals with the release of radioactivity.

Complainants charged:

> The statements made about the water near Maxey Flats were absolutely absurd. There is no possible way in which the very tiny amounts of radioactivity in the drinking water could have changed its color or appearance—every scientist in the world would agree on this.

And also:

> In fact, the producer was told that the "strange milky material" was clay being washed down the stream by bulldozing operations nearby.

And NBC responded:

> It was stated that the streams coming from the Maxey Flats site appeared milky. Other streams in the area are clear. It did not say the milky material was radioactive, only that the stream was being used to carry away material from the site. Several former workers said in an interview not included in the program that they had witnessed contaminated water from Maxey Flats being dumped directly into the stream at times, so there is some reason to at least listen to the fears of the people in the area.

Further, the staff's investigation revealed that, as to the "unexplained problems" with the herd of cattle, a veterinarian had diagnosed the problem as a copper and phosphorus deficiency; the cattle had been treated for the same and had responded; the veterinarian had so testified at a public hearing on Maxey Flats which NBC crew had attended and, in part at least, taped. Asked why testimony which explained the animals' problems was not included, the producer said that she was reporting fears and doubts of the community and did not intend that portion of the program to stand for the proposition that the problems were caused by radiation.

Transient Worker

NARRATION: The company also made use of transient workers who were hired for short periods of time to work in the most highly radioactive areas of the plant. They received burnout doses of radiation, that is, the maximum amount allowable in a year. The practice enabled regular workers to keep their exposures down. Jerry Brown was a transient worker at the plant from July to September 1972. Subsequently he and his wife had two children, who have a rare genetic disease called Hurler's syndrome.

JERRY BROWN: Working conditions were, I would say, quite substandard. There was supposed to be a health and safety man on the job at all times, which there were several jobs that were on that—I would be in a room that you could only get into from the outside. There was no inside latch, so you were stranded in this room until the health and safety man decided to come back and let you out.

NARRATION: Ralph Deuster, president of NFS, appeared on a panel and later at a news conference. Producer Joan Konner was there.

JOAN KONNER: How can you justify the use of transient workers and exposing them to burnout doses of radiation, doses that you would not allow your regular workers to be exposed to?

RALPH DEUSTER: It's a practice that the industry has used. I think it's a logical thing to do.

JERRY BROWN: They'll eventually go blind around the, at the age of five, blind and deaf. (Sound effects—babies) And later on in life, they'll have problems with their internal organs—the heart, the lungs, the liver, the kidneys—and the end result is death at the age of ten.

NARRATION: Jerry Brown is not sure the radiation caused his children's illness.

JERRY BROWN: I can't say definitely, then I think I'd probably be liable, and I do have a strong feeling that's what it was caused from, but I can't find a doctor that would definitely say so.

DR. BROSS: This is one industry where health is a limiting factor—

the health of the persons either exposed directly as workers or involved with the, in the environment of the plants or in transport or in other ways.

NARRATION: There are other limiting factors at West Valley. The Nuclear Regulatory Commission required modifications in the plant design because of the threat of earthquakes in the area. Also community pressure built up against expansion of the facility. West Valley is now left with six hundred thousand gallons of the long-lived deadly liquid waste. . . .

Complainants charged:

The most offensive example [of an unrelated emotional scene] was the heartless exploitation of a former nuclear worker who has two sons born with a genetic disease (Hurler's syndrome). NBC did not present any evidence relating this disease to radiation. The father admitted that no doctor had established any connection. . . . This tactic, using deformed children to scare the public, is not unknown to the irresponsible fringe of the nuclear opposition.

To which NBC responded:

Dr. Irwin Bross of the Roswell Park Memorial Institute said there is no way of finding out whether the Brown children's illness was caused by the burnout dose of radiation given to Mr. Brown. He did say it was a possibility, and he carefully outlined how.

AEC reports show that the West Valley facility exceeded acceptable levels of radiation on many occasions. In addition, the effluents from the plant made a nearby stream one of the most radioactive in the state.

And variously:

The man who has two children with Hurler's syndrome was a transient worker. It cannot be proved that the disease was caused by his exposure, which he and the script stated. However, Dr. Irwin Bross of the Roswell Park Memorial Institute in Buffalo, who is acquainted with the case, said that the exposure could have caused the genetic damage. Dr. Bross has done and published studies showing that radiation, medical and otherwise, causes an increase in leukemia, genetic defects, and other diseases.

Staff investigation further revealed that, according to Ralph Deuster, president of the company that employed the transient workers, Jerry Brown had been subjected to 25 percent of the allowable dosage of radiation. According to Dr. Bross this would be roughly the equivalent of an ordinary x-ray dosage (1 rad). He told the staff that his studies show that serious genetic defects occur in children of those exposed to this dosage. Other scientists with whom the staff spoke and who are studying the biological effects of radiation challenge the validity of Dr. Bross's findings. None of these scientists appeared on the program. Nor for that matter did the portion of Dr. Bross's interview which was used reflect his position as relied upon by NBC in its response to complainants. (It should be noted that the producer told staff investigators that she had copies of Mr. Brown's records indicating he had received a higher dosage. Mr. Deuster explained this as an error on her part in having inappropriately added together unrelated figures.)

What we have is a series of "mights." A radiation dosage equivalent to an x-ray *might* be sufficient to cause human genetic defects. Hurler's syndrome *might* be one of the genetic defects produced by radiation. Workers *might* be exposed to dosages which *might* be harmful to the extent that genetic damage *might* occur that *might* be manifested in their children. And so forth. We find the NBC response in this regard inadequate, what we consider to be the result of tortured logic.

In conclusion and on the record before us, we believe that the presentations on these two matters were not consistent with good journalism. Both stories must necessarily have had strong impacts on the audience, but with dubious relevance to the subject at hand. In both instances and as far as the transcript goes there was no evidence of cause and effect. Indeed the conclusion on both stories is nothing more than that there *might* be a connection. The use of this material would seem to betoken scare tactics, beyond the limits of sound journalism. The complaints in this regard are found to be warranted.

Finally, we consider the allegations of gimmickry, heavy-handed editing, manipulative sound effects and other so-called "production tricks." Without regard to whatever personal feelings we may have on these assertions, we believe that this Council should not substitute its producing judgment for that of a news organization. One allegation, that of staging (*i.e.,* using a "dead fish"), is serious and, if true, would be beyond the bounds of journalistic discretion. We note that we found no evidence to support this contention. (The reference is apparently to a government slide—one of several pictures—taken under water where there was an apparent leakage from drums. These seem to have been actual photographs and it is not even clear that the fish was dead. It was just still—which isn't surprising since it was a still photograph.) The complaints in this regard are found unwarranted.

Partial dissent by Sylvia Roberts: It is my opinion that the complaint with respect to the portion of the documentary showing the children afflicted with Hurler's syndrome is unwarranted. In all other respects, I concur with the majority.

Partial dissent by Norman Isaacs: I agree with the central thrust of The Council's findings on the NBC program dealing with atomic wastes. However, I find myself compelled to voice disagreement over The Council's method of treating all parts of the determination in equal manner—warranted or unwarranted—regardless of the degrees of importance.

For me, the program was in the tradition of crusading journalism. It took on an issue of profound national importance. In the main, it did the job with skill and fairness. Unhappily, in two places the presentation became flawed—flawed enough to carry the impression of possible unfairness. To lift these two segments to the importance of the over-all focus and effect of the program strikes me as unbalanced on The Council's part.

My basic argument is that journalism does not lend itself to unvarying standard determinations. There are times when a journalistic effort can be defended for over-all purpose and still found wanting. The Council majority maintains that it has done this in this instance. I respectfully disagree. The two flaws do not seem to me to merit equal standing with a judgment on the totality of the program.

Appendix V

Major Corporate Subsidiaries: RCA, ABC, and CBS

RCA Corporation Subsidiaries

(as of December 31, 1976)

	State of Incorporation	Percentage of Voting Securities Owned by RCA Corporation
Banquet Foods Corporation	Delaware	100
Coronet Industries, Inc.	Delaware	100
National Broadcasting Company, Inc.	Delaware	100
Random House, Inc.	New York	100
RCA Alaska Communications, Inc.	Alaska	100
RCA American Communications, Inc.	Delaware	100
RCA Distributing Corporation	Illinois	100
RCA Global Communications, Inc.	Delaware	100
RCA International Development Corporation	Delaware	100
RCA Limited	Canada	100
RCA International Finance Ltd.	Delaware	100
RCA Limited	England	100
Oriel Foods Limited	England	100
Morris & David Jones Limited	England	100
RCA Sales Corporation	Delaware	100
The Hertz Corporation	Delaware	100

Each of the above subsidiaries is included in the consolidated financial statements of the registrant.

The names of a number of subsidiaries have been omitted. Such subsidiaries, considered in the aggregate as a single subsidiary, would not constitute a significant subsidiary.

American Broadcasting Companies, Inc., Subsidiaries

(as of January 1, 1977)

	State or Country of Incorporation	Percentage of Voting Securities Owned by Immediate Parent
American Broadcasting Companies, Inc. (Parent)		
ABC DISC, Inc.	N.Y.	100
ABC Entertainment, Inc.	Del.	100
ABC-FM Spot Sales, Inc.	N.Y.	100
ABC International Television, Inc.	N.Y.	100
ABC Leisure Magazines, Inc.	Del.	100
ABC Schwann Publications, Inc.	Del.	100
ABC News, Inc.	Del.	100
ABC News Intercontinental, Inc.	Del.	100
ABC Picture Holdings, Inc.	N.Y.	100
ABC Record and Tape Sales Corp.	Del.	100
ABC Records, Inc.	N.Y.	100
ABC/Dunhill Music, Inc.	N.Y.	100
ABC Record Distributors, Inc.	Del.	100
ABC Recording Studios, Inc.	Del.	100
American Broadcasting Music, Inc.	N.Y.	100
Anchor Music, Inc.	N.Y.	100
Blue Thumb Records, Inc.	Calif.	100
Westminster Recording Co., Inc.	N.Y.	100
ABC Scenic and Wildlife Attractions, Inc.	Fla.	100
Silver Springs, Inc.	Fla.	100
Weeki-Wachee Spring, Inc.	Fla.	100
ABC Scenic and Wildlife Attractions, Incorporated (Delaware)	Del.	100
ABC Family Entertainment, Inc.	Texas	100
Historic Smithville Inns, Inc.	Del.	100
Smithville Airfield, Inc.	N.J.	100
Smithville Theatre, Inc.	N.J.	100
ABC Sports, Inc.	N.Y.	100
ABC Television Spot Sales, Inc.	N.Y.	100
ABC Theatre Holdings, Inc.	Del.	100
ABC Florida State Theatres, Inc.	Fla.	100
ABC Interstate Theatres, Inc.	Del.	100
Modern Sales and Service, Inc.	Texas	100
ABC Southeastern Theatres, Inc.	Del.	100
Miami Florida Theatre Building, Inc.	Fla.	100
Smyrna Halifax Theatre, Inc.	Fla.	100

American Broadcasting		
Theatres, Inc.	Fla.	100
Arcade Investment Company	Fla.	100
Augusta Rialto Corporation	Del.	75
Calpar Theatres, Inc.	Calif.	100
Hollywood Amusements, Inc.	Fla.	85.71
Marion Advertising Agency, Inc.	Fla.	100
Wil-Kin, Inc.	Del.	100
Ambro Distributing Corp.	N.Y.	100
Ambro Western Hemisphere		
Releasing Corp.	N.Y.	100
Ambroad, Inc.	Del.	100
American Broadcasting Company		
Merchandising, Inc.	N.Y.	100
Anchor Records, Inc.	Del.	100
Anchor Records Limited	U.K.	100
Anchor Music Limited	U.K.	100
Anchor Record Production		
Limited	U.K.	100
CT Industries, Inc.	Del.	100
KQV, Inc.	Pa.	100
KXYZ, Inc.	Texas	100
Liberty Pictures Corporation	Del.	100
Selmur Productions, Inc.	Del.	100
The Prairie Farmer Publishing Company	Ill.	100
Prairie Farmer Insurance		
Services, Inc.	Ill.	100
Indiana Prairie Farmer Insurance		
Services, Inc.	Ind.	100
Wallace Homestead Co.	Iowa	100
Wallaces Farmer Insurance		
Services, Inc.	Iowa	100
Wallace-Homestead Book		
Company	Iowa	100
Wisconsin Farmer Company, Inc.	Wisc.	78.75
Wisconsin Agriculturist Insurance		
Services, Inc.	Wisc.	100
WLS, Inc.	Del.	100
WMAL, Inc.	Del.	100
Word, Incorporated	Texas	100
Personal Growth Resources, Inc.	Texas	100
Whittemore Associates, Inc.	Mass.	100
Word Direct Marketing		
Services, Inc.	Texas	100
Word Music, Inc.	Texas	100
Word (U.K.) Limited	U.K.	100
WXYZ, Inc.	Mich.	100

Columbia Broadcasting System, Inc., Subsidiaries

(as of December 31, 1976)

	State or Country of Incorporation	Percentage of Voting Securities Held by Immediate Controlling Parent
A & A Records and Tapes Limited	Canada	100	
A & A Franchise System Ltd.	Canada		100
Glenn's Music Limited	Canada		100
Glenn's Music (Western) Limited	Canada		100
April House A.B.	Sweden	100	
April Music Belgium S.A./N.V.	Belgium	100	
April Music Inc.	Connecticut	100	
April Music Publishing Company (Proprietary) Limited	South Africa	50	
A.R.S. (Atlantic) Limited	Canada	100	
Better Publications of Canada Limited	Canada	100	
Blackwood Music Inc.	Connecticut	100	
CBS/Arbiter Limited	England	51	
Dallas Music Industries Limited	England		100
Dallas Musical Limited	England		100
Vox Sound Limited	England		100
CBS/Arbiter G.m.b.H.	Germany	51	
CBS Australia Pty. Limited	Australia	100	
April Music Pty. Ltd.	Australia		100
Australian Record Club Pty. Limited	Australia		100
Australian Record Company Limited	Australia		100
Arcol Distribution & Services Pty. Limited	Australia		100
Fender Sound House Pty. Limited	Australia		100
Music Publishing Co. of Australia Pty. Limited	Australia		50
CBS Films Pty. Limited	Australia		100
CBS Columbia C.A.	Venezuela	100	
CBS Columbia A.G.	Switzerland	100	
April Musikverlag G.m.b.H.	Germany		100
CBS Disques/Grammofoonplaten S.A./N.V.	Belgium		100
CBS Grammofoonplaten B.V.	Holland		100
April Music Holland B.V.	Holland		100
CBS Records A.B.	Sweden		100
Cupol-Starton A.B.	Sweden		100
CBS Records ApS	Denmark		100
Grammofonselskabs Distribution Centralen A/S	Denmark		33.3

	State or Country of Incorporation	Percentage of Voting Securities Held by Immediate Controlling Parent
CBS Records A/S	Norway	100
Plate-Sentralen A/S	Norway	50
CBS Records Inc. (Zug)	Switzerland	100
CBS Records Ltd.	Israel	75
April Music Ltd.	Israel	100
CBS Schallplatten G.m.b.H.	Germany	100
Discos CBS, S.A.	Spain	100
Funckler B.V.	Holland	100
Industria de Discos Centroamericana, S.A.	Costa Rica	100
Distribuidora Salvadorena de Discos, S.A.	El Salvador	100
Distribuidora Panamena de Discos, S.A.	Panama	100
Distribuidora Guatemalteca de Discos, S.A.	Guatemala	100
Mundo Musical, S.A.	Costa Rica	100
CBS/Columbia Internacional, S.A.	Mexico 100	
Mundo Musical, S.A.	Mexico	100
CBS/EVR Inc.	New York 100	
CBS International S.A.	France 100	
CBS Disques S.A.	France	85
Société-Freycinet Wilson, S.A.	France	49
Les Editions April Music S.A.R.L.	France	100
CBS Musical Instruments, Ltd.	Canada 100	
CBS Records Canada, Ltd.	Canada 100	
April Music (Canada) Ltd.	Canada	100
A.R.S. Records Canada Limited	Canada	100
Blackwood Music (Canada) Ltd.	Canada	100
Columbia Records Distributors Canada, Ltd.	Canada	100
CBS Records Ltd., Cyprus	Cyprus 75	
CBS Records OY	Finland 100	
CBS Records S.S.K.	Iran 66	
CBS Schallplattengesellschaft m.b.H.	Austria 100	
CBS/SONY Inc.	Japan 50	
CBS/SONY Family Club, Inc.	Japan	100
CBS/SONY Records Inc.	Japan	100
April Music Inc.	Japan	100
CBS/SONY California, Inc.	California	100
CBS-SUGAR Compagnia Generale del Disco S.p.A.	Italy 50	

	State or Country of Incorporation	Percentage of Voting Securities Held by Immediate Controlling Parent
CBS Television Network Sales of Canada Limited	Canada	100
CBS United Kingdom Limited	England	100
April Music Limited	England	100
Holt Saunders Limited	England	100
Realm Record and Tape Club Limited	England	100
Shorewood Packaging Company Limited	England	80
Colfax Inc.	New York	100
Columbia Recording Corporation	New York	100
Blackwood Music Publishing, Limited Liability Company	Greece	97
Columbia Television, Inc.	New York	100
Daylight Productions, Inc.	New York	100
Discos CBS Industria e Comercio Ltda.	Brazil	100
Editora Latino Americana de Musica "ELAM" Ltda.	Brazil	100
Editora Mundo Musical Ltda.	Brazil	100
Discos CBS S.A.I.C.F.	Argentina	100
Ediciones Mundo Musical S.R.L.	Argentina	90
Melograf S.R.L.	Argentina	75
Discos CBS, S.A.	Colombia	100
DISKI CBS AEBE	Greece	100
Distribuidora Interamericana, S.A.	Spain	100
Editora Interamericana S.A.	Uruguay	100
Editora Interamericana Ltda.	Brazil	100
Editorial Interamericana C.A.	Ecuador	100
Editorial Interamericana Inc.	Delaware	100
Editorial Interamericana S.A.	Argentina	100
Editorial Interamericana S.A.	Colombia	100
Editorial Interamericana S.A.	Peru	100
Editorial Interamericana de Venezuela, C.A.	Venezuela	100
Edizioni April Music S.R.L.	Italy	50
Epic Records, Inc.	New York	100
5152 Ground Floor, Inc.	New York	100
Frank Music Corp.	New York	100
Andrew Music Corp.	New York	100
Audubon Music, Inc.	New York	100
Boston Music Company	West Virginia	100
Frank Distributing Corp.	Massachusetts	100
Carmichael Publications Inc.	New York	50
Desilu Music Corp.	New York	50

	State or Country of Incorporation	Percentage of Voting Securites Held by Immediate Controlling Parent
Desilu Songs, Inc.	New York	100
Empress Music Inc.	New York	100
Frank Management Corp.	New York	100
Remsen Music Corp.	New York	100
Frank Music (Canada) Limited	Canada	97
Frank Music West, Inc.	California	100
Saunders Publications, Inc.	New York	100
Complex IV Music Corporation	New York	50
Tosci Music Corp.	New York	50
Union Record Co., Inc.	New York	100
The Walter Reade Music Corporation	New York	49
Gramophone Record Company (Proprietary) Limited	South Africa	49.99
Shenbourne Distributors, Ltd.	England	100
Gulbransen International, Inc.	Delaware	100
Holt, Rinehart & Winston of Canada, Limited	Canada	100
HRW Publications Ltd.	Canada	100
Holt-Saunders Pty. Limited	Australia	100
Interamericana Commercial, S.A.	Mexico	100
Nueva Editorial Interamericana, S.A. de C.V.	Mexico	100
Jare Ventures Inc.	New York	100
Kriven Inc.	New York	100
Movie Book Club, Inc.	New York	100
National Cablevision Limited	Canada	20
National Handcraft Institute, Inc.	Iowa	100
Pakhsh Ahang Iran S.S.K.	Iran	66
Riverfront Redevelopment Corporation	Missouri	100
Premier Cablevision Limited	Canada	18.54
Shorewood Packaging Corp. of Canada Limited	Canada	60
Solo Products Limited	Canada	50
Esty Limited	Canada	100
Solestil Limited	Canada	50
Steinway & Sons	New York	100
Stephens & Towndrow Co. Limited	Canada	20
Newsradio Limited	Canada	100
Tartini Musical Imports Ltd.	Canada	50
Audio-Tec Music Services Ltd.	Canada	100
The Klingbeil Company	Ohio	29.7
Tuna Fish Music Inc.	New York	100
Vista Marketing Inc.	New York	100
W. B. Saunders Company Canada Limited	Canada	100

	State or Country of Incorporation	Percentage of Voting Securities Held by Immediate Controlling Parent
Winston Press Inc.	Minnesota	100
Winterland Press Inc.	New York	100

Appendix VI

List of Conglomerates in FCC Study

American Broadcasting Companies, Inc.
Capital Cities Communications, Inc.
Columbia Broadcasting System, Inc.
Columbia Pictures Industries, Inc.
Corinthian Broadcasting Corporation
Deseret Management Corporation
Downe Communications, Inc.
General Electric Company
Hughes Tool Company
Jefferson-Pilot Corporation, Inc.
Kaiser Industries Corporation
Kansas City Southern Industries, Inc.
Lamb Communications, Inc.
Levin-Townsend Computer Corporation
Liberty Corporation
Lin Broadcasting Corporation
Meredith Corporation
Metromedia, Inc.
Nationwide Corporation
Outlet Company
RCA Corporation
Reeves Telecom Corporation
Rollins, Inc.
Rust Craft Greeting Cards, Inc.
Schering-Plough Corporation
Signal Companies, Inc. (*also* Golden West Broadcasting, Inc.)
Storer Broadcasting Company
Time, Inc.
TransAmerica Corporation
Twentieth Century-Fox Film Corporation
Westinghouse Electric Corporation

Conglomerates Selected for the Preliminary Inquiry

AVCO Corporation
Chris-Craft Industries, Inc.
Cox Enterprises, Inc.
Fuqua Industries, Inc.
E. W. Scripps Company
Travelers Corporation

Appendix VII

CBS Rules on Terrorist Coverage

Guidelines issued by CBS News President Richard S. Salant on April 7, 1977.

Because the facts and circumstances of each case vary, there can be no specific self-executing rules for the handling of terrorist/hostage stories. CBS News will continue to apply the normal tests of news judgment and if, as so often they are, these stories are newsworthy, we must continue to give them coverage despite the dangers of "contagion." The disadvantages of suppression are, among [other] things, (1) adversely affecting our credibility ("What else are the news people keeping from us?"); (2) giving free rein to sensationalized and erroneous word of mouth rumors; and (3) distorting our news judgments for some extraneous judgmental purpose. These disadvantages compel us to continue to provide coverage.

Nevertheless, in providing for such coverage there must be thoughtful, conscientious care and restraint. Obviously, the story should not be sensationalized beyond the actual fact of its being sensational. We should exercise particular care in how we treat the terrorist/kidnapper.

More specifically:

(1) An essential component of the story is the demands of the terrorist/kidnapper and we must report those demands. But we should avoid providing an excessive platform for the terrorist/kidnapper. Thus, unless such demands are succinctly stated and free of rhetoric and propaganda, it may be better to paraphrase the demands instead of presenting them directly through the voice or picture of the terrorist/kidnapper.

(2) Except in the most compelling circumstances, and then only with the approval of the President of CBS News, or in his absence, the Senior Vice President of News, there should be no live coverage of the terrorist/kidnapper since we may fall into the trap of providing an unedited platform for him. (This does *not* limit live on-the-spot

reporting by CBS News reporters, but care should be exercised to assure restraint and context.)

(3) News personnel should be mindful of the probable need by the authorities who are dealing with the terrorist for communication by telephone and hence should endeavor to ascertain, wherever feasible, whether our own use of such lines would be likely to interfere with the authorities' communications.

(4) Responsible CBS News representatives should endeavor to contact experts dealing with the hostage situation to determine whether they have any guidance on such questions as phraseology to be avoided, what kinds of questions or reports might tend to exacerbate the situation, etc. Any such recommendations by established authorities on the scene should be carefully considered as guidance (but not as instruction) by CBS News personnel.

(5) Local authorities should also be given the name or names of CBS personnel whom they can contact should they need further guidance or wish to deal with such delicate questions as a newsman's call to the terrorists or other matters which might interfere with authorities dealing with the terrorists.

(6) Guidelines affecting our coverage of civil disturbances are also applicable here, especially those which relate to avoiding the use of inflammatory catchwords or phrases, the reporting of rumors, etc. As in the case of policy dealing with civil disturbances, in dealing with a hostage story reporters should obey all police instructions but report immediately to their superiors any such instructions that seem to be intended to manage or suppress the news.

(7) Coverage of this kind of story should be in such overall balance as to length, that it does not unduly crowd out other important news of the hour/day.

Appendix VIII

Excerpt from "The Police Tapes": Interview with Anthony Bouza, N.Y.P.D.

BOUZA: You look at the average policeman, and he comes from the lower-middle class or upper-lower class, and suddenly he's going to become a policeman. He wants security; he wants a nice paying job; he wants to work out-of-doors; he wants to help people. He's willing to don this uniform, and he's going to go out into the streets of our city, and he's going to help people. And that is the psychology.

And he goes to the Police Academy, and he is told that he's going to be helping people. And he's taught how to help people. He's going to be preserving the fabric of our society. He's going to be preserving life and property and maintaining peace, and doing all the noble purposes.

And then he gets out there and he suddenly discovers that he's regulating human behavior, that he is bitterly resented. And he's shocked. The police officer's reaction to this is absolute shock— that a citizen, and I mean the citizen generically, should resent his presence. And he does. And it is resented. And it is resented rightly. We all bridle at control.

The policeman has great difficulty assimilating this knowledge. He becomes a bit cynical. He becomes a bit hardened. He cannot permit every emotional contact to drain him—he has to have emotions for his life and for his family. So like the prostitute that cannot afford to become emotionally, romantically, involved with every client, the policeman cannot afford to become emotionally or romantically involved with every client. And the result is that he develops calluses over his emotions.

As a matter of fact, that hardness and that cynicism permits him to cope with what he encounters. I think that if you maintain the involvement of the philosopher in the ghetto in a policeman, I think he'd disintegrate after a very little while.

INTERVIEWER: Do you think that there are degrees to which policemen become hardened, that perhaps go over into another areas.

BOUZA: Absolutely, absolutely. And this is reflected in names like
Fort Apache. Here we are, surrounded by a bunch of hostiles, we
are an island of heroes in a sea of hostility. It is us and them.
They're all a bunch of animals out there. The insularity grows.
The parochialism grows. And they become an island. So we have
the outside world and we have the police world. And we experience our reality, and the real world experiences its reality. And
it is terribly difficult for any citizen to understand the complexities involved in police work.

The policeman fundamentally has a ringside seat on the greatest show on earth. One of the beautiful things about being a
policeman is that you're at the center of action all the time. You
are seeing people, sometimes famous people, under most incredible circumstances. You're in on every secret of society in a sense.
And that's very exciting.

The public doesn't understand everything that you see. You
can't even explain it. Most policemen have a tighter relationship
with their partners than they do with their wives, which is a
whole different situation. So the insularity grows, the secretive-
ness grows, the parochialism grows. Society doesn't understand.
The policeman is shocked that society doesn't appreciate him
sufficiently, and they are driven apart. And this really creates a
kind of ineluctable drift that I don't know how to combat. . . .

Just as in Clockwork Orange, a dehumanized and impersonal
society is brutalizing and conditioning its citizens. . . . We have
poverty, the lack of education, the inability to articulate, alcohol-
ism, unemployment, inadequate housing, and all of the desperate
conditions of the ghetto fundamentally conditioning the citizens
in that ghetto to resolve their disputes violently.

We have a sub-culture in our society, and it resides in the
ghetto. And we are conditioning this sub-culture, and their reaction is very predictable. B. F. Skinner would have no difficulty
identifying what is happening there. We are conditioning people
to fail. We are conditioning people to become alcoholics. We are
conditioning them to be violent. And we give them no other
mechanisms with which to cope.

There is nothing inevitable about it. It is a process that is
taking place because of forces that are conditioning this response,
just as forces are conditioning my response to educate my children effectively—make sure they get a good education. I pay my

mortgage, pay my taxes. I resolve my disputes with my wife orally or with my colleagues through communications. In the ghetto I'd be stabbing and punching and kicking and scratching and doing everything else that everybody else is doing—simply because I'm a human being, and I'm conditionable. And they're conditionable.

INTERVIEWER: So often the violence stems from such a trifling matter. You know, somebody neglected to return something they borrowed, and the person decides to go shoot them.

BOUZA: The levels of rage and frustration have created an emotional gorge that people are permanently endowed with in the ghetto. So it may take quite a while for me to get you angry enough to be violent; if you were walking around with an emotional gorge up to here it would only take another fraction of an inch to get you to respond.

And that's really what is happening. The frustrations that I'm talking about—the heat, the misery, the lack of rest, the whole miserable condition of poverty. And Aristotle did say 2,500 years ago that poverty is the parent of revolution and crime. It is still true. And when you're going around with that gorge and those levels of frustration and permanent anger, and you don't even know what you want, the first available target becomes the focus of the violence.

America attacks the problems that it sees. It doesn't see these problems. They're now under the rug. The fact is that we have ignored them. They are being more ignored now than they ever have been. They're poorer than they ever have been. There hasn't been a significant redistribution of income in this nation for 30 years. The bureaucracy and the government are failing, and fundamentally, the Federal Government has simply got to look at what is happening in the city ghetto and address it. And one of the reasons it hasn't done so is because it has been invisible. No one is filming it, no one is writing about it, no one is doing stories about it. It is just invisible, and if you go out into the streets of the Bronx, you will see a lot of Black and Hispanic energetic young men and women all dressed up, no place to go, nothing to do, no jobs, no point in living, and seeking any form of escape that they can find, whether that form is drugs or alcohol or whatever. Most frequently it's alcohol, and thank God that it's so freely available.

To the degree that I succeed in keeping it cool—in keeping the ghetto cool—to the degree that I can be effective, to that degree, fundamentally, am I deflecting America's attention from discovering this cancer? And the longer it is deferred—the discovery —as in Viet Nam, the greater the moral dilemma, the greater the moral problem when it is ultimately discovered. So maybe I would be better off failing. Maybe I'd be better off not working quite as hard. Maybe I'd be better off not being as effective as I presume myself to be.

And that way America would be confronting the problem as it had to do during the urban riots of the sixties and so on. The fact of the matter is that we are manufacturing criminals. We are manufacturing brutality out there. We are very efficiently creating a very volatile and dangerous sub-element of our society. And we are doing it simply because we don't want to face the burdens and the problems and the responsibilities that their existence imposes on any society with conscience. So rather than awaken your conscience to the problem, you're far better off just ignoring it.

And that's what we are doing. And I am very well paid, almost, to be the commander of an army of occupation in the ghetto. And that is a great tragedy, I think, and I don't know that anyone's useful life ought to be employed in that kind of a pursuit, however well paid one is. So that's where my sense of defeat and frustration comes from.

Appendix IX

Summary of ERA Research Techniques

THIS IS a short summary of the five techniques that ERA uses to probe for understanding that delicate relationship between a news department and its audience.

Field Research

We do large-sample field surveys. Face-to-face and/or mail interviews study viewing patterns versus socioeconomic patterns versus attitudinal data. This is a complete research project in itself, developing a very large body of information.

Perception Measurements

We use diverse behavioral measurement techniques to measure the many facets of human communication.

A. Emotional Response Measurement

We assess the quantity and quality of emotional response to news product. Electro-dermal response measurements are made while target audience test panels are viewing videotape airchecks.

B. Real Time Conscious Opinion Measurement

A second line of data is collected from the panels as they view the tapes. Each panel member expresses his moment-to-moment opinion via a scaled voting machine. This is nonverbal, memory-independent data.

C. Personality Perception Measurement

Audience perceptions of news personality traits are measured immediately after the panels have viewed their performances.

D. Focus Group Opinion Measurement

In-depth discussion groups are conducted, using "soft" encounter techniques and multiple-track recording/transcription. This technique doubles focus data.

E. EVDT

Electronic Voting Discussion Technique quantifies focus inputs, and adds the "secret ballot" to the group interaction of the focus groups.

Custom Combinations

Any one or any combination of these techniques may be applied to specific problems. Recent market changes, the impact of new personalities, promotional campaigns, etc., can be quickly assessed by an EVDT/Focus study. State-of-the-market benchmarks can be established quickly and relatively inexpensively with a large-sample field study.

What Does It All Mean?

When you receive your ERA report, the findings are clearly and concisely presented. The many elements of your (and your competition's) news product are evaluated and scored for audience effectiveness. Detailed diagnostic observations are made. When a news element is effective, we tell you what made it so. When something fails, we tell you what went wrong. The ERA report becomes a primer for improving your newscasts.

ERA Recommendations

Our research report includes wide-ranging and specific recommendations. An ERA principal presents the report to you in person, and a dialogue is opened to assure that the findings of the research are communicated accurately.

The Last Word

We at ERA are all broadcasters. We all share the experience of being frustrated by inadequate research, patched up with vague generalizations and strange conclusions. We put this company together to create an alternative.

Appendix X

Investigation of Publication of Select Committee on Intelligence Report, Hearings Before the Committee on Standards of Official Conduct, House of Representatives, Ninety-fourth Congress. Testimony of Daniel Schorr, Reporter, CBS, Inc.

September 15, 1976

Mr. Chairman, I appear before this committee today under protest, in response to a subpena whose issuance I deeply deplore.

I had hoped that this committee, which has already learned a great deal about congressional procedures for handling intelligence information, could have completed these hearings without crossing that constitutional Great Divide which separates the roles of the Congress and the press.

Whatever happens hereafter at this hearing, it is my belief that your subpena, commanding the appearance of a reporter to discuss his journalistic activities, its effect can only be to establish an atmosphere of intimidation for the press.

Now, this subpena requires me to produce all records, papers, documents, correspondence, et cetera, and this is not inclusive, "which relate in any way" to the subject of your inquiry. It's a broad statement and I have tried to interpret it, and I will divide the material in my possession into four general categories.

First, many of the records in my possession are material in the public domain, such as speeches that I have made, newspaper articles and I guess copies of [the] Village Voice containing the report of the House Intelligence Committee.

To the extent that these public materials are not already available to the committee and are desired by the committee, I am willing to provide them.

Second, since the publication of the report in the Village Voice I have received several thousand letters and telegrams. If the committee feels a need for such correspondence, I should like first to seek the permission of the persons involved out of respect for their privacy.

Third, I have notes taken during the coverage of the House Intelligence Investigation and I have draft scripts that were written in preparation for broadcasts.

Now, because of the internal news decisionmaking and the editing process, some of those scripts vary from what I actually did broadcast, and in fact, others were not broadcast at all.

All of this work product I must respectfully decline to submit. I believe that it falls under the category of reporters' notes, protected by the first amendment. I take now the same position that Dr. Frank Stanton, who was then President of CBS, Incorporated, took in 1971.

He refused to comply with the House Commerce Committee subpena demanding the scripts and the so-called out-takes of interviews filmed in preparation for the CBS television documentary, "The Selling of the Pentagon."

His position and mine today is that the internal process of preparing news for publication or for broadcast cannot be subjected to the compulsory process of subpena without subverting the purposes of the first amendment.

Now fourth, the subpena specifically demands "all drafts and copies of the report of the Select Committee on Intelligence which were in existence prior to January 29, 1976."

I cannot comply with that demand. The examination of the document could conceivably help to lead to discovery of the source, and as must now be manifest, if it has not been manifest before, I consider it a matter of professional conscience as well as a constitutional right not to assist you in discovering that source.

Now, this also means, obviously, and we may as well say it now, that I shall not respond to direct questioning about confidential sources, for in some 40 years of practicing journalism I have never yielded to a demand for a disclosure of a source that I had promised to protect, and I cannot do so now.

At the appropriate time, Mr. Chairman, Mr. Califano is ready to explain why, given the circumstances of this case, my role in the publication of the report, and my right to withhold the source, are indeed, protected by the Constitution.

But let me add that even if our legal position were not as strong as I believe it is, I could still not tell you my source, because for me this is a personal matter, and almost a visceral matter.

Mr. Chairman and members of the committee, we all build our lives around certain principles, and without those principles our careers simply lose their meaning.

For some of us, doctors, lawyers, clergymen, and yes, journalists, it is an article of faith that we must keep confidential those matters entrusted to us only because of the assurance that they would remain confidential.

Now, for a journalist, the most crucial kind of confidence is the identity of a source of information. To betray a confidential source would mean to dry up many future sources for many future reporters.

The reporter and the news organization would be the immediate losers, but I would submit to you that the ultimate losers would be the American people and their free institutions.

And if you will permit me one last personal word, without all of this constitutional argument, I would like to go beyond all of this. To betray a source would be for me to betray myself, my career, and my life, and to say that I refuse to do it isn't quite saying it right.

I cannot do it.

That concludes my statement.

Some Information About the Alfred I. duPont-Columbia University Awards for 1977-78

EACH YEAR the awards are based upon research done in conjunction with the annual DuPont-Columbia Survey of Broadcast Journalism. There is no set number of awards, nor are there permanent categories for the awards, which will vary according to evidences of outstanding performance in news and public affairs during the year. Local and network radio, local and network television, as well as syndicated material, will be surveyed.

Although categories for the awards will not be set in advance, concerned parties are encouraged to suggest to the jurors examples of broadcast journalism which they feel are particularly worthy of attention. They are also invited to suggest subjects for research.

Suggestions for those wishing to participate:

1. Any concerned person, group, organization, or broadcast station may bring to the DuPont jury's attention material dealing with performance in broadcast news and public affairs.

2. If such information concerns a specific program, it should include the following particulars: (a) the time, the date, and the station carrying the program, (b) the subject of the program, (c) the reason the program is being singled out. If possible, there should be notification enough in advance of air time to permit jurors to view or hear the program at the time of the original broadcast. In any event, supporting material such as tapes, films, or scripts should be retained as documentation. *However, films, tapes, and other supporting material should not be submitted unless expressly asked for by the Director.*

3. If information submitted concerns long-term performance of an individual, a station, or other institution, names or call letters should be given, as well as a full statement of the reasons for the submission.

4. Nominations may be made throughout the year for programs aired between July 1, 1977, and June 30, 1978. Nominations must be postmarked no later than midnight, July 2, 1978.

5. All materials submitted will become the property of Columbia University.

6. All inquiries and correspondence should be addressed to:
Director
The Alfred I. duPont–Columbia University
   Survey and Awards
Graduate School of Journalism
Columbia University
New York, N.Y. 10027

Acknowledgments

THE EDITOR AND JURORS ARE, as in the past, grateful to all those organizations and individuals who have offered us generous assistance in the putting together of this volume. Unfortunately, it is not possible to list them all. However, we would particularly like to express our gratitude to the news directors and newsmen and women from the networks and individual stations who answered questionnaires, furnished tapes and films, and produced the news and public affairs with which this volume and the DuPont-Columbia Awards are particularly concerned.

We would also like to thank the awards and public information departments of the commercial and public networks, as well as individual radio and television stations upon whose help, as always, we depended heavily.

Each year the volume of material to be handled in judging the awards and compiling this report increases with a commensurate broadening of reportorial and research chores. My assistant director, Barbara Eddings, once again, has been in charge of the formidable logistics involved in this process. Assisting us was DuPont Fellow Ann Rauma. Columbia School of Journalism graduates Steve Long and Tom Sawicki have also performed major reporting and research chores.

Thanks are due to our special consultants John C. Schultz and Harry Arouh, as well as Women in Communications, Incorporated, for their generous assistance.

Again, the reporters of *Variety, Advertising Age, Broadcasting,* the *New York Times,* the *Wall Street Journal, Television/Radio Age, TV Guide, More,* and the *Columbia Journalism Review* furnished both individual insights and continuous coverage of the broadcast scene which were invaluable to the editor and jurors.

We are particularly grateful this year to the John and Mary R. Markle Foundation for providing additional financial help toward the publication of this volume.

Finally, the network of DuPont correspondents across the country have been invaluable in providing those specific insights into local television which are so important a part of the overall picture of broadcast journalism which we hope this book provides.

Index